Extradition law

a practitioner's guide

Rebecca Niblock is a partner at Kingsley Napley LLP. **Edward Grange** is a partner at Corker Binning. Ranked as 'Star Individuals' by Chambers & Partners, they are both recognised as leaders in the field of extradition law. Together, they established the Defence Extradition Lawyers' Forum (DELF) and were founding Chairs. They are members of the Legal Experts Advisory Panel (LEAP) that was established by Fair Trials.

The Legal Action Group is a national, independent charity which campaigns for equal access to justice for all members of society. Legal Action Group:

- provides support to the practice of lawyers and advisers
- inspires developments in that practice
- campaigns for improvements in the law and the administration of justice
- stimulates debate on how services should be delivered.

Extradition law

a practitioner's guide

THIRD EDITION

Edward Grange and Rebecca Niblock

LAG the access to justice charity
Legal Action Group
2021

Third edition published in Great Britain 2021
by LAG Education and Service Trust Limited
2nd floor, Gatehouse Chambers, 1 Lady Hale Gate, London WC1X 8BS
www.lag.org.uk

First edition 2013
Second edition 2015

British Library Cataloguing in Publication Data. A CIP catalogue record for this book is available from the British Library.

FSC
www.fsc.org
MIX
Paper | Supporting responsible forestry
FSC® C020438

This book has been produced using Forest Stewardship Council (FSC) certified paper. The wood used to produce FSC certified products with a 'Mixed Sources' label comes from FSC certified well-managed forests, controlled sources and/or recycled material.

print ISBN: 978 1 913648 13 8
eBook ISBN: 978 1 913648 14 5
bundle (print and eBook) ISBN: 978 1 913648 15 2

Typeset by Refinecatch Ltd, Bungay, Suffolk
Printed in Great Britain by Hobbs the Printer, Totton, Hampshire

Foreword

By Mrs Justice Arbuthnot DBE

This book may be short but it packs a big punch. It takes you by the hand and guides you through the pitfalls that await the unwary, whether it is the complexities of the many challenges that may be mounted, a case management form, legal aid, certificate for counsel or skeleton arguments. The 260 or so pages will take a new practitioner on a step-by-step voyage through the first extradition hearing with bail considerations, on to a contested hearing, followed, if the worst comes to the worst (and you are defending), by an appeal hearing. It considers Part 1 (Arrest Warrant) and Part 2 cases.

The book is not just for new practitioners, however. This is the third edition and builds on the earlier two. It is an up-to-date textbook on the various arguments raised and decisions made by judges at Westminster Magistrates' Court and the guidance given by the Divisional Court in the last few years, but it also includes the older cases. The footnotes are very helpful and will allow readers to continue their in-depth learning and may perhaps allow them to discover an entirely new argument which will enthral the courts in the years to come.

This book is also for the judges. Each new judge, or 'appropriate judge' I should say, should be given a copy of this book. It provides the perfect introduction to the complexities of the work ahead.

For all practitioners and judges, the book brings them up to date with the latest arguments on various sections of the Extradition Act 2003. Most importantly, the timing of the publishing of this book has been carefully thought through. The approach to Arrest Warrants under the Trade and Cooperation Agreement is a new area of work which will be of particular significance in the months and years to come. The book sets out the law for those arrested after 11pm on 31 December 2020.

Ed and Rebecca have many years of experience in the extradition field and we should all be grateful that they have spared the time to write this invaluable tool. This book will be very much needed in the months and years ahead.

Mrs Justice Arbuthnot DBE
(Senior District Judge (Chief Magistrate) between 2016 and 2021)

August 2021

Preface

After six years, a new edition of *Extradition law: a practitioner's guide* has been published. The first edition was published in 2013, updated to a second edition in 2015. The gap of six years since the second edition was, of course, as a consequence of the June 2016 UK vote to leave the European Union. In the early days following the Brexit vote it had been assumed (wrongly) that all would become clear by 29 March 2019. As it turned out, we had four and a half years to speculate on what the UK's extradition arrangements with the EU27 would be, with much time and many words wasted along the way. The final agreement in the form of the surrender provisions of the Trade and Cooperation Agreement (TCA) came as a surprise to many (including the authors): given the length of time taken to negotiate the Norway and Iceland extradition agreement with the EU, both Schengen Area countries (unlike the UK), it seemed highly unlikely that anything like the EAW would remain. Documents preparing for a no-deal Brexit (specifically, the Law Enforcement and Security (Amendment) (EU Exit) Regulations 2019) provided a framework for the future of cross-border co-operation for the UK in the form of a reversion to the 1957 European Convention on Extradition. Despite the predictions of many experts in the field, it appears that political pragmatism prevailed in the end; the current arrangements replicate the features of the EAW to a very large extent.

In terms of the practical arrangements at court, little has changed since the last edition, although important changes with regards to how cases are presented and heard have of course occurred as a result of the Coronavirus pandemic. There have, of course, been momentous events taking place outside the courtroom, which have had and will have an impact inside it.

The third edition has been fully updated to take into account the changes brought about by the TCA. As with the second edition, we resolved to ensure that the information provided within these pages was as practical as possible, whilst remaining of a size that sits comfortably into the advocate's bag. We hope that the information contained within these pages will be of comfort to those without prior experience of extradition, including duty solicitors and new appropriate judges as well as being of practical use to the more seasoned extradition practitioner.

The book begins by looking at practical considerations in chapter 2. Chapter 3 goes on to examine the TCA Arrest Warrant in detail. A guide to the areas which should be covered when meeting the client for the first time is provided in chapter 4. The book then gives an overview of ways in which extradition can be challenged, looking first at the bars to extradition and then at human rights considerations in chapters 5 and 6. The initial hearing in TCA cases is covered in chapter 7 and chapter 8 deals with requests for extradition from outside the European Union.

The preparation required for the contested extradition hearing is considered in chapter 9. An explanation of the steps which will be taken in the full contested extradition hearing is dealt with in chapter 10. The book then goes on to provide a guide to the appeals process in chapter 11 providing up to date guidance from the Administrative Court. The final chapter looks at various ancillary matters, such as compromising a warrant, temporary surrender and transfer of sentenced prisoners.

Rebecca Niblock
Edward Grange
August 2021

Acknowledgements

We are eternally grateful to Rosemary Davidson and Ben Lloyd of 6KBW College Hill, who pored over our proofs with their customary grace and precision and undoubtedly significantly improved this book.

Our thanks to others who have given their precious time to provide us with their wisdom (and tell us where we have gone astray): Jyoti Gill, Katy Smart, Katherine Tyler, Simon Dulake, Susan Watt, and Senior District Judge Goldspring.

To Esther Pilger and others at LAG for encouraging a third edition and for tolerating our constant amendments.

Danielle Reece Greenhalgh at Corker Binning, Áine Kervick, Maeve Keenan and Will Hayes of Kingsley Napley; each of whom gave up their time to proofread our manuscript.

Since the second edition, George and Renée have arrived in our lives. Although they have offered little by way of insight into extradition law, we have them to thank for much light and laughter. And finally, to Natalie and Rob for holding the reins to allow us to write.

Ed and Rebecca
August 2021

Contents

Table of cases

HH v Italy [2012] UKSC 25, [2013] 1 AC 338, [2012] 3 WLR 90, [2012] 4 All ER 539, [2012] 6 WLUK 423, [2012] HRLR 25, (2012) 156(25) SJLB 31, (2012) Times, July 2	6.47, 6.48, 6.49, 6.50
Hamburg Public Prosecutor's Office v Altun *See* Germany v Altun—	
Harkins and Edwards v United Kingdom (Application Nos 9146/07 and 32650/07) [2012] 1 WLUK 236, [2012] 6 Costs LO 733, (2012) 55 EHRR 19, (2012) Times, February 13, ECtHR	6.15
Haynes v Malta [2009] EWHC 880 (Admin), [2009] 3 WLUK 698, [2009] Extradition LR 189	5.113
Hilali v Spain [2006] EWHC 1239 (Admin), [2007] 1 WLR 768, [2006] 4 All ER 435, [2006] 5 WLUK 711, [2006] Extradition LR 154, [2006] ACD 92	5.27, 5.28, 5.56, 7.23
Hoholm v Norway [2009] EWHC 1513 (Admin), [2009] 6 WLUK 736, (2009) Times, October 13	11.105, 11.106
Huczko v Governor of Wandsworth Prison [2012] EWHC 4134 (Admin), [2012] 6 WLUK 200	7.18
IM v Regional Prosecutor's Office of Ruse, Bulgaria [2019] EWHC 602 (Admin), [2019] 3 WLUK 349	6.27
Iacob v Romania [2017] EWHC 155 (Admin), [2017] 2 WLUK 95	3.57
Ilia v Appeal Court in Athens, Greece [2015] EWHC 547 (Admin), [2015] 3 WLUK 184, [2015] ACD 89	6.59, 9.49, 11.158
India v Chawla [2018] EWHC 1050 (Admin), [2018] 5 WLUK 633	11.131
Ismail, Re [1999] 1 AC 320, [1998] 3 WLR 495, [1998] 3 All ER 1007, [1998] 7 WLUK 592, (1999) 163 JP 154, (1999) 11 Admin LR 37, (1998) 95(35) LSG 35, (1998) 148 NLJ 1302, (1998) 142 SJLB 246, (1998) Times, August 20, HL	3.43
JK v District Court of Lublin, Poland [2018] EWHC 197 (Admin), [2018] 1 WLUK 259, [2018] ACD 25	5.93
JZ v Prokuratura Rejonowa Łódź (Case C-294/16 PPU), 28 July 2016, CJEU	4.18, 4.19
Jane v Westminster Magistrates' Court [2019] EWHC 394 (Admin), [2019] 4 WLR 95, [2019] 2 WLUK 367	11.188, 11.190, 11.191
Janovic v Lithuania [2011] EWHC 710 (Admin), [2011] 3 WLUK 838	6.31
Jansons v Latvia [2009] EWHC 1845 (Admin), [2009] 3 WLUK 495	5.106
Kaderli v Turkey [2021] EWHC 1096 (Admin), [2021] 4 WLUK 312	6.10
Kakis v Cyprus [1978] 1 WLR 779, [1978] 2 All ER 634, [1978] 5 WLUK 130, [1978] Crim LR 489, (1978) 122 SJ 400, HL	5.39, 5.44, 5.101

Table of statutes

Table of statutory instruments

Table of European legislation

Table of international agreements

Abbreviations

ACO	Administrative Court Office
AW	arrest warrant
CCF	Commission for the Control of INTERPOL's files
CJA 1967	Criminal Justice Act 1967
CJEU	Court of Justice of the European Union
CJPOA 1994	Criminal Justice and Public Order Act 1994
CLAS	Criminal Law Accreditation Scheme
CoE	Council of Europe
CPS	Crown Prosecution Service
CrimPD	Criminal Practice Directions
CrimPR	Criminal Procedure Rules 2015
CVP	Cloud Video Platform
DELF	Defence Extradition Lawyers' Forum
DPP	Director of Public Prosecutions
DUC	Document Upload Centre
EA 2003	Extradition Act 2003
EAW FD	Framework Decision on the European Arrest Warrant
EC	European Convention on Extradition
ECBA	European Criminal Bar Association
ECE	European Convention on Extradition
ECHR	European Convention on Human Rights and Fundamental Freedoms
ECRIS	Exchange of information on criminal records
ECtHR	European Court of Human Rights
ELA	Extradition Lawyers' Association
E(PA)A 2020	Extradition (Provisional Arrest) Act 2020
EU	European Union
EVie	Evidence via the internet hearings
FD	Framework Decision on the European Arrest Warrant
GLD	Government Legal Department
HMCTS	Her Majesty's Courts and Tribunals Service
HRA 1998	Human Rights Act 1998
ICC	International Criminal Court
IJO	International Jurisdiction Office
INTERPOL	International Criminal Police Organization
LAA	Legal Aid Agency
LASPO 2012	Legal Aid, Sentencing and Punishment of Offenders Act 2012

LCJ	Lord Chief Justice
MoU	memorandum of understanding
NCA	National Crime Agency
NCB	National Central Bureau
NEU	National Extradition Unit
NGO	non-governmental organisation
NRM	National Referral Mechanism
PACE 1984	Police and Criminal Evidence Act 1984
PNC	Police National Computer
PSI	prison service instruction
QC	Queen's Counsel
RPA 1984	Repatriation of Prisoners Act 1984
SCCO	Senior Courts Cost Office
SIS II	Schengen Information System II
SSHD	Secretary of State for the Home Department
TCA	Trade and Cooperation Agreement
UKHTC	UK Human Trafficking Centre
WMC	Westminster Magistrates' Court

CHAPTER 1

Introduction

What is extradition?

1.1 Extradition is the formal process whereby a *requesting state* asks a *requested state* to return an individual who is in the requested state in order to stand trial or to serve a custodial sentence imposed in the requesting state. While extradition hearings are heard at first instance in the magistrates' court and are subject to the Criminal Procedure Rules (CrimPR), they do not involve the determination of a criminal charge and are therefore exceptional.[1]

Extradition arrangements

1.2 The Extradition Act (EA) 2003 governs extradition proceedings in the United Kingdom (UK). It came into force on 1 January 2004. It was enacted to address the increasingly international nature of crime,[2] giving effect to the Framework Decision on the European Arrest Warrant (EAW FD) of 13 June 2002[3] and bringing about significant changes to the way extradition was dealt with in respect of requests from outside the European Union (EU). Since its enactment, it has been amended several times. The most recent change was brought about as a result of the UK's departure from the EU, in the European Union (Future Relationship) Act 2020. This book sets out the law that applies to persons arrested after 11 pm on 31 December 2020. For those arrested pursuant to requests from the EU prior to that, the previous EAW arrangements will apply.[4]

1.3 The only court of first instance that hears extradition cases is Westminster Magistrates' Court (WMC). There is a separate extradition rota for duty solicitors at the court. Each day, three duty solicitors[5] are allocated and they are expected to represent those produced at court who have not arranged their own representation following arrest.

1 See Dr Paul Arnell, 'What an extradition hearing is and why it matters' (2018) 4, *Juridical Review* 250–268 which designates extradition hearings as 'sui generis, quasi-criminal proceedings affected by international considerations' at p251. The CrimPR and Criminal Practice Directions (CrimPD) are available here: www.gov.uk/guidance/rules-and-practice-directions-2020#rules-and-practice-directions-contents.

2 EA 2003 Explanatory Notes at para 6.

3 2002/584/JHA: Council Framework Decision of 13 June 2002 on the European Arrest Warrant and the surrender procedures between member states.

4 For such cases, practitioners are referred to earlier editions of this book.

5 Correct at the time of writing.

Extradition controversy

1.4 The EA 2003 has not been without its controversies. In particular, the EAW scheme was criticised for overuse. It was said to have been abused, with instances of EAWs being issued for 'trivial' offences. The new arrangements under the 2021 Trade and Cooperation Agreement[6] (TCA) introduce a foundational principle of proportionality[7] in what appears to be an attempt to address these criticisms. The removal of the principle of 'mutual trust and recognition' which was a cornerstone of the EAW scheme will also be welcomed by some of its critics. At the time of writing, the effects of the changes wrought by the TCA are yet to be fully understood, but it is worth noting that although these changes may be seen as significant, the reality is that the new arrangements under the TCA will be very familiar to extradition practitioners: the surrender provisions of the TCA required very few amendments to the EA 2003, and many of the provisions in the TCA are effectively unchanged from those set out in the EAW FD.

1.5 The US–UK extradition arrangements have also come under attack from opponents who maintain that they are one-sided and do not afford British citizens sufficient protection. The controversy follows the absence of the prima facie case requirement (not just for the US, but also for a number of other countries – see para 8.79), along with the perception of an exorbitant jurisdiction on the part of US prosecutors and criticisms of both the plea bargaining system and harsh sentencing practice in the US. The introduction of the forum bar in October 2014 was an attempt to address these concerns, however complaints about an imbalance remain, and the forum bar has been subject to considerable criticism.[8]

1.6 A further area of significant controversy is the practice of accepting diplomatic assurances from requesting states where doubt has been raised about their ability to ensure a requested person's fundamental rights are protected. While assurances are seen as vital in

6 Trade and Cooperation Agreement between the European Union and the European Atomic Energy Community, of the one part, and the United Kingdom of Great Britain and Northern Ireland, of the other part, Document 22021A0430(01), 30 April 2021, https://eur-lex.europa.eu/legal-content/EN/TXT/?uri=uriserv:OJ.L_.2021.149.01.0010.01.ENG.

7 See TCA Article 597.

8 See, for example: Paul Arnell and Gemma Davies: 'The forum bar in UK extradition law: an unnecessary failure' (2020) 84(2) *Journal of Criminal Law* 142–162.

allowing the extradition system to continue to function, they have been widely criticised on both legal and policy grounds. Some commentators have pointed to the fact that assurances in effect give states permission to continue to violate human rights standards, and create a two-tier system of protection of fundamental rights.[9] Nevertheless, there is no doubt that assurances are firmly entrenched: in a recent Supreme Court decision, they were said to be 'not merely normal but indispensable in the operation of English law'.[10] Moreover, the TCA includes an express provision for the use of assurances in cases where there are substantial grounds for believing that there is a real risk to the fundamental rights of the requested person.

Extradition Act 2003

Overview

1.7 The EA 2003 is split into five parts and contains five schedules. The parts are:

Part 1 – Extradition to category 1 territories (known as 'Part 1 cases' or 'arrest warrant (AW) cases');
Part 2 – Extradition to category 2 territories (known as 'Part 2 cases');
Part 3 – Extradition to the UK;
Part 4 – Police powers;
Part 5 – Miscellaneous and general provisions.

Part 1 and Part 2 requests for extradition

1.8 The UK has extradition arrangements with over 100 territories. EA 2003 Part 1 warrants (referred to as 'AW cases') are the most common types of request.

1.9 The following territories have been designated category 1 territories and all issue AWs:

9 See, for example, the 'Report of the Special Rapporteur on torture and other cruel, inhuman or degrading treatment or punishment, UN Doc A/HRC/37/50, 23 November 2018 at para 47: 'even if diplomatic assurances were to be faithfully implemented by the receiving State, they reflect the expectation that the receiving State will comply only selectively with the prohibition of torture and ill-treatment, and the deporting State's acquiescence in this regard, thus severely jeopardizing one of the most fundamental norms of international law and squarely contradicting the principles and purposes of the United Nations'.

10 *Zabolotnyi v Mateszalka District Court, Hungary* [2021] UKSC 14.

Austria, Belgium, Bulgaria, Croatia, Cyprus, Czech Republic, Denmark, Estonia, Finland, France, Germany, Gibraltar, Greece, Hungary, Ireland, Italy, Latvia, Lithuania, Luxembourg, Malta, Netherlands, Poland, Portugal, Romania, Slovakia, Slovenia, Spain and Sweden.

1.10 Part 2 territories include the following:

Albania, Algeria, Andorra, Anguilla, Antigua and Barbuda, Argentina, Armenia, Aruba, Australia, Azerbaijan, The Bahamas, Bangladesh, Barbados, Belize, Bermuda, Bolivia, Bonaire, Bosnia and Herzegovina, Botswana, Brazil, British Antarctic Territory, British Indian Ocean Territory, Brunei, Canada, Cayman Islands, Chile, Colombia, Cook Islands, Cuba, Curaçao, Dominica, Ecuador, El Salvador, Falkland Islands, Faroe Islands, Fiji, The Gambia, Georgia, Ghana, Greenland, Grenada, Guatemala, Guyana, Hong Kong Special Administrative Region, Haiti, Iceland, India, Iraq, Israel, Jamaica, Kenya, Kiribati, Kosovo, Kuwait, Lesotho, Liberia, Libya, Liechtenstein, Malawi, Malaysia, Maldives, Mauritius, Mexico, Moldova, Monaco, Montenegro, Montserrat, Morocco, Nauru, New Zealand, Nicaragua, Nigeria, North Macedonia, Norway, Panama, Papua New Guinea, Paraguay, Peru, Philippines, Pitcairn, Henderson, Ducie and Oeno Islands, Republic of Korea, Russian Federation, Saba, Saint Christopher and Nevis, St Helena, Ascension and Tristan da Cunha, Saint Lucia, Saint Vincent and the Grenadines, San Marino, Serbia, Seychelles, Sierra Leone, Singapore, Sint Eustatius, Sint Maarten, Solomon Islands, South Africa, South Georgia and the South Sandwich Islands, The Sovereign Base Areas of Akrotiri and Dhekalia, Sri Lanka, Swaziland, Switzerland, Tanzania, Thailand, Tonga, Trinidad and Tobago, Turkey, Turks and Caicos Islands, Tuvalu, Uganda, Ukraine, United Arab Emirates, United States, Uruguay, Vanuatu, Virgin Islands, Western Samoa, Zambia, Zimbabwe.

1.11 It is a common misconception that extradition cannot take place in the absence of an extradition treaty. This is not the case. If a country does not appear above in the above lists, an extradition request can still be made. Those countries that are not extradition treaty partners with the UK can make extradition requests and be treated as if they were a category 2 territory by entering into a memorandum of understanding (MoU) with the UK. These arrangements are known as 'ad hoc arrangements' (see chapter 8, paras 8.5–8.7).

Extradition proceedings: participants

1.12 The following key participants play a part in extradition proceedings in England and Wales:

- Crown Prosecution Service (CPS) Extradition Unit;
- National Crime Agency (NCA);
- Home Office;
- Government Legal Department (GLD);
- National Extradition Unit (NEU);
- WMC;
- Administrative Court;
- Supreme Court; and
- extradition defence lawyers.

Crown Prosecution Service

1.13 The Director of Public Prosecutions (DPP) has a duty to conduct extradition proceedings.[11] The CPS acts as the representative of the requesting state. The Extradition Unit is part of the International Justice and Organised Crime Division. It need not apply the Code for Crown Prosecutors in extradition proceedings.

1.14 The role of the CPS can include providing advice to foreign states on the preparation of an extradition request; advising foreign states on the content and validity of an extradition request received from the NCA/Home Office; representing judicial authorities/requesting states in proceedings before WMC, the High Court and the Supreme Court; and advising foreign states on the merits of an appeal. Those representing the requesting state/judicial authority are referred to in the CrimPR as 'presenting officers'.[12]

1.15 It is possible for the requesting state to instruct a private firm of solicitors to act on its behalf under Prosecution of Offences Act 1985 s3(2A). At the time of writing, this has only happened once since the EA 2003 came into force.[13]

National Crime Agency

1.16 The NCA is the central authority designated to receive AWs. The NCA certifies AWs in accordance with EA 2003 s2 (including a

11 Prosecution of Offences Act 1985 s3(2)(ea).

12 CrimPR 50.2.

13 *Ukraine v Kononko* [2014] EWHC 1420 (Admin).

proportionality exercise in accusation cases) and facilitates communication between the CPS and the issuing judicial authority. The NCA will also arrange for the surrender of those whose extradition has been ordered by the courts in AW cases.

1.17 The National Central Bureau of INTERPOL (the International Criminal Police Organization) is part of the NCA. The NCA is the designated authority for issuing a certificate in part 2 cases to allow for a provisional arrest to take place without a warrant (see chapter 8, para 8.10).

Home Office – Extradition Section, UK Central Authority (for Part 2 cases)

1.18 The Secretary of State for the Home Department (SSHD) is responsible for certifying extradition requests from Part 2 territories and all extradition requests are received at the Home Office Extradition Section for processing. The Extradition Section will facilitate requests for further information. They are also responsible for arranging removal in Part 2 cases. The SSHD plays an important role in Part 2 cases.

Government Legal Department

1.19 The GLD is a non-ministerial government department that provides legal services to the majority of central government departments.[14] The GLD acts as private solicitor for the SSHD in extradition cases when the SSHD is a party to the proceedings.

The National Extradition Unit

1.20 The NEU takes responsibility for all new extradition requests. The NEU will liaise with local police forces in the arrests of those whose extradition are sought. Any correspondence for the NEU (for example, to arrange for voluntary attendance for arrest) should be sent to nationalextradition@met.police.uk. The main office number for the NEU is 0300 790 0000.

14 See: www.gov.uk/government/organisations/government-legal-department and can be contacted by emailing westminster.ij@justice.gov.uk.

Westminster Magistrates' Court

1.21 Extradition proceedings can be conducted at any court where an 'appropriate judge' is sitting. However, at the time of writing, all cases are heard at WMC. The International Jurisdiction Office (IJO) at WMC deals with the administration of extradition cases and can be contacted by emailing westminster.ij@justice.gov.uk.

1.22 Extradition hearings will always be heard before specially trained district judges (known as 'appropriate judges'). A district judge is designated an appropriate judge by the Lord Chief Justice of England and Wales after consulting the Lord Chancellor.[15] The current Senior District Judge (Chief Magistrate) is Paul Goldspring and the Deputy Senior District Judge (Deputy Chief Magistrate) is Tanweer Ikram.

Administrative Court

1.23 Appeals under the EA 2003 are heard in the Administrative Court, Royal Courts of Justice, London. Appeals are heard by a single judge or by a Divisional Court made up of two or three judges, one of whom will be a Lord/Lady Justice. The Lord Justice with overall supervision of extradition appeals is Lord Justice Holroyde.[16]

1.24 Each appeal case is allocated to a lawyer at the Administrative Court who will be the initial contact for enquiries regarding the case. The Administrative Court also hears appeals against the refusal/grant of bail by WMC.

Supreme Court

1.25 In October 2009, the Supreme Court superseded the Appellate Committee of the House of Lords as the highest court in the UK. An appeal can only be brought to the Supreme Court if the High Court has certified that there is a point of law of general public importance and where the High Court or the Supreme Court has granted leave to appeal.

1.26 The Supreme Court has 12 justices and the President of the Supreme Court is Lord Reed.[17]

15 EA 2003 s139(1)(a).
16 As at time of writing.
17 Since 20 January 2020.

Extradition defence lawyers

1.27 Those arrested under the EA 2003 are very often represented at the first court appearance by the duty solicitor. It is imperative that they receive competent advice and representation from a solicitor who is knowledgeable in extradition law.

1.28 The following chapters will go some way to providing practitioners with the foundations needed to adequately represent 'requested persons'[18] in extradition proceedings.

Practitioners' associations

1.29 There are several useful networks of extradition lawyers from which practitioners may benefit, including the Defence Extradition Lawyers' Forum (DELF: www.delf.org.uk), the Extradition Lawyers' Association (ELA: www.extradition-lawyers.co.uk) and the European Criminal Bar Association (ECBA: www.ecba.org).

18 Crim PR 50.1(5)(c) refers to 'requested persons' as the 'defendant'. This book will use the phrase 'requested person' to refer to those arrested under EA 2003 Part 1 or Part 2.

CHAPTER 2

Practical considerations

Introduction

2.1 This chapter looks at practical matters for lawyers acting on behalf of those making their first appearance at the magistrates' court in extradition cases and, in particular, duty solicitors. It looks first at police powers and the arrest of a requested person, and goes on to describe a typical day of the duty solicitor in the extradition courts.

Arrest

2.2 A solicitor will often have minimal involvement when a requested person is first arrested. Police powers in extradition cases are governed by Part 4 of the Extradition Act (EA) 2003. The EA 2003 Codes of Practice[1] set out the police powers that may be relied upon in extradition cases, additional to the common law powers of the police. On arrest, the police have the power to search both the person (section 163) and the premises (section 162) and to seize and retain material (sections 162 and 165) for material specified within those sections. The police may also apply for a warrant for search and seizure (section 156). They have a power to enter and search premises to effect an arrest (section 161).

2.3 The police will generally ask the requested person to identify themselves and seek to obtain evidence of their identity. Upon arrest, the police will caution the requested person. Anything that the requested person says (for example, 'Oh yes, I know all about this, it's the burglary that I committed in Krakow in 2018') will be noted and may be used in subsequent proceedings.

2.4 The right of access to legal advice at the police station under Police and Criminal Evidence Act 1984 (PACE) s58 applies to those arrested in extradition cases.[2] However, for the vast majority of those requested persons who are unable to pay for legal advice, this will be limited to telephone advice. Given that the police do not interview requested persons, it is unlikely that physical attendance at the police station would pass the 'sufficient benefit' test as set out in the 2017 Standard Crime Contract provisions. The requested person will also

1 Home Office, February 2021, https://assets.publishing.service.gov.uk/government/uploads/system/uploads/attachment_data/file/963549/CCS001_CCS0221079802-001_Extradition_Act_2003_CoP_Web_Accessible.pdf.

2 EA 2003 s171(3)(d).

have the right to have someone informed of their arrest, and, if necessary, will have access to an interpreter.

2.5 A person cannot be granted bail by the police when arrested on an arrest warrant (AW), however the police may grant bail to a person arrested under EA 2003 Part 2 (EA 2003 ss72(4)(a) and 74(4)(a)). Where a person is held in custody following arrest, they must be brought before a court as soon as practicable.[3]

The duty solicitor's day

2.6 Unlike general criminal matters, it is unusual for those making their first appearance after an arrest under the EA 2003 to have their own solicitor. Many arrested will require the assistance of an interpreter.

2.7 The duty solicitor's day in the extradition courts can be a busy one. It is not unusual for the duty solicitor to be fully occupied throughout the day and until or after 6 pm. There are four extradition court rooms at Westminster Magistrates' Court (WMC) and some have different functions. The court's work is generally separated as follows:

- court 1 – full extradition hearings;
- court 2 – full extradition hearings;
- court 3 – video-link remand hearings, short hearings and initial hearings;
- court 4 – full extradition hearings.

2.8 The magistrates' court at Westminster sits at 10 am. Duty solicitors should arrive at 9 am and sign in at the first-floor enquiries counter. Although the first hour or so may be quiet, requested persons arrive throughout the day, and any preparation that has been done before the court begins to sit will be useful later on in the day when it is likely to be very busy. It is important that duty solicitors make themselves known to the list caller in court 3 and to the Crown Prosecution Service (CPS) so that all the extradition work is handed to them. While those arrested on an AW or extradition request will occasionally have their own solicitor, the majority will not. It is therefore advisable to obtain the AWs/extradition requests from the CPS early on in the day to allow time to properly consider them (see chapter 3 and chapter 8). The CPS should also provide a statement from the

3 EA 2003 s4(3) for Part 1 cases and s72(3) for Part 2 cases (s74(3) for provisional arrest requests).

arresting officer and the requested person's record of previous convictions. The prosecution may be found in the extradition courts, or outside the courtrooms just before they open. They also have an unmarked office on the first floor of the courthouse in the corridor opposite courts 3 and 4, which is attended throughout the day by CPS caseworkers.

2.9 It is good practice for the duty solicitor to make themselves known to the jailers. By attending the cells, one can garner a considerable amount of information from the whiteboard that shows who is in custody and who is expected to be brought in to custody. The whiteboard displays information that can help in this regard. In particular, it will show the police station or prison from which the person is coming. If a person is coming from a police station or prison that is not in London, it is very likely that the person will have been arrested pursuant to an extradition request/AW. The gaolers should be able to give an indication of when the person is expected to arrive. Once the person has arrived, the gaolers will ask them whether an interpreter is required, and will note that information on the board. The cells are closed between 1 pm and 1.45 pm. This time can usefully be used for reading AWs, speaking to family members about bail arrangements or completing legal aid forms.

2.10 Because requested persons are arrested all over the country, they will arrive throughout the day until the 'referral time',[4] which is 3.30 pm. Any persons arriving after that time will be referred to the judge, who will decide whether or not they will be accepted by the jailers, or whether they will be detained in a local police station overnight to appear at court the following day. It is possible, therefore, to have a very quiet morning as duty solicitor, but to have a number of clients in the afternoon. Generally, if there are more than four extradition clients per duty solicitor who require advice and representation, the court will ask another duty solicitor to assist. If it is apparent that there are a large number of cases to deal with, it is wise to seek assistance at an early stage. In every case, there is a significant amount of important information to convey to, and obtain from, the requested person and, particularly where an interpreter is required, this can take some time. In addition, it will often take time to obtain the information required for a bail application, such as a bail surety or security, a suitable address, location of identity documents, or the nearest police station for a reporting condition. Some

4 While sometimes called the 'cut-off time', 'referral time' is a more accurate description: not all those arriving after 3.30 pm will be turned away.

of this information may come from third parties, such as family members. Duty solicitors should allow a minimum of 45 minutes for every client, allowing time for completion of legal aid and case management forms. Although there is sometimes pressure from the court, it is important that the necessary time is spent looking at the warrant and advising the client. A failure to explain something at this stage, or to ask a particular question, could mean that a person is wrongly extradited.

2.11 If it is apparent that a client requires an interpreter for a language other than Polish, Lithuanian or Romanian, it is important that this is made known to the list caller as soon as possible. In theory, the court should be notified by the arresting police officers that an interpreter is needed, but this frequently fails to happen and, for more unusual languages, it can take hours for an interpreter to arrive. If no interpreter has been booked, the legal adviser should make arrangements to book one by notifying the International Jurisdiction Office (IJO). At the time of writing, all interpreters are provided to the court by one company under contract. The quality of interpreters varies greatly, and solicitors should be alive to the possibility that the interpreter that has been provided may be inexperienced or unfamiliar with the terminology used in extradition cases.

2.12 New cases are likely to be heard in court 3 after the video-link remand hearings have been concluded. Any overflow will go to any other available extradition court room.

2.13 Legal aid forms can be submitted online, on the Legal Aid Agency (LAA) portal. They should be submitted on the day of the requested person's first appearance to ensure that any work done thereafter is covered. A requested person in custody should not have to provide evidence of income and, as long as the form is fully completed and they are financially eligible,[5] legal aid will be granted in the interests of justice for all extradition cases.

2.14 Ideally, following the hearing the client should be seen and the outcome explained. This is often impracticable when dealing with several clients in succession in court. One may find at the end of the day that the client has been taken to prison before it has been possible to see them again. For this reason it is important to ensure that all matters, including appeal procedures, are covered before the court appearance.

5 Occasionally, the LAA may query how a requested person was supporting him or herself before being remanded in custody.

Live-link hearings

2.15 During the coronavirus pandemic of 2020, live-links were heavily relied upon to keep the courts running. Temporary powers[6] to direct live link attendance in extradition cases were given to the court by way of Coronavirus Act 2020 s54 and Sch 24, amending EA 2003 ss206A–206C. A direction for live-link attendance may be made on application or of the court's own motion,[7] where the judge is satisfied that it is not contrary to the interests of justice to give a direction.[8] See appendix G for procedural guidance issued by the Chief Magistrate.

Essential materials

2.16 Duty solicitors in the extradition court should have access to:

- a sufficient number of forms CRM14, CRM15 and the declaration for online submissions;
- an updated copy of the EA 2003, Criminal Procedure Rules (CrimPR) 2020 and Criminal Practice Directions (CrimPD);[9]
- this book;
- copies of checklists as set out in appendices D–F.

6 For the two years starting from 25 March 2020.
7 EA 2003 s206A(4).
8 EA 2003 s206A(5).
9 The CrimPR and CrimPD are available here: www.gov.uk/guidance/rules-and-practice-directions-2020#rules-and-practice-directions-contents.

CHAPTER 3

Looking at a Trade and Cooperation Agreement arrest warrant

continued

Introduction

3.1 The purpose of the Framework Decision (FD) of 2002, which created the European Arrest Warrant (EAW) scheme, was to simplify and facilitate extradition procedures across European Union (EU) countries. When the implementation period following the departure of the United Kingdom (UK) from the EU ended, on 31 December 2020, an arrangement which broadly follows the EAW scheme (and required minimal amendment to the Extradition Act (EA) 2003 and the model warrant form) replaced it.

3.2 The new arrangements can be found in the Trade and Cooperation Agreement (TCA) (see appendix B), Part III, Title VII entitled 'Surrender'.[1] The model TCA arrest warrant (AW) form is annexed to the TCA at Annex 43 'Arrest Warrant'. Like the EAW form, its purpose is to ensure that all of the relevant information required is included by the judicial authority. It should, however, be noted that if the form is incorrectly filled out – for example, if there are boxes that are not filled in – this does not in itself invalidate the warrant.[2]

3.3 This chapter will look at the warrant and at each box of the form as set out in appendix C. It will look at challenges to the validity of the warrant, along with extradition offences.

EAW case-law

3.4 The new AW arrangements largely follow those in place for the EAW, and much of the significant body of case-law in relation to the EAW will apply to AWs. Practitioners should, however, approach this case-law with caution: the mutual trust under which the EAW FD operated was frequently relied on by the court as a basis for ordering

1 Trade and Cooperation Agreement between the European Union and the European Atomic Energy Community, of the one part, and the United Kingdom of Great Britain and Northern Ireland, of the other part, Document 22021A0430(01), 30 April 2021, https://eur-lex.europa.eu/legal-content/EN/TXT/?uri=uriserv:OJ.L_.2021.149.01.0010.01.ENG. TCA is an international agreement and its provisions have not been directly incorporated into domestic law. Where there are differences between the provisions set out in the TCA and the EA 2003 as amended, it is the domestic legislation which is the correct starting point for any legal analysis (*Polakowski v Westminster Magistrates' Court and others* [2021] EWHC 53 (Admin)).

2 See para 3.31 and following below, for the circumstances in which a warrant may be held to be invalid.

extradition in spite of factual errors or omissions in an EAW.[3] The TCA contains no explicit reference to mutual trust or mutual recognition, but states that cooperation 'is based on the ... long-standing respect for democracy, the rule of law and the protection of fundamental rights and freedoms of individuals'.[4] The extent to which, in the absence of an explicit reference to mutual trust or mutual recognition, the courts will be willing to order extradition in respect of AWs with errors and/or omissions is something to keep under review.

The TCA Arrest Warrant

Certification by the National Crime Agency

3.5 AWs in the UK are received by the National Crime Agency (NCA) as the designated authority under EA 2003 s2(9). The NCA has the function of certifying the AW; the certificate is then attached to the front of the warrant.

3.6 According to EA 2003 s2, the NCA must check that the warrant has been issued by a judicial authority of the requesting state and that it contains the following information:

- a statement that the person in respect of whom the warrant is issued is accused/convicted of an offence specified in the warrant and that it has been issued with a view to their arrest and extradition for the purpose of conducting a prosecution or executing a custodial sentence;
- particulars of the person's identity;
- (in the case of a conviction warrant) particulars of the conviction;
- particulars of any other warrant issued in the category 1 territory for the person's arrest in respect of the offence;
- (in the case of an accusation warrant) particulars of the circumstances in which the person is alleged to have committed the offence, including the conduct alleged to constitute the offence, the time and place at which they are alleged to have committed the offence and any provision of the law of the category 1 territory under which the conduct is alleged to constitute an offence;

3 See, for example, *Zakrzewski v The Regional Court in Lodz, Poland* [2013] UKSC 2 at para 10.

4 TCA Article 524(1).

- particulars of the sentence that may be imposed under the law of the category 1 territory in respect of the offence if the person is convicted of it/has not been sentenced; and
- (in the case of a sentenced person) particulars of the sentence that has been imposed.

3.7 If the warrant contains this information and the NCA believes that the authority which issued the AW has the function of issuing arrest warrants in the category 1 territory,[5] the NCA may issue a certificate. See para 3.39 regarding the definition of 'judicial authority'.

3.8 The NCA must not certify an AW if the Secretary of State for the Home Department (SSHD) believes that the conditions set out in EA 2003 s208(2)–(4) relating to national security are satisfied.

3.9 The certificate will give the date on which the requesting state issued the AW and the date on which it was certified by the NCA. It should also be signed and dated; an electronic signature, or the initials of the person certifying, are sufficient for this purpose. Once the warrant has been certified, it may be executed by a police officer or a customs officer in any part of the UK.[6]

Proportionality check by the National Crime Agency

3.10 The NCA must refuse to certify an AW if it would be clear to them that a judge proceeding under EA 2003 s21A would be required to order a person's discharge on the basis that extradition would be disproportionate (see para 6.64 regarding EA 2003 s21A). While the TCA emphasises the principle of proportionality in general, and provides for it as a ground for non-execution of an AW, the EA 2003 currently confines the consideration of proportionality to accusation warrants.[7]

3.11 In determining this question, the NCA must apply any general guidance issued by the Lord Chief Justice ('LCJ guidance').[8] This guidance sets out the type of offences for which a judge (absent exceptional circumstances) should generally determine that extradition would be disproportionate. The table of offences can be found at Criminal Practice Direction (CrimPD) 50A.5 and is set out opposite.

5 EA 2003 s2(7).
6 EA 2003 s3.
7 EA 2003 s2(7A).
8 EA 2003 s2(7C). Note, however, that proportionality may be raised in conviction cases where Article 8 ECHR is engaged: see para 6.53.

Table 3.1 Offences for which extradition will normally be disproportionate

Category of offence	Examples
Minor theft – (not robbery/burglary or theft from the person)	Where the theft is of a low monetary value and there is a low impact on the victim or indirect harm to others, for example: (a) Theft of an item of food from a supermarket (b) Theft of a small amount of scrap metal from company premises (c) Theft of a very small sum of money
Minor financial offences (**forgery**, **fraud** and **tax** offences)	Where the sums involved are small and there is a low impact on the victim and/or low indirect harm to others, for example: (a) Failure to file a tax return or invoices on time (b) Making a false statement in a tax return (c) Dishonestly applying for a tax refund (d) Obtaining a bank loan using a forged or falsified document (e) Non-payment of child maintenance
Minor **road traffic**, **driving** and related offences	Where no injury, loss or damage was incurred to any person or property, for example: (a) Driving whilst using a mobile phone (b) Use of a bicycle whilst intoxicated
Minor **public order** offences	Where there is no suggestion the person started the trouble, and the offending behaviour was for example: (a) Non-threatening verbal abuse of a law enforcement officer or government official (b) Shouting or causing a disturbance, without threats (c) Quarrelling in the street, without threats
Minor **criminal damage**, (other than by fire)	For example, breaking a window
Possession of controlled substance (other than one with a high capacity for harm such as heroin, cocaine, LSD or crystal meth)	Where it was possession of a very small quantity and intended for personal use

3.12 The exceptional circumstances (referred to in CrimPD 50A.3) are listed at CrimPD 50A.4 and include:

- vulnerable victim;
- crime committed against someone because of their disability, gender-identity, race, religion or belief, or sexual orientation;
- significant premeditation;
- multiple counts;
- extradition also sought for another offence;
- previous offending history.

3.13 Practitioners will be aware that at least one of the last three factors will very frequently be present. If any of these circumstances are present, the NCA is likely to certify the AW despite the offence being one that falls within the LCJ's guidance.

Statement of purpose and Box A

3.14 The first page of the TCA AW will usually contain the statement of purpose along with information required to identify the requested person, which is set out in box A.

(a) Information regarding the identity of the requested person:

Name:

Forename(s):

Maiden name, where applicable:

Aliases, where applicable:

Sex:

Nationality:

Date of birth:

Place of birth:

Residence and/or known address:

Language(s) which the requested person understands (if known):

Distinctive marks/description of the requested person:

Photo and fingerprints of the requested person, if they are available and can be transmitted, or contact details of the person to be contacted in order to obtain such information or a DNA profile (where this evidence can be supplied but has not been included).

3.15 In theory, the statement of purpose will be different for accused or convicted persons (see EA 2003 s2(3) and (5)), but in practice warrants will contain the standard statement set out in the pro forma, which states:

> This warrant has been issued by a competent judicial authority. I request that the person mentioned below be arrested and surrendered for the purposes of conducting a criminal prosecution or executing a custodial sentence or detention order.

In order to determine whether the AW has been issued for an accusation or following conviction, it will, therefore, be necessary to look at the warrant as a whole, but in particular boxes B and C. Practitioners should note that a failure to delete the inapplicable part of the pro forma does not invalidate the AW. For the principles to be applied by the court when seeking to characterise a case as an accusation or a conviction case, see *Konecny v District Court in Brno-Venkov, Czech Republic*[9] at para 50.

3.16 Box A sets out information that enables the authorities to identify the requested person. Frequently some fields in this box will be left blank. This will not invalidate the warrant, but the name of the requested person and the date of birth will clearly be essential in order to ensure that the correct person is arrested.

Box B

(b) Decision on which the warrant is based:

1. Arrest warrant or judicial decision having the same effect:

....

Type:

....

2. Enforceable judgment:

....

Reference:

....

3.17 Box B requires the judicial authority to state the decision on which the warrant is based, and will either be:

9 [2019] UKSC 8.

- an 'arrest warrant or judicial decision having the same effect' (in the case of an accusation warrant); or
- an 'enforceable judgment' (in the case of a conviction warrant).

It is from this box, therefore, that it will usually be possible to determine whether the requested person is being accused or has been convicted. An AW may be issued for multiple offences and the Extradition Act 2003 (Multiple Offences) Order 2003 SI No 3150 provides that any reference in the EA 2003 to 'an offence' is to be construed as a reference to 'offences', unless the context requires otherwise. In some cases, the requested person will be wanted for both accusation and conviction offences and the judicial authority will, therefore, have to provide both sets of information. These AWs are known as 'hybrid warrants'.

3.18 The judicial authority should state the type of decision along with its date and the case reference. See para 3.57 below, and the decision in *Edutanu v Romania*.[10]

Box C

> **(c) Indications on the length of the sentence:**
>
> 1. Maximum length of the custodial sentence or detention order which may be imposed for the offence(s):
>
> ....
>
> 2. Length of the custodial sentence or detention order imposed:
>
> ....
>
> Remaining sentence to be served:
>
> ....

3.19 Box C will contain information regarding either (in the case of (1) above) the maximum custodial sentence or, in the case of (2) above, the length of the sentence imposed and the remaining sentence to be served. As with box B, it is divided into two sections, which should correspond with those in the box above (ie if (1) is completed in box B, it should also be (1) that is filled in for box C).

3.20 The function of this box is to ensure that the offences for which the warrant has been issued meet the minimum requirements for the punishment threshold: that is, for those yet to be sentenced, an

10 [2016] EWHC 124 (Admin).

offence that carries imprisonment of 12 months or more, or, in the case of requested persons who have been sentenced, an offence for which the person has been sentenced to a term of four months' imprisonment or more. It is the sentence that will be imposed in the requesting state that is determinative, and not the sentence in the requested state. This means that, unlike in Part 2 cases, a person can be extradited for an offence that does not carry a sentence of imprisonment in this country, as long as the minimum sentence in the requesting state is 12 months (for those yet to be sentenced) and four months (for sentenced persons).[11]

3.21 Box C also allows the judicial authority to state the remaining sentence to be served.[12] The idea of an outstanding sentence to be served may be unfamiliar to many UK criminal practitioners who see their clients serving sentences immediately and then being released at the halfway point without returning to prison (apart from in very specific circumstances, such as breach of licence, or bail granted pending an appeal).

3.22 Many European countries, however, allow those sentenced for offences to be released part-way through their sentence, with a requirement to return to prison at a date in the future. Some countries do not imprison people immediately following a sentence, but require them to surrender themselves to serve a sentence when notified. A very large proportion of Polish EAWs were issued in respect of those who breached the Polish equivalent of a suspended sentence or licence, and were therefore required to serve a sentence of imprisonment. While the minimum period of imprisonment required for a warrant to be issued for sentenced prisoners is four months, there is no requirement for a minimum period to remain (of a sentence to be served) in order for an AW to be issued. It is, therefore, theoretically possible for a person's extradition to be sought in order to serve a remaining sentence of, for example, one month as long as the original sentence was longer than four months. Such a case, however, may be open to challenge on the grounds that it would amount to a disproportionate interference with the requested person's rights under European

11 TCA Article 599(4) provides a list of offences for which dual criminality will not be required, if either the UK or the EU make a notification. Different minimum sentence periods will apply to those offences, if such a notification is made (see para 3.64 below).

12 In relation to EAWs, a failure to complete this part of box C or an error as to the amount of time left to serve did not invalidate the warrant: *Banasinski v District Court in Sanok, Poland* [2008] EWHC 3626 (Admin), approved in *Lis v Regional Court in Rzeszow, Poland* [2014] EWHC 3226 (Admin).

Convention on Human Rights (ECHR) Article 8 (right to respect for one's private and family life, home and correspondence). See para 3.53 below regarding the requirement to state particulars of the sentence.

Box D

(d) Indicate if the person appeared in person at the trial resulting in the decision:

1. ☐ Yes, the person appeared in person at the trial resulting in the decision.

2. ☐ No, the person did not appear in person at the trial resulting in the decision.

3. If you have ticked the box under point 2, please confirm the existence of one of the following, if applicable:

☐ 3.1a the person was summoned in person on ... (day/month/year) and thereby informed of the scheduled date and place of the trial which resulted in the decision and was informed that a decision may be handed down if he or she does not appear for the trial;

OR

☐ 3.1b the person was not summoned in person but by other means actually received official information of the scheduled date and place of the trial which resulted in the decision, in such a manner that it was unequivocally established that he or she was aware of the scheduled trial, and was informed that a decision may be handed down if he or she does not appear for the trial;

OR

☐ 3.2 being aware of the scheduled trial the person had given a mandate to a legal counsellor, who was either appointed by the person concerned or by the State, to defend him or her at the trial, and was indeed defended by that counsellor at the trial;

OR

☐ 3.3 the person was served with the decision on ... (day/month/year) and was expressly informed about the right to a retrial or appeal, in which he or she has the right to participate and which allows the merits of the case, including fresh evidence, to be re-examined, and which may lead to the original decision being reversed, and

☐ the person expressly stated that he or she does not contest this decision;

OR

☐ the person did not request a retrial or appeal within the applicable timeframe;

OR

☐ 3.4 the person was not personally served with the decision, but

– the person will be personally served with this decision without delay after the surrender; and

– when served with the decision, the person will be expressly informed of his or her right to a retrial or appeal, in which he or she has the right to participate and which allows the merits of the case, including fresh evidence, to be re-examined, and which may lead to the original decision being reversed; and

– the person will be informed of the timeframe within which he or she has to request a retrial or appeal, which will be ..... days.

4. If you have ticked the box under point 3.1b, 3.2 or 3.3 above, please provide information about how the relevant condition has been met:

....

3.23 Box D is used in conviction cases only to give details of the requested person's right to a retrial where they have been convicted in absentia (see para 5.88). It will be necessary for the court to be satisfied to the criminal standard that a requested person who was not deliberately absent but convicted in absence will have a right to a retrial.

Box E

(e) Offences:

This warrant relates to in total: .... offences.

Description of the circumstances in which the offence(s) was (were) committed, including the time, place and degree of participation in the offence(s) by the requested person:

....

Nature and legal classification of the offence(s) and the applicable statutory provision/code:

....

I. The following applies only in case both the issuing and executing State have made a notification under Article 599(4) [Scope] of the Agreement: if applicable, tick one or more of the following offences, as defined by the law of the issuing State, punishable in the issuing State by a custodial sentence or detention order of a maximum of at least three years:

☐ participation in a criminal organisation,

☐ terrorism as defined in Annex 45 of the Agreement,

☐ trafficking in human beings,

☐ sexual exploitation of children and child pornography,

☐ illicit trafficking in narcotic drugs and psychotropic substances,

☐ illicit trafficking in weapons, munitions and explosives,

☐ corruption, including bribery,

☐ fraud, including that affecting the financial interests of the United Kingdom, of a Member State or of the Union,

☐ laundering of the proceeds of crime,

☐ counterfeiting of currency,

☐ computer-related crime,

☐ environmental crime, including illicit trafficking in endangered animal species and in endangered plant species and varieties;

☐ facilitation of unauthorised entry and residence,

☐ murder, grievous bodily injury,

☐ illicit trade in human organs and tissue,

☐ kidnapping, illegal restraint and hostage-taking,

☐ racism and xenophobia,

☐ organised or armed robbery,

☐ illicit trafficking in cultural goods, including antiques and works of art,

☐ swindling,

☐ racketeering and extortion,

☐ counterfeiting and piracy of products,

☐ forgery of administrative documents and trafficking therein,

☐ forgery of means of payment,

☐ illicit trafficking in hormonal substances and other growth promoters,

☐ illicit trafficking in nuclear or radioactive materials,

☐ trafficking in stolen vehicles,

☐ rape,

☐ arson,

☐ crimes within the jurisdiction of the International Criminal Court,

☐ unlawful seizure of aircraft, ships or spacecraft;

☐ sabotage

II. Full description of offence(s) not covered by section I above:

....

....

3.24 Box E is a particularly important part of the AW. It is essential to examine it carefully to ensure that the warrant complies with both EA 2003 ss2 and 10. As shown below, it requires the requesting state to provide information regarding the circumstances of the offence. Failure to provide sufficient detail here may invalidate the warrant (see para 3.47 below).

3.25 Dual criminality will, at the time of writing, be required in respect of all offences. Should the UK and a requesting state make a notification to the Specialised Committee on Law Enforcement and Judicial Cooperation under Article 599(4), it will not be necessary to show dual criminality in respect of the 32 offences listed in box E ('TCA list offences') (see para 3.61 regarding dual criminality). Note that such notification must be reciprocal and must be accompanied by amendment of the EA 2003 to take effect in the UK.

3.26 TCA list offences must be punishable in the requesting state with at least three years' imprisonment. While it is not necessary to establish dual criminality for TCA list offences, the description of the offence must contain sufficient detail to establish that the conduct in question amounts to an offence in the UK (see para 3.58 below for more information on extradition offences).

Box F

(f) Other circumstances relevant to the case (optional information):
(NB: This could cover remarks on extraterritoriality, interruption of periods of time limitation and other consequences of the offence)
....

3.27 Box F is used where the requesting state has identified potential problems with the execution of the warrant. It can be used, in the examples given within the box, or for example, where temporary surrender (see para 7.38) is anticipated. It often also provides information on any attempts made to locate the requested person and statements about their knowledge of the proceedings.

Box G

(g)
This warrant pertains also to the seizure and handing over of property which may be required as evidence:
This warrant pertains also to the seizure and handing over of property acquired by the requested person as a result of the offence:
Description of the property (and location) (if known):
....

3.28 Box G allows for the seizure and return of evidence to the requesting state in pre-trial cases, or, post-conviction, for property which is the subject of a confiscation order. It is, at present, unusual for this box to be completed, however given that the UK no longer participates in the European Investigation Order, it is foreseeable that this box may see greater use in the future.

Box H

(h)

The offence(s) on the basis of which this warrant has been issued is(are) punishable by / has(have) led to a custodial life sentence or lifetime detention order:

the issuing State will upon request by the executing State give an assurance that it will:

☐ review the penalty or measure imposed – on request or at least after 20 years,

and/or

☐ encourage the application of measures of clemency to which the person is entitled to apply for under the law or practice of the issuing State, aiming at non-execution of such penalty or measure.

3.29 TCA Article 604(a) allows countries to make execution of an AW subject to guarantees if it is issued for an offence punishable by a life sentence. Article 604(b) and (c) allow countries to seek guarantees in other circumstances, however boxes which allow the requesting state to provide details regarding these assurances have not been incorporated into the AW form.

Box I

(i) The judicial authority which issued the warrant:

Official name: ....

Name of its representative: ....

Post held (title/grade): ....

File reference: ....

Address: ....

Tel. No.: (country code) (area/city code) (...) ....

Fax No.: (country code) (area/city code) (...) ....

E-mail: ....

Contact details of the person to contact to make necessary practical arrangements for the surrender:

....

Where a central authority has been made responsible for the transmission and administrative reception of European arrest warrants:

Name of the central authority: ....

Contact person, if applicable (title/grade and name): ....

Tel. No.: (country code) (area/city code) ....

Fax No.: (country code) (area/city code) ....

E-mail: ....

Signature of the issuing judicial authority and/or its representative:

....

Name: ....

Post held (title/grade): ....

Date: ....

Official stamp (if available):

3.30 It is necessary for the information in box I to be provided so that practical arrangements can be made where extradition has been ordered. Practitioners should refer to it in order to determine whether the warrant has been issued by a 'judicial authority' (see para 3.39 below).

Challenging the validity of a TCA Arrest Warrant

Extradition Act 2003 s2

3.31 While the NCA is initially responsible for checking that the information required by EA 2003 s2 is included, it is vital that the AW is carefully checked for compliance with section 2. Failure to comply with section 2 may mean that the warrant is invalid, and that the requested person should therefore be discharged. Note that, where multiple offences are alleged, the Extradition Act 2003 (Multiple Offences) Order 2003 requires the court to consider the validity of each of the individual offences in the warrant.[13] Where insufficient detail is provided in relation to one or more, this will not invalidate

13 See *Taylor v Germany* [2012] EWHC 475 (Admin).

the entire AW but may lead to a discharge for the offences for which the particulars are insufficient.[14]

Key principles for challenges under Extradition Act 2003 s2

3.32 There is a significant body of case-law relating to the validity of EAWs under section 2. In dealing with EAWs, the courts would generally take a 'cosmopolitan' approach and favour a purposive construction when looking at whether the requirements of section 2 are satisfied, in order to accommodate differences in legal systems across member states.

3.33 The legislation itself has not changed as a result of the TCA, and, as noted in *Polakowski*,[15] the correct starting point is the domestic legislation. Nevertheless, the EAW case-law on validity placed great emphasis on the principle of mutual trust, described by Lord Sumption as 'the first and the main [safeguard against an unjustified extradition]' where a warrant contains a factual error.[16] While mutual trust is not a foundational principle of the TCA AW scheme, cooperation is based on the 'long-standing respect for democracy, the rule of law and the protection of fundamental rights and freedoms of individuals'[17] between the EU and the UK. Furthermore, like the Framework Decision, the TCA uses the term 'surrender' rather than 'extradition'. Beyond the TCA, general principles of international comity and reciprocity still apply, as does the public interest in upholding an effective system of extradition. Although the concept of mutual trust has disappeared, it appears likely, therefore, that the courts will continue to read the domestic legislation purposively, and on the basis that requesting states are acting in good faith, unless the contrary can be shown. Below, EAW case-law regarding section 2 challenges is cited, however it must be treated with some caution, bearing in mind the changes brought about by the TCA.

14 Extradition Act 2003 (Multiple Offences) Order 2003 SI No 3150; and see *Zengota v Poland* [2017] EWHC 191 (Admin).

15 *Polakowski v Westminster Magistrates' Court and others* [2021] EWHC 53 (Admin).

16 *Zakrzewski v Regional Court in Lodz, Poland* [2013] UKSC 2 at paras 9–10.

17 TCA Article 524(1).

Further / extraneous information

3.34 An AW must conform to the requirements set out in EA 2003 s2. If it does not, it will not be an AW within the meaning of that section.[18] The approach of the court as to whether all of the required information must be included in the AW or whether this information can be provided at a later date, has changed in recent years. In *Dabas v High Court of Justice, Madrid, Spain*[19] Lord Hope stated that a judge conducting an extradition hearing:

> ... must first be satisfied that the warrant with which he is dealing is a Part 1 warrant within the meaning of section 2(2). A warrant which does not contain the statements referred to in that subsection cannot be eked out by extraneous information. The requirements of section 2(2) are mandatory. If they are not met, the warrant is not a Part 1 warrant and the remaining provisions of that Part of the Act will not apply to it.

3.35 In relation to extraneous information, the Supreme Court departed from the approach taken in *Dabas* in the case of *Goluchowski and Sas*[20] and found that further information could rectify omissions in the particulars of an EAW. *Goluchowski and Sas* followed the Supreme Court judgment in *Zakrzewski v Regional Court in Lodz, Poland*[21] in which the court held that, where statements made in a Part 1 warrant cease to be true (for example, where a sentence is subsequently altered) or where the statement is wrong by way of omission, this could be cured by the provision of further information from the requesting state.[22] Subsequent case-law has distinguished between cases in which the omission of particulars amount to 'wholesale failures' which cannot be cured by the provision of further information, and, in the alternative cases in which gaps in the particulars can be filled by supplementary information.[23] It should be noted that the provisions of the EAW FD were central in *Zakrzewski* and *Goluchowski and Sas*, and that, in respect of the latter case, the court

18 *Office of the King's Prosecutor, Brussels v Cando Armas* [2005] UKHL 67 at para 28.

19 [2007] UKHL 6 at para 50.

20 *Goluchowski v District Court in Elblag, Poland* [2016] UKSC 36.

21 [2013] UKSC 2.

22 At para 10.

23 See *Alexander v Public Prosecutor's Office, Marseille District Court of First Instance, France; Di Benedetto v Court of Palermo, Italy* [2017] EWHC 1392 (Admin) and *M and others v Preliminary Investigation Tribunal of Napoli, Italy* [2018] EWHC 1808 (Admin).

relied on the Court of Justice of the European Union (CJEU) decision of *Bob-Dogi*[24] in reaching its conclusion.

Incorrect information

3.36 Practitioners should note that, where an EAW contained information that was demonstrably incorrect, but was nevertheless valid at face value, the correct challenge was an abuse of process rather than under section 2, following the principles set out by Lord Sumption in *Zakrzewski v The Regional Court in Lodz, Poland*.[25] The court, however, had to be satisfied that the abuse of process would cause prejudice to the requested person, either in the extradition process or in the requesting state if extradited.[26]

Grounds of challenge

3.37 The main grounds of challenge under section 2 are as follows:

- whether the authority that issued the AW is a 'judicial authority';
- lack of clarity as to the purpose of the warrant;
- deficient particulars of circumstances;
- deficient particulars of other warrants; and
- deficient particulars of sentence.

3.38 This chapter will go on to look at each of these headings in turn.

Judicial authority

3.39 The definition of 'judicial authority' was, under the EAW scheme, an autonomous concept of EU law and whether particular issuing judicial authorities met the definition was the subject of a significant body of case-law, both domestically and emanating from the CJEU. According to that case-law, 'the meaning and scope of ["judicial authority"] cannot be left to the assessment of each Member State'.[27] The TCA at Article 598, however, provides a definition of 'judicial authority' as:

> ... an authority that is, under domestic law, a judge, a court or a public prosecutor. A public prosecutor is considered a judicial authority only to the extent that domestic law so provides.

24 *Parchetul de pe lângă Curtea de Apel Cluj v Bob-Dogi* (Case C-241/15).

25 At para 13.

26 *Belbin v The Regional Court in Lille, France* [2015] EWHC 149 (Admin).

27 *OG and PI* (Joined Cases C-508/18 and C-82/19 PPU) at para 48.

3.40 The definition provided above suggests that a different approach may now be warranted under the TCA, given the specific reference to domestic law, although, at the time of writing, the UK courts are yet to deal with this issue. It is presumed that the domestic law referred to is the domestic law of the issuing judicial authority, meaning that, where AWs have been issued by a public prosecutor, it will be necessary to consider their status under the law of that state.

Lack of clarity as to the purpose of the warrant

3.41 By virtue of EA 2003 s2(5), the warrant must contain a statement that it has been issued in respect of an accused or convicted person (see para 3.14 above regarding the statement of purpose). Where, read as a whole, it is unclear from the warrant (and alongside any further information provided by the requesting state; see para 3.34 above), whether a person is wanted as an accused or a convicted person, or where it appears that the person is wanted as a suspect and not for prosecution, there may be grounds to challenge the validity of the warrant under section 2.

3.42 Section 2(3) requires the warrant to contain a statement that it has been issued 'with a view to [the] arrest and extradition [of the requested person] to the category 1 territory for the purpose of being prosecuted for the offence'. To seek a person's extradition in order to conduct an investigation with a view to possible prosecution is not a legitimate purpose. It may, in some circumstances, be necessary to obtain expert evidence addressing the stage the proceedings have reached and the classification of the requested person under the law of the requesting state (although see point 7 in the list below). A helpful summary of the principles deriving from the case-law is set out by Aikens LJ in *Asztaslos v Szekszard City Court, Hungary*:[28]

> (1) The court will look at the warrant as a whole to see whether it is an 'accusation case' warrant or a 'conviction case' warrant. It will not confine itself to the wording on the first page of the warrant, which may well be equivocal.
> (2) In the case of an 'accusation case' warrant, issued under Part 1 of the Act, the court has to be satisfied, looking at the warrant as a whole,

28 [2010] EWHC 237 (Admin) at para 38. This case was decided before the Supreme Court's decisions in *Goluchowski v District Court in Elblag, Poland* [2016] UKSC 36 and *Zakrzewski v Regional Court in Lodz, Poland* [2013] UKSC 2 which considered the admissibility of additional evidence in the context of arguments under EA 2003 s2(6).

that the requested person is an 'accused' within *section 2(3)(a)* of the Act.

(3) Similarly, the court will look at the wording of the warrant as a whole to decide whether the warrant indicates, unequivocally, that the purpose of the warrant is for the purpose of the requested person being prosecuted for the offences identified.

(4) The court must construe the words in *section 2(3)(a)* and *(b)* in a 'cosmopolitan' sense and not just in terms of the stages of English criminal procedure.

(5) If the warrant uses the phrases that are used in the English language version of the EAW annexed to the Framework Decision, there should be no (or very little scope) for argument on the purpose of the warrant.

(6) Only if the wording of the warrant is equivocal should the court consider examining extrinsic evidence to decide on the purpose of the warrant. But it should not look at extrinsic material to introduce a possible doubt as to the purpose where it is clear on the face of the warrant itself.

(7) Consideration of extrinsic factual or expert evidence to ascertain the purpose of the warrant should be a last resort and it is to be discouraged. The introduction of such evidence is clean contrary to the aspiration of the Framework Decision, which is to introduce clarity and simplicity into the surrender procedure between member states of the European Union. Therefore the introduction of extrinsic factual and expert evidence must be discouraged, except in exceptional cases.

3.43 Although *Asztaslos* was a case decided in relation to an EAW, the courts have been applying a 'cosmopolitan' approach in relation to this question since before the EA 2003 (see *In Re Ismail*)[29] and it therefore appears inevitable that they will continue to do so under TCA.

3.44 In *Assange*,[30] the High Court examined the question of whether a person who had not been charged could properly be said to be an accused person. In such cases, it was said, the court must 'ask whether the case against him has moved from where he can be seen only as a suspect where proof may be lacking or whether there is an accusation against him supported by proof'.[31]

3.45 The fact that an investigation is continuing does not mean a decision to charge has not been made: see *Puceviciene v Lithuanian*

29 [1999] 1 AC 320.

30 *Assange v Swedish Prosecution Authority* [2011] EWHC 2849 (Admin).

31 At para 152.

Judicial Authority.[32] Further, a request to seize evidence does not necessarily mean that an arrest warrant has been issued for investigation rather than prosecution.[33] A request for a person to face a hearing to determine whether to activate a suspended sentence is properly categorised as a conviction warrant.[34]

3.46 There is significant overlap between the requirements of section 2 and the bar to extradition at section 12A which prevents extradition in the absence of a prosecution decision. See para 5.13.

Deficient particulars of circumstances

3.47 The requirements for particulars of accusation and conviction warrants are set out at EA 2003 s2(4)(c) and (6)(b) respectively. It is not necessary to describe in great detail the circumstances surrounding the offence in respect of either a conviction or an accusation warrant. Provided the particulars give sufficient information to enable a point on a bar to be taken or a defence to the warrant to be raised, they will suffice for accusation and conviction cases.[35] The level of particularity will depend on the circumstances of the case.

3.48 In accusation cases, section 2(4)(c) requires that the circumstances of the alleged offence are set out, including the conduct, time, place and the relevant provision of law. The language of this section is 'not obscure and ... should be given its plain and ordinary meaning'.[36] The particulars of the offence must provide a person with 'a clear understanding of why his extradition is being sought'.[37] Thus, 'a broad omnibus description of the alleged criminal conduct, "obtaining property by deception", to take an English example, will not suffice'.[38] The conduct must be fairly, accurately and properly set

32 [2016] EWHC 1862 (Admin) at para 40.

33 See, for example: *Amandeep Kapoor v Juzagado De Instruccion No.4 De Las Palmas De Gran Canaria, Spain* [2020] EWHC 590 (Admin); or *Shiraz Ahmed v Swedish Economic Crime Authority* [2017] EWHC 345 (Admin).

34 *Miroslav Murin v District Court in Prague, Czech Republic* [2018] EWHC 1532 (Admin).

35 *Anthony King v Public Prosecutors of Villefranche Sur Saone, France* [2015] EWHC 3670 (Admin) at para 22. Note that while this decision was made on the basis of FD Article 8, the requirements for an AW set out in TCA mirror the FD requirements precisely.

36 *Von Der Pahlen v The Government of Austria* [2006] EWHC 1672 (Admin) at para 21.

37 *Naczmanski v Regional Court in Wloclawek, Poland* [2010] EWHC 2023 (Admin) at para 17.

38 *Von der Pahlen v The Government of Austria* [2006] EWHC 1672 (Admin) at para 21.

out in the warrant. Guidance was given by Cranston J in *Ektor v National Public Prosecutor of Holland*,[39] who said:

> ... the person sought by the warrant needs to know what offence he is said to have committed and to have an idea of the nature and extent of the allegations against him in relation to that offence. The amount of detail may turn on the nature of the offence. Where dual criminality is involved the detail must also be sufficient to enable the transposition exercise to take place.[40]

Successful challenges have been made to warrants that do not contain sufficient particulars of time or place. In general, however, the courts do not require precision as to these particulars.[41]

3.49 If the information communicated by the requesting state is found to be insufficient to allow it to decide on surrender, TCA Article 613(2) stipulates that supplementary information shall be requested by the executing judicial authority. In many cases, errors or omissions going to the validity of an AW may be cured by the provision of further information by the requesting state. See para 3.34 above. Extradition cannot be properly achieved on the basis of a 'bit of paper' – there must be a document in the prescribed form, and setting out to address the information required by EA 2003.[42] Where there is a wholesale failure to provide particulars, the court is relieved of the obligation to seek further information from the requesting state.[43] For an example of a case where the court was faced with a wholesale failure to provide particulars, rather than lacunae in the warrant which could be filled by further information, see the case of *M and another v Preliminary Investigation Tribunal of Napoli, Italy*.[44]

3.50 In many cases where there is doubt as to the sufficiency of the particulars of conduct set out, there may be a parallel challenge as to whether the conduct amounts to an extradition offence (see para 3.58 below).

39 [2007] EWHC 3106 (Admin).

40 [2007] EWHC 3106 (Admin) at para 7.

41 *Fofana and another v Deputy Prosecutor Thubin Tribunal de Grande Instance de Meaux, France* [2006] EWHC 744 (Admin); *Crean v Ireland* [2007] EWHC 814 (Admin) at para 17.

42 *Alexander v Public Prosecutor's Office, Marseille District Court of First Instance, France; Di Benedetto v Court of Palermo, Italy* [2017] EWHC 1392 (Admin) at para 75. While this case looked at FD Article 15, this provision is replicated in its entirety in TCA Article 613(2).

43 *Tifrac v Romanian Judicial Authority* [2018] EWHC 1909 (Admin), following *M and another v Preliminary Investigation Tribunal of Napoli, Italy* [2018] EWHC 1808 (Admin).

44 [2018] EWHC 1808 (Admin).

Deficient particulars of other warrants

3.51 The requirement to provide particulars of 'any other warrant' in EA 2003 s2(4)(b) and (6)(c) (accusation and conviction respectively) requires the requesting state to provide particulars of the domestic warrant (or enforceable judicial decision having the same effect[45]) on the basis of which the AW was issued.[46] The rationale for this is that it enables the court 'to ascertain that there are criminal proceedings in the requesting state'.[47]

3.52 In *Goluchowski v District Court in Elblag, Poland*[48] the Supreme Court examined the meaning of 'warrant', looking at EAW FD Article 8.1 which underlay the EA 2003 provisions. EAW FD Article 8.1 is replicated in TCA Article 606(1)(c) and requires the arrest warrant to provide 'evidence of an enforceable judgment, an arrest warrant or any other enforceable judicial decision having the same effect'. The court looked at the difference in practice between accusation and conviction cases: in an accusation case, the arrest warrant will normally be based on a domestic arrest warrant, whereas in a conviction case, the natural basis of the arrest warrant will be 'an enforceable judgment' or 'any other enforceable judicial decision having the same effect'.[49] The court in that case found that conviction warrants which did not provide particulars of domestic warrants issued to secure the requested person's surrender to custody were nevertheless valid as they particularised an enforceable judgment and the sentenced passed and due to be served in respect of it.

Deficient particulars of sentence

3.53 The AW must set out either the sentence that may be imposed (where a person is yet to be sentenced), or the sentence that has been imposed (where a person has been sentenced). It is necessary to state the particulars of sentence to enable the court to determine whether the offence is an extradition offence under sections 64 and 65 of the

45 *Goluchowski v District Court in Elblag, Poland* [2016] UKSC 36 at para 28.

46 It does not amount to a requirement to include details of previous AWs that have been withdrawn: *Louca v A German Judicial Authority* [2009] UKSC 4.

47 *Louca v Office of Public Prosecutor in Bielefeld, Germany* [2008] EWHC 2907 (Admin) at para 26.

48 [2016] UKSC 36.

49 *Goluchowski v District Court in Elblag, Poland* [2016] UKSC 36 at paras 25–26. See also para 27 for an example of a conviction case where a domestic warrant may be required.

Act. In an accusation case, the maximum sentence for each offence must be stated.[50]

3.54 Practitioners will find that a large number of Polish clients are subject to a sentence of imprisonment which does not take immediate effect, or a suspended sentence that has been activated, although this may not be clear from the warrant. Although the EA 2003 contains no mention of the possibility of sentences of imprisonment which do not take immediate effect, the Supreme Court in *Goluchowski* indicated that the legislation should be understood and made to work in a manner which will cater for such sentences.[51] Failure to state that a sentence has been suspended will not invalidate the warrant.[52]

3.55 Complications arise in relation to the requirement where a person's extradition is sought for multiple offences and in particular, where the sentence for these offences is 'merged' or 'aggregated'. In a conviction case, if there are several offences that are dealt with by way of an aggregate penalty, it is enough for the warrant to state the aggregate sentence.[53] Conversely, while it is necessary to state the sentence that has been imposed, if there is more than one offence there is no requirement to state the aggregate penalty.[54] Indeed, a warrant will still be valid even if it can be shown that the sentence has been aggregated after the warrant has been issued (meaning that there is a different sentence to serve than that set out in the warrant).

3.56 Where a conviction warrant sets out an aggregate sentence comprising a sentence for the index offence along with a suspended sentence that has been activated by the commission of the index offence, the AW must contain the particulars of each conviction and particulars of both offences in order to be a valid AW.[55]

3.57 Further complications can arise where a conviction warrant seeks a person's return for an offence but the sentence imposed has been merged with other offences that have not been particularised, or have only been partially particularised. In *Edutanu v Romania*,[56] the Divisional Court looked at several such cases. In relation to EAWs,

50 *Taylor v Public Prosecutor's Office, Berlin* [2012] EWHC 475 (Admin).

51 *Goluchowski v District Court in Elblag, Poland* [2016] UKSC 36 at para 30.

52 *Bulkowski (Kamil) v Regional Court of Elblag, Poland* [2012] EWHC 381 (Admin).

53 *Pilecki v Circuit Court of Legnica, Poland* [2008] UKHL 7, [2008] 1 WLR 325.

54 *Bartkowiak v Judicial Authority of Poland* [2012] EWHC 333 (Admin).

55 See *Echimov v Court of Babadag, Romania* [2011] EWHC 864 (Admin) and *Presecan v Cluj-Napoca Court, Romania* [2013] EWHC 1609 (Admin).

56 [2016] EWHC 124 (Admin).

the court in *Iacob v Romania*[57] drew some useful principles from *Edutanu*, namely:

- Box B of the EAW is important but not conclusive as to what the total sentence reflects.
- The issue of substance is whether the requested person has sufficient details of the offences to understand of what they have been convicted or sentenced and whether any bars to extradition apply. That must be determined in the light of the warrant as a whole.
- Provided that underlying principle can be respected, the EAW should be given a broad purposive construction in order to reflect the principles of mutual trust.
- Where it appears from the terms of an EAW read as a whole that either a return which would expose the requested person to serve a longer sentence than the sentences for the offences for which extradition is sought, or where the total sentence relates to offences which have not been particularised, the EAW will not be valid.
- The fact that the EAW refers to a total sentence to be served that is longer than the sentence for the particularised offences is a strong pointer towards regarding the sentence as originating from unparticularised conduct;
- Care has also to be taken where there is a possibility that the requested person will serve a disaggregated shorter sentence in respect of an un-particularised offence.

Extradition offences

3.58 EA 2003 ss64 and 65 define extradition offences, drawing a distinction between sentenced persons and those who have not been sentenced (whether or not convicted), with different minimum periods of sentence applying in both cases. These sections are complicated and are by no means a direct transposition of the relevant provisions of the TCA, which are covered under the heading 'Scope' at Article 599.[58]

57 [2017] EWHC 155 (Admin) at para 20.

58 In relation to EAWs, see J R Spencer 'Implementing the European Arrest Warrant: a tale of how not to do it' (2009) 30(3) *Statute Law Review* 184 at pp191–192. Note that this article predates the amendments made by the Anti-social Behaviour, Crime and Policing Act 2014.

3.59 The conduct alleged should be carefully analysed to determine whether it satisfies the dual criminality requirement, ie that the acts constitute an offence under the law of the relevant part of the UK, as well as the requesting state. This is the primary area of challenge under these sections. This chapter will go on to look at the minimum periods of sentence, and will then cover dual criminality and the relevance of the location of the offence.

Minimum periods of sentence for extradition offences

3.60 If the offence would have constituted an offence had it taken place in the UK, it will be an extradition offence if it is punishable by at least 12 months' imprisonment (for persons not sentenced) or a sentence of four months' imprisonment was imposed (where a person has been sentenced). This can be contrasted with Part 2 cases, where the offence must be punishable in the UK by a minimum of 12 months' imprisonment.[59] These minimum periods of sentence apply not only to imprisonment but also to other forms of detention.

Dual criminality

3.61 In order to determine whether an offence satisfies the dual criminality requirement, it is necessary to look at the conduct complained of in the warrant and, if the judicial authority has provided it, any further information.[60] The court must transpose the conduct alleged into legal terms for the purpose of seeing whether such conduct would constitute a crime in England & Wales.[61] It would be wrong to look at whether the elements of the offence have a precise equivalent in this country.[62] If the conduct set out in the warrant and any further information would not amount to an offence in England and Wales,

59 EA 2003 ss137 and 138.

60 See para 3.58 above regarding the admission of extraneous material. Whilst the Divisional Court in *Assange v Swedish Prosecution* [2011] EWHC 2849 (Admin) stated that such material should only be admitted in exceptional circumstances, this was both prior to the 'sea change' resulting from the decision in *Goluchowski v District Court in Elblag, Poland* [2016] UKSC 36 and was a decision explicitly based on the principle of mutual recognition under the EAW FD. See also *Alexander v Public Prosecutor's Office, Marseille District Court of First Instance, France, Di Benedetto v Court of Palermo, Italy* [2017] EWHC 1392 (Admin).

61 *Al Fawwaz v Governor of Brixton Prison* [2001] UKHL 69, [2002] 1 AC 556 at para 110.

62 *Norris v United States of America* [2008] UKHL 16; and *Zak v Regional Court of Bydgoszcz, Poland* [2008] EWHC 470 (Admin) at para 5.

the offence is not an extradition offence and the requested person should be discharged.

3.62 An issue may arise where the particulars as set out in the warrant lack a description of an element of the domestic equivalent. This occurs most frequently where the court is seeking to transpose conduct which requires particular intent in English law. The case-law distinguishes between situations in which (a) the offence in the requesting state does not include an element which is essential to establish liability in England and Wales (as in the facts of *Assange*);[63] and (b) the particulars of conduct do not address an ingredient of an equivalent English law offence.[64] In relation to the former, the test in *Assange* applies, ie the facts set out must be such as to impel the inference in relation to the missing element ('the inevitable inference test') in order for the court to find dual criminality.[65] In relation to the latter, however, there is no legal justification for applying the 'inevitable inference' test. Instead, the issue is whether the particulars contained in the warrant are sufficient to enable an offence under English law to be identified.[66] For an illustration of this distinction, see *Cleveland v Government of the United States of America*.[67]

3.63 Note that, where part of the conduct described in the warrant would not meet the test of dual criminality, it is open to the judge to excise any such conduct.[68]

3.64 An exception to the dual criminality requirement can be found in TCA Article 599(3) which requires states not to refuse extradition for joint participation in terrorist offences, drug trafficking and serious offences against the person. A further exception may be introduced by way of Article 599(4), which effectively re-introduces the FD list of offences for which it was not necessary to show dual criminality, however at the time of writing, a notification that Article 599(4) would

63 [2011] EWHC 2849 (Admin).

64 *Cleveland v Government of the United States of America* [2019] EWHC 619 (Admin) at para 61.

65 See *Kechedzhiev v Gdansk Regional Court, Poland* [2020] EWHC 3021 (Admin) for an example of a case in which the court applied the inevitable inference test following *Cleveland*.

66 *Cleveland v Government of the United States of America* [2019] EWHC 619 (Admin) at para 61.

67 [2019] EWHC 619 (Admin) at paras 61–64.

68 See *Dabas v High Court of Justice, Madrid, Spain* [2007] UKHL 6 at para 51 and *Osunta v Public Prosecutor's Office in Dusseldorf, Germany* [2007] EWHC 1562 (Admin).

be applied has not been made by the UK.[69] Should a notification be made, it will be necessary for the EA 2003 to be amended before the waiver of dual criminality for those offences in the TCA list takes effect.

3.65 In looking at dual criminality, the courts will follow the same principles that apply to EA 2003 s2, that is, a cosmopolitan approach will be taken.

Location of conduct

3.66 In many cases, the location of the conduct will not be an issue: the conduct will take place, either in whole or in part, within the territory of the requesting state. Where the conduct takes place outside the requesting state but has an intended effect within it, the court will consider that the conduct took place in that state and the conduct will constitute an extradition offence, subject to certain minimum sentence requirements – see EA 2003 ss64(3) and 65(3). This is the case irrespective of where the person was when doing the acts constituting the conduct.[70]

3.67 Where, however, the criminal conduct occurs outside the territory of the requesting state, the court must be satisfied that the conduct in question would constitute an extra-territorial offence under the law of the UK in order for it to constitute an extradition offence, subject again to the minimum sentence requirements – see EA 2003 ss64(4) and 65(4). For an example of a case in which the court dealt with this issue, see *Kalinowski v Circuit Court in Todz, Poland*.[71] In cases where the conduct took place outside the requesting state and there are questions around the extent to which any harm is or is not felt within that state, it may be possible to argue that it is not an extradition offence.

69 As of 5 March 2021, 15 member states have indicated their willingness to waive the requirement to establish dual criminality in respect of the Framework list of offences (Belgium, Ireland, Greece, Spain, France, Italy, Cyprus, Lithuania, Luxembourg, Hungary, the Netherlands, Austria, Poland, Portugal and Romania): http://data.parliament.uk/DepositedPapers/Files/DEP2021-0194/Letter_Kevin_Foster_to_Lord_Ricketts_UK_EU_security_cooperation.pdf.

70 *Office of the King's Prosecutor, Brussels v Cando Armas* [2005] UKHL 67 at para 35.

71 [2019] EWHC 3734 (Admin).

CHAPTER 4

Attending on the requested person

Introduction

4.1 Often the first interaction the requested person will have with a lawyer following arrest will be in the cells at Westminster Magistrates' Court (WMC). Although entitled to have free telephone advice at the police station following arrest, it is unlikely that the duty solicitor (particularly those based outside of London) will be versed in extradition law.

4.2 At court, time will often be limited, particularly for the duty solicitor who may be dealing with multiple cases. It is therefore important to be able to obtain the necessary information as quickly as possible in order to appropriately advise the requested person at the initial hearing. This chapter looks at what should be covered in the first meeting with the requested person, in particular how to explain the law and procedure. It also looks at the information that should be obtained at the first meeting in order to be in a position to effectively represent the requested person at the initial hearing in Extradition Act (EA) 2003 Part 1 arrest warrant (AW)[1] cases. The initial hearing for AW cases will be discussed in chapter 7. The initial hearing in EA 2003 Part 2 cases is explored in chapter 8.

Seeing the requested person

4.3 Requested persons are unlikely to be familiar with the extradition process. When acting for those arrested on AWs, it is important to explain the nature of the fast-track extradition procedure, specifically that the court's primary concern will be to ensure that procedural requirements have been met, and that the purpose of the extradition proceedings is not to decide whether and by whom the offence was committed: guilt or innocence are for the court in the requesting state to determine. Given that time will often be limited, this should be explained at the outset.

4.4 It is important for requested persons to be given a realistic assessment of their prospects of success: they should be informed of the difficulties inherent in contesting extradition, and that most requested persons are eventually extradited.

1 References to 'AW cases' mean cases brought under Part 1 of the EA 2003 involving category 1 territories.

4.5 Requested persons arrive in the cells throughout the day (subject to a cut-off time of 3.30 pm[2]) and it is therefore imperative that the practitioner obtains estimated times of arrival so that they can apportion their time accordingly. Ordinarily, new arrest cases will be heard in the afternoon court session. Practitioners should be aware that generally, the cells at WMC allow access from 9 am until 1 pm and from 1.45 pm until the courthouse closes.

4.6 Before seeing the requested person, the defence lawyer should obtain the papers from the Crown Prosecution Service (CPS) representative and ensure that they include: (a) the arrest warrant; (b) the arrest statement; and (c) the Police National Computer (PNC) record of convictions of the requested person. These documents should be considered carefully before seeing the requested person and as much of appendix D completed as possible. The views of the CPS representative should be ascertained as to whether they are objecting to bail and if so, what the specific objections are.

Extradition Act 2003 ss4 and 7

4.7 Using the procedure that the court will follow at the initial hearing as a way of structuring the interview, the preliminary points regarding the question of production, service of the warrant (EA 2003 s4) and identity (EA 2003 s7) should be covered with the requested person. The law in relation to these areas is set out in chapter 7. In brief, however, the requested person must be given a copy of the AW as soon as practicable after arrest; failure to comply means a judge *may* grant their discharge. In addition, the requested person must be produced before WMC as soon as practicable; failure to comply means a judge *must* discharge the requested person.

4.8 While it will often be clear from the arrest statement whether or not the AW has been served and whether the requested person has been produced as soon as practicable following their arrest, it is always worth checking with the requested person. If it is apparent from the arrest statement that the AW has not been served, or that the person has not been produced as soon as practicable, these points will need to be covered in more detail. In particular, should there have been any obvious delay in the requested person being produced, a full chronology of events should be taken from the requested person, along with their understanding of any cause for the delay.

2 The referral time is court practice and practitioners should check from time to time that it remains 3.30 pm.

Attempts should be made to obtain the custody record from the police station where the requested person was detained, which will often reveal the efforts that were made to transport the requested person to court and when.

4.9 In relation to section 7, the judge must decide, on a balance of probabilities, whether the person before them is the person in respect of whom the warrant was issued. The requested person should be informed that a challenge as to identity does not relate to whether or not they have been correctly identified as the person who has committed the offence or not. The question of identity will often have been resolved by the arresting officer asking the person to confirm their name and date of birth, and seizing any identity documents in their possession. If the requested person disputes that they are the person who is the subject of the warrant, it will be necessary to take further instructions. Fingerprints may have been taken at the police station in order to confirm identity.

4.10 Requested persons should be warned that disputing identity could have an impact upon their credibility at the extradition hearing and on their prospects of obtaining bail if the issue of identity is determined against them.

Persons facing charges in the UK

4.11 If the requested person has been produced at the initial hearing from a prison, they will either be on remand or a serving prisoner. The court will need confirmation of the early release date if the requested person is serving a sentence of imprisonment, as the extradition hearing *may* be adjourned while that sentence is served. Adjournments can be for a period of up to six months.

4.12 In the case of persons facing charges in England and Wales, the court *must* adjourn proceedings until the domestic case is disposed of.[3] Adjournments will be for a period of 28 days if the requested person is remanded in custody. Relevant dates should be established with the requested person regarding the domestic proceedings.

4.13 There is no requirement to adjourn extradition proceedings for those under investigation and subject to police bail.

3 EA 2003 s214 states that a charge is disposed of when a person is either acquitted of it, or, if convicted, when there is no further possibility of an appeal against conviction.

Consent to extradition

4.14 A requested person may consent to extradition at any time. The advantage of consenting to extradition is that it will result in an expedited process: a person who has consented cannot appeal, and they will not, therefore, have to wait until the end of the seven-day appeal period following the making of the extradition order for removal to take place.[4] Consenting to extradition may also have its benefits in the requesting state, for example, being granted bail in the requesting state may be more achievable if extradition is not challenged.

4.15 Consent must be given in writing and is irrevocable.[5] The legal adviser will have a form that can be completed during the hearing for those who wish to consent.[6] The requested person must have had the opportunity to receive legal advice before giving consent. Consent to extradition is not to be taken as a waiver of specialty rights.[7]

4.16 It is worth noting that, if the requesting state does wish to prosecute an extradited person for offences for which they have not been extradited, it is possible for that state to seek consent from the UK to deal with the person for those offences after extradition has taken place.[8] Consent will be sought at a hearing where the person is unlikely to be represented. The grounds for refusing consent are limited.

Time spent in custody awaiting extradition

4.17 In AW cases, requested persons should be advised that any time spent in custody as a result of extradition proceedings should count towards any sentence in the requesting state.[9] The requested state has the responsibility under the TCA for transmitting information

4 A person that consent to their extradition should be extradited within 10 days of the order being made although this period can be extended (EA 2003 s47).

5 EA 2003 ss45/127.

6 For those that consent over the video-link, the practice of the court is to send the consent form via fax to the prison for the requested person to sign it in the presence of the judge over the video-link.

7 Anti-social Behaviour, Crime and Policing Act 2014 s163.

8 EA 2003 ss54/129.

9 Article 624(1) of the Trade and Cooperation Agreement (TCA) between the European Union and the European Atomic Energy Community, of the one part, and the United Kingdom of Great Britain and Northern Ireland, of the other part, Document 22021A0430(01), 30 April 2021, https://eur-lex.europa.eu/legal-content/EN/TXT/?uri=uriserv:OJ.L_.2021.149.01.0010.01.ENG.

about the duration of detention to the requesting state at the time of surrender of the requested person.[10] To fulfil this requirement, the National Crime Agency (NCA) should provide the requesting state with a notice detailing the days spent in detention on the day that they are returned to the requesting state.

Time spent subject to a curfew

4.18 In some situations, time spent subject to a curfew may count towards a sentence in the requesting state, but this will vary according to the specific circumstances of the requested person and the jurisdiction. Practitioners should note the Court of Justice of the European Union (CJEU) decision in the case of *JZ*[11] in which the court held that:

> ... the concept of 'detention' within the meaning of Article 26(1) of Framework Decision 2002/584 must be interpreted as covering not only imprisonment but also any measure or set of measures imposed on the person concerned which, on account of the type, duration, effects and manner of implementation of the measure(s) in question deprive the person concerned of his liberty in a way that is comparable to imprisonment.[12]

4.19 However, when considering whether the bail conditions imposed in the UK on a Polish national awaiting extradition were so restrictive so as to fall within the meaning of Article 26(1) of Framework Decision 2002/584 the court answered the referred question as follows:

> Article 26(1) of Council Framework Decision 2002/584/JHA of 13 June 2002 on the European arrest warrant and the surrender procedures between Member States, as amended by Council Framework Decision 2009/299/JHA of 26 February 2009, must be interpreted as meaning that measures such as a nine-hour night-time curfew, in conjunction with the monitoring of the person concerned by means of an electronic tag, an obligation to report to a police station at fixed times on a daily basis or several times a week, and a ban on applying for foreign travel documents, are not, in principle, having regard to the type, duration, effects and manner of implementation of all those measures, so restrictive as to give rise to a deprivation of liberty comparable to that arising from imprisonment and thus to be classified as 'detention' within the meaning of that provision, which it is nevertheless for the referring court to ascertain.[13]

10 TCA Article 624(2).

11 *JZ v Prokuratura Rejonowa Łódź* (Case C-294/16 PPU), 28 July 2016.

12 *JZ v Prokuratura Rejonowa Łódź* at para 47.

13 *JZ v Prokuratura Rejonowa Łódź* at para 58.

4.20 It is therefore necessary, in those cases, to check with a lawyer in the requesting state whether time spent subject to a curfew will count towards a sentence.

Personal circumstances

4.21 Details of the requested person's personal circumstances should be obtained. If it is clear that extradition will be contested, completion of the legal aid forms will provide a good deal of necessary background information.[14] An interview with a requested person will inevitably be determined by the facts of the case. However, the below questions should assist in providing a starting point, both in advising as to any grounds on which the requested person may challenge the extradition proceedings and in preparing for a bail application:

General instructions

4.22 When did the requested person come to the UK and why?

- Have they been back to the requesting state?
- Is the requested person aware of the criminal proceedings (see para 4.25 below)?
- Were they present at the trial (conviction cases)? If not, why not?
- Do they have family in the UK/requesting state? Do they have any dependents, and if so, do the dependents have any health concerns?
- Are they employed? If so, what are the hours of work? Is it possible to contact the employer?
- What is their housing situation? How long have they been at the present address?
- Where were they arrested? At home/work?
- Has the requested person instructed lawyers in the requesting state?
- What is their immigration status in the UK (see para 4.27 below)?
- Do they have any health problems?
- Why does the requested person think that they should not be extradited?

14 Time should, however, not be wasted on completion of the legal aid form if it is clear that an extradition order will be made that day or that the requested person will not pass the means test for obtaining legal aid.

Bail instructions

4.23 Is any security or surety available? Contact numbers will need to be obtained.

- What is the nearest police station to the requested person's address? If possible, attempt to find out the opening hours prior to the hearing.
- Where are the identity documents of the requested person? Is it possible to obtain those that have not been seized by the police in order to surrender them?
- Does the requested person have any commitments that would make compliance with a curfew or a condition to report to the police station difficult?
- What are the circumstances of any offending whilst on bail/ failure to surrender as listed within the PNC's record of convictions? Are the details within the PNC correct?

4.24 See chapter 7 for further information on making a bail application and refer to the checklists at appendices E and F.

Awareness of proceedings

4.25 The question of whether the requested person had been aware of the allegation or conviction prior to their arrest will be relevant for any passage of time challenge to extradition as well as bail: their knowledge of any outstanding proceedings will go to the question of the requested person's status as a fugitive. In the case of a conviction warrant, it will be crucial to ascertain for the purpose of EA 2003 s20 whether or not they were present upon conviction (see para 5.38 in relation to EA 2003 s14).

4.26 The requested person should be made aware that assertions they make are likely to be the subject of requests for further information from the judicial authority.

Immigration status

4.27 The large majority of those facing AWs will be exercising their right to reside in the UK under the EU Settlement Scheme.[15]

15 The deadline for applying was 30 June 2021 and the applicant must usually have started living in the UK by 31 December 2020.

4.28 EA 2003 ss39 and 121[16] prevent the extradition of a person who has claimed asylum (whether before or after the issue of the warrant), until the determination of that claim. See para 5.118.

Challenges to extradition

4.29 It is worth explaining the most common bars and challenges to extradition to the requested person. Not only will this assist the requested person's understanding of the extradition process (and the limited grounds on which it is possible to contest extradition), it will also ensure that no possible grounds of challenge are overlooked. The list below sets out those most commonly relied upon:

- rule against double jeopardy (EA 2003 s12);
- absence of a decision to charge or try (section 12A) (accusation cases only);
- extraneous considerations (section 13);
- passage of time (section 14);
- forum (accusation cases only) (section 19B);
- conviction in absence (section 20);
- human rights considerations (section 21) under the European Convention on Human Rights (ECHR):
  - Article 2 – right to life;
  - Article 3 – prohibition of torture and ill-treatment;
  - Article 5 – right to liberty and security;
  - Article 6 – right to a fair trial;
  - Article 8 – right to respect for private and family life;
- proportionality (accusation cases only) (section 21A); and
- physical or mental health (section 25).

Case management form

4.30 The case management form should be completed with the requested person if extradition is going to be challenged. The case management form can be found at appendix H. The form warns the requested person that 'the information you provide must be accurate as it may be checked, and it may be referred to at a later hearing'. The form must therefore be completed accurately. The requested person is required to sign the case management form as well as the advocate.

16 As amended by Anti-social Behaviour, Crime and Policing Act 2014 s162.

Compromising the arrest warrant

4.31 In some jurisdictions, it will be possible to persuade the judicial authority to withdraw the warrant by negotiating a voluntary return to the issuing state. This is known as 'compromising the warrant' (see chapter 12). In order to pursue this route, it will be necessary for the requested person to instruct (and, unless legal aid is available, pay for) lawyers in the requesting state, who may be able to secure the withdrawal of the domestic warrant and AW on condition that the requested person will, for example, pay a bail security in the issuing state and return voluntarily or enter a guilty plea.[17] In general, the courts are reluctant to adjourn extradition proceedings to allow the requested person to attempt to compromise the warrant. However, practitioners should familiarise themselves with EA 2003 s21B (see para 12.6) as this allows for the requested person who faces an accusation AW to request to speak to the prosecutor in the requesting state.[18] See also para 12.16 and following on transfer of sentenced prisoners.

Procedure if extradition is ordered

4.32 Requested persons should be advised of the timescales that apply if extradition is ordered. EA 2003 s35 provides that a requested person must be extradited before the end of a ten-day period, starting with either the day on which extradition is ordered (if the person has consented to be extradited) or on the eighth day after extradition has been ordered (ie after the period in which a person can lodge an application for leave to appeal has passed, for those who have not consented to be extradited). Section 35 does, however, allow the judge and the issuing authority to agree a later date. In practice, extensions of time are frequently sought and requested persons are rarely returned within the time limits set out in section 35. Where a person has not been removed within the required period, an application for discharge should be made: see chapter 11, para 11.181.

17 This is sometimes referred to as an 'iron letter'. See para 12.12.
18 EA 2003 s21B(2)(b) only applies to accusation cases.

CHAPTER 5

Bars to extradition

continued

Introduction

5.1 There are a limited number of grounds (often referred to as 'bars to extradition') that can be relied upon to resist extradition. This chapter will consider the statutory bars to extradition, which are set out in Extradition Act (EA) 2003 ss11/79. It will then go on to look at the other grounds for resisting extradition, namely: conviction in absence; physical or mental condition; and abuse of process. The judge will follow these in the order set out in the statute in looking at each ground during the extradition hearing (if raised). The structure of the Act envisages a 'step-by-step' approach by the judge. Finally, the chapter will look at grounds for refusal to extradite under the 2021 Trade and Cooperation Agreement (TCA).[1]

Statutory bars to extradition – Extradition Act 2003

Overview

5.2 Under EA 2003 s11 (Part 1 cases) and s79 (Part 2 cases) the judge must decide whether a person's extradition is barred by reason of:

- the rule against double jeopardy (sections 12/80[2]);
- absence of prosecution decision (Part 1 cases only) (section 12A);
- extraneous considerations (sections 13/81);
- passage of time (sections 14/82);
- the person's age (Part 1 cases only) (section 15);
- hostage-taking considerations (Part 2 cases only) (section 83);
- death penalty (Part 2 cases only) (section 94);
- specialty (sections 17/95);
- earlier extradition from territory or by the International Criminal Court (ICC) (sections 18, 19 and 19A/96 and 96A); and
- forum (sections 19B/83A).

5.3 Having considered these bars (where raised), the judge will go on to look at conviction in absence (EA 2003 ss20/85); human rights (and, in Part 1 cases only, proportionality) (sections 21A/87) and whether a person's mental or physical condition should prevent extradition

1 *Mihai Sonea v Mehedinti District Court, Romania* [2009] EWHC 89 (Admin) at para 16.

2 Where EA 2003 Parts 1 and 2 set out the same bar to extradition, this is indicated using '/', for example sections 12/80.

(sections 25/91). This chapter will follow the statutory numbering in considering each of these in turn, and end by looking at abuse of process, which, although not a statutory bar, is within the court's jurisdiction and has on occasion prevented a person's extradition. Human rights considerations are discussed in chapter 6.

5.4 In addition to these statutory bars to extradition, there is also the possibility of making a request for either temporary transfer to the requesting territory or for arrangements to be made for discussions with investigators/prosecutors from the requesting territory under EA 2003 s21B. See para 12.6 for further detail.

Double jeopardy (sections 12/80)

5.5 This bar may arise in cases where there is an element of cross-border activity, such that one country has already taken action against the requested person. A person, for example, carrying out a customs fraud may commit an offence in two jurisdictions. It may be that a prosecution in jurisdiction A deals with one part of the conduct and that jurisdiction B then seeks to prosecute for another part of the conduct or indeed a larger conspiracy that subsumes the element that has already been prosecuted. Depending on the particular facts of the case, this may give rise to an argument that the requested person's extradition falls within the double jeopardy bar.

5.6 Section 12 'Rule against double jeopardy' provides that:

> A person's extradition to a category 1 territory is barred by reason of the rule against double jeopardy if (and only if) it appears that he would be entitled to be discharged under any rule of law relating to previous acquittal or conviction.

5.7 In order for the bar to apply, the requested person must previously have been put in 'peril of conviction' for the offence for which they now face extradition.[3] Any conviction or acquittal must be final, and finality 'is to be judged by the process in the requesting state'.[4]

5.8 In Part 1 cases, the judge is required to proceed on the basis of two statutory assumptions, that:

3 *Connelly v DPP* [1964] AC 1254, HL, *Mitchell v High Court of Boulogne sur mer, France* [2007] EWHC 2006 (Admin), *Zdinjak v Croatia* [2012] EWHC 1554 (Admin).

4 *R (Oncel) v Governor of Brixton Prison, Government of the Republic of Turkey* [2001] EWHC 1142 (Admin) at para 32.

- the UK courts had jurisdiction to try them for those offences; and
- they were facing trial for the offences in that part of the UK.[5]

The court then has to ask itself whether English rules of law on double jeopardy would apply.[6]

5.9 In *Fofana and Belise v Deputy Prosecutor Thubin, Tribunal de Grande Instance de Meaux, France*[7] the Divisional Court reviewed the authorities and summarised the two circumstances in English law that offend the rule against double jeopardy as follows:

1) following an acquittal or conviction for an offence, which is the same in fact and law – autrefois acquit or convict; and
2) following a trial for any offence which was founded on 'the same or substantially the same facts', where the court would normally consider it right to stay the prosecution as an abuse of process and/or unless the prosecution can show 'special circumstances' why another trial should take place.[8]

5.10 In relation to the second limb above, the defence bear the burden of establishing an abuse of process on the balance of probabilities. A stay of proceedings on the grounds of abuse of process is an exceptional remedy, and only rarely granted.[9] It is imperative to scrutinise the factual foundation of both the first 'offence' and the second, and see whether they are, in truth 'founded on the same incident'.[10] Each case will turn on its own facts.[11] Note, however, that the fact that the same evidence is used, or there is a significant overlap in conduct, does not necessarily mean that the test under the second limb is met. See, for example, *Kulibaba v United States*[12] where conduct which was

5 In relation to Part 2 cases, the judge is not required to make these assumptions (EA 2003 s80). For Part 1 cases, also see TCA Article 600(b) which sets out the terms of the mandatory bar under the TCA (Trade and Cooperation Agreement between the European Union and the European Atomic Energy Community, of the one part, and the United Kingdom of Great Britain and Northern Ireland, of the other part, Document 22021A0430(01), 30 April 2021, https://eur-lex.europa.eu/legal-content/EN/TXT/?uri=uriserv:OJ.L_.2021.149.01.0010.01.ENG).

6 *Hamburg Public Prosecutor's Office v Altun* [2011] EWHC 397 (Admin) at para 19.

7 [2006] EWHC 744 (Admin).

8 [2006] EWHC 744 (Admin) at para 18.

9 *Zada v Italy* [2017] EWHC 513 (Admin) at para 32.

10 *R v Z* [2000] 1 AC 483 at 498.

11 *Ninedeys v District Prosecutor's Office of Varna, Bulgaria* [2014] EWHC 4416 (Admin) at para 9.

12 [2014] EWHC 176 (Admin).

'essentially the same' did not operate to prevent extradition under the double jeopardy bar. See also *Boudhiba v Central Examining Court No 5 of the National Court of Justice, Madrid, Spain;*[13] *Maxwell-King v United States;*[14] *and Purcell v High Court in Dublin, Ireland.*[15]

5.11 To establish this bar, evidence from both lay and expert witnesses is usually required.

5.12 The double jeopardy bar to extradition does not apply to prevent extradition where a requested person has already been discharged on an extradition request in another country.

Absence of prosecution decision (section 12A)

5.13 This bar, inserted by the Anti-social Behaviour, Crime and Policing Act 2014, prevents the extradition of a person where the requesting state has not made a decision to charge or try the requested person. It applies only to Part 1 requests. The purpose of the insertion of the provision was described in *Puceviciene v Lithuanian Judicial Authority*[16] as follows:

> ... The mischief at which the section is directed is the possibility of a person being surrendered and then languishing in custody whilst the alleged crime continued to be the subject of lengthy investigation without decision to charge and try having been made. It was not designed to enable a requested person to remain in the United Kingdom for as long as possible by forcing the requesting judicial authority to carry out part of its processes in this jurisdiction. The application of the provisions of s.12A secures that the requesting judicial authority will be in a position to get on immediately with the next step in its prosecution process as soon as the requested person is surrendered. The purpose of s.12A is served by confining it to the issues it actually raises.[17]

5.14 It will be apparent that there is some overlap between this bar and the provisions of EA 2003 s2(3) which require a warrant to contain a statement that the person in respect of whom the warrant is issued is accused of the commission of an offence and that the warrant has been issued with a view to their arrest and extradition for the purpose of being prosecuted for the offence (see paras 3.14–3.15). Familiar principles apply to the judge's task under section 12A. The judge

13 [2006] EWHC 167 (Admin).
14 [2006] EWHC 3033 (Admin).
15 [2012] EWHC 3325 (Admin).
16 [2016] EWHC 1862 (Admin).
17 At para 73.

must take 'a cosmopolitan approach' and avoid '[approaching] the construction of the phrases "decision to charge" and "decision to try" in section 12A by reference solely to the domestic law and practice of criminal procedures in England and Wales'.[18]

5.15 There are two distinct stages to the application of this section.

First stage

5.16 Under the first stage of EA 2003 s12A, the judge must have reasonable grounds for believing that:

a) the competent authorities in the category 1 territory have not made a decision to charge or have not made a decision to try (or have made neither of those decisions); and
b) the person's absence from the category 1 territory is not the sole reason for that failure.[19]

5.17 The default position at the first stage is that the two decisions have been taken. The requested person must raise a challenge based on something more than mere assertion in order for the questions to be asked.[20]

5.18 In considering this first stage, the judge must begin by looking at the warrant as a whole. If it is clear from the warrant that the decisions have been taken, the judge should look no further.[21] If there is a lack of clarity, the judge will be entitled to consider extraneous evidence.[22] The court in *Kandola* disapproved, however, of the deployment of 'elaborate "expert" evidence' and indicated that it would not, at this stage, be necessary or appropriate for enquiry to be made of the requesting state.[23]

18 *Kandola and others v Generalstaatwaltschaft Frankfurt, Germany and others* [2015] EWHC 619 (Admin) at para 27.

19 EA 2003 s12A(1)(a).

20 *Kandola and others v Generalstaatwaltschaft Frankfurt, Germany and others* [2015] EWHC 619 (Admin) at para 30. Note that in *Puceviciene v Lithuanian Judicial Authority* [2016] EWHC 1862 at para 68, the Divisional Court disapproved the judgment in *Kandola* with regard to the relevance of mutual legal assistance to section 12A.

21 See *Litwinczuk v The Circuit Court in Szczecin, Poland* [2019] EWHC 2745 (Admin) at paras 22–26 in which the High Court took into account the reasoning in *Goluchowksi v District Court in Elblag, Poland* [2016] UKSC 36 in relation to further information provided by the judicial authority in coming to the conclusion that looking at the warrant 'as a whole' included any further information provided by the judicial authority.

22 At para 31. See also *Puceviciene v Lithuanian Judicial Authority* [2016] EWHC 1862 (Admin) at para 51.

23 At para 32.

5.19 It will also be for the requested person to provide sufficient evidence to raise a case that their absence is not the sole reason for the lack of a decision to charge or to try that person.[24] In practice, this is likely to require evidence from a lawyer in the requesting state.

Second stage

5.20 If the requested person is able to satisfy the judge as to both (a) and (b) above, the judge must then move on to consider the second stage. Under section 12A(1)(b) the requested person's extradition will be barred unless the prosecution is able to prove to the criminal standard that:

a) the competent authorities in the category 1 territory have made a decision to charge and a decision to try; or
b) in a case where one of those decisions has not been made (or neither of them has been made), the person's absence from the category 1 territory is the sole reason for that failure.

5.21 Relevant guidance from the Divisional Court can be found in *Puceviciene*[25] and *James Fox v Public Prosecutor's Office of Frankfurt am Main Germany*.[26] The use of the terms 'decision to charge'" and 'decision to try' does not imply that the case must be trial ready.[27] The decision to charge is 'the decision which is made when there is sufficient evidence under the relevant procedural system to make an allegation that the defendant has committed the crime alleged'.[28] A decision to try need not be formal and may be conditional. The Divisional Court provided the following explanation:

> ... simply a decision where the relevant decision maker ... has decided to go ahead with the process of taking to trial the defendant against whom the allegation is made ... that decision may be conditional or contingent upon other matters. Again ... a decision is a decision even if informal.[29]

5.22 In *Puceviciene* the court emphasised that the real focus of the section is on whether there has been a decision to try. If there has been no decision to try, the question of whether there has been a decision to charge is irrelevant.[30]

24 At para 33.
25 [2016] EWHC 1862 (Admin).
26 [2017] EWHC 3396 (Admin).
27 [2016] EWHC 1862 (Admin) at para 50.
28 *Puceviciene v Lithuanian Judicial Authority* [2016] EWHC 1862 (Admin) at para 55.
29 At para 56. See also *Fox v Germany* [2017] EWHC 3396 (Admin) at para 48.
30 At para 50.

Extraneous considerations – sections 13/81

5.23 EA 2003 s13 states:

> A person's extradition to a category 1 territory is barred by reason of extraneous considerations if (and only if) it appears that–
> (a) the Part 1 warrant issued in respect of him (though purporting to be issued on account of the extradition offence) is in fact issued for the purpose of prosecuting or punishing him on account of his race, religion, nationality, gender, sexual orientation or political opinions; or
> (b) if extradited he might be prejudiced at his trial or punished, detained or restricted in his personal liberty by reason of his race, religion, nationality, gender, sexual orientation or political opinions.

5.24 Section 81 uses precisely the same formulation in relation to Part 2 requests. As can be seen from the above, there are two separate limbs within the extraneous considerations bar that are set out as alternatives: it is enough to show one or the other.

5.25 The bar prevents the extradition of a person if, broadly, the 'extraneous considerations' have resulted in the issue of the warrant or request, or will prejudice the person upon their return. The first limb (subsection (a)) looks at the reasons behind the issue of the warrant or request: it prevents extradition where a country has ostensibly sought the return of a person for a particular offence, but where the real motive for seeking their return is to prosecute or punish that person because of the 'extraneous considerations'. This limb requires the court to assess the state of mind of the judicial authority at the time the request was made.[31] The second limb (subsection (b)) is directed at what might happen to the person in the future if they are extradited. If the person will suffer prejudice at trial,[32] punishment or detention or restriction of liberty by reason of the 'extraneous considerations', then extradition will be barred. It is not necessary to identify precisely how prejudice will manifest itself.[33] The requirement to 'predict prejudice' is a reference to a need to identify the risk of such

31 *Slepcik v Governor of HMP Brixton* [2004] EWHC 1224 (QB) at para 23 see also *Adamescu v Romania* [2020] EWHC 2709 (Admin) in which the parties agreed that the court was not limited to considering the precise moment when the judge issued the European Arrest Warrant (EAW), but was required to have regard to the underlying process which led to the decision (at para 66).

32 *Turkey v Ozbek* [2014] EWHC 3469 (Admin): there are four forms of mistreatment set out in subsection (b), however, the only context in which prejudice is relevant is at trial.

33 *Turkey v Tanis* [2021] EWHC 1675 (Admin) at para 45.

treatment being accorded by reason of one of the protected factors set out in subsection (b).[34]

5.26 There is an obvious overlap between this bar and human rights considerations, in particular European Convention on Human Rights (ECHR) Articles 3 (prohibition of torture and ill-treatment), 5 (right to liberty and security) and 6 (right to a fair trial), and in practice they are often argued in parallel (see chapter 6).[35]

Test

5.27 The test is set out in the pre-EA 2003 case of *Fernandez v Government of Singapore*,[36] which was summarised by Scott-Baker LJ in *Hilali v The National Court in Madrid and another*[37] as follows:

> The burden is on the appellant to show a causal link between the issue of the warrant, his detention, prosecution, punishment or the prejudice which he asserts he will suffer and the fact of his race or his religion. He does not have to prove on the balance of probabilities that the events described in s.13(b) will take place, but he must show that there is a 'reasonable chance' or 'reasonable grounds for thinking' or a 'serious possibility' that such events will occur ...[38]

5.28 The test was reaffirmed in the case of *Adamescu v Bucharest Appeal Court Criminal Division, Romania*:[39]

> In relation to section 13(b), the court is concerned with what may happen in the future if the requested person is extradited. The burden was on the appellant to show that there is a reasonable chance (alternatively expressed as reasonable grounds for thinking, or a serious possibility) that he might be prejudiced at his trial or punished, detained or restricted in his personal liberty on account of his political opinions: see *Hilali* at [62]. In *Antonov & Barauskas*, at [27], the court emphasised that a requested person must establish the necessary causal link, and that–
>
> '... the "serious possibility" test applies to both what might happen and the reason for it happening.'

5.29 The test distinguishes between the first limb, which requires the requested person to show a causal link on the balance of

34 At para 47.

35 Different tests do, however, apply. See *Nikolics v The City Court of Szekszard (a judicial authority in Hungary)* [2013] EWHC 2377 (Admin) para 14.

36 [1971] 1 WLR 987, HL.

37 [2006] EWHC 1239 (Admin).

38 [2006] EWHC 1239 (Admin) at para 62.

39 [2020] EWHC 2709 (Admin) at para 67.

probabilities,[40] and the second, which requires the requested person to show 'a serious possibility' that the events listed in (b) will occur and that there is a causal link.[41] As such, while it may appear that the test is easily satisfied, in reality it is difficult to succeed on this bar to extradition because of the problems one may face in adducing evidence to show the causal link between the issue of the warrant, the person's detention, prosecution, punishment or the prejudice the person asserts they will suffer and any extraneous considerations.

5.30 By way of example, it may be helpful to consider a case in which reliance was unsuccessfully placed on this bar alongside a case in which extraneous considerations did bar a person's extradition.

5.31 In *Tamarevichute v Russian Federation*[42] the defence sought to argue that there was a 'reasonable chance' or a 'serious possibility' that, as a person of Roma origin, the appellant might be prejudiced at her trial in Kaliningrad on account of her race. The Administrative Court found that the appellant had 'adduced powerful evidence of widespread discrimination against the Roma within the Russian Federation ... [which included] attacks on Roma people and their property, the voicing of anti-Roma sentiments in the media and in political speeches, and human rights abuses by the law enforcement authorities'.[43]

5.32 This, however, was not enough to bar her extradition. The judge said (at para 99):

> The fact that, if returned to the Russian Federation, the appellant would be at risk of suffering general prejudice as a result of her Roma origin is not, however, sufficient to constitute a bar to her extradition under the provisions of section 81(b) of the Act. She must demonstrate that there exists a 'reasonable chance' or a 'serious possibility' of her being prejudiced at her trial, or 'punished, detained or restricted in her personal liberty' by reason of her race.

In deciding that the causal link had not been demonstrated, the judge looked at whether the appellant had actually suffered prejudice when in Russia on account of her Roma origin, and found that she had not.

5.33 This can be contrasted with the case of *Government of the Republic of Serbia v Ejup Ganić*,[44] in which the district judge found that extradition was barred under both subsections (a) and (b) of EA 2003 s81.

40 See *Adamescu* at para 65.

41 *Antonov v Prosecutor General's Office, Lithuania* [2015] EWHC 1243 (Admin) at para 27.

42 [2008] EWHC 534 (Admin) (DC).

43 At para 98.

44 [2010] EW Misc 11 (EWMC).

In that case, the return of the former acting President of Bosnia was sought for war crimes. The requested person had been subject to two international investigations, both of which had found that there was no case to answer. The defence called a number of witnesses who gave evidence to say that the prosecution was politically motivated, resulting in the discharge of the requested person under both section 81(a) and (as a result of evidence called to show that he would be prejudiced at trial on account of his race) section 81(b).

5.34 This bar is most commonly invoked in cases where it is argued that persons are sought in respect of a politically motivated request.[45]

5.35 As can be seen from the above examples, a requested person will need to obtain a significant body of evidence from experts and others to persuade a judge that extraneous considerations should bar the person's extradition.

5.36 See para 5.129 below regarding the political offence exception in the TCA, and note the difference between the extraneous considerations bar and the political offence exception as set out in the magistrates' court decision of *Government of the USA v Assange*[46] at paras 50–55.

Passage of time – sections 14/82

5.37 Passage of time is frequently raised by requested persons seeking to resist their extradition. Under EA 2003 Part 1 s14, or Part 2 s82, a person's extradition is barred if it appears that it would be *unjust or oppressive* to extradite them by reason of the passage of time since they are alleged to have committed the offence or since they are alleged to have become unlawfully at large. The bar under sections 14/82 operates differently depending on whether the person is categorised as an accused person under subsection (a), when the person will be able to rely on the passage of time since the date of the commission of the offence; or as a person unlawfully at large following conviction under subsection (b), in which case the person may

45 In respect of imputed political opinions, see the Supreme Court judgment in *RT (Zimbabwe) and others v Secretary of State for the Home Department* [2012] UKSC 38 at paras 53 and 55. In the extradition context, see, for example, *Russian Federation v Azarov*, Westminster Magistrates' Court, 19 December 2007; and *Russian Federation v Nikitin and Skarga*, Westminster Magistrates' Court, 8 December 2008.

46 Westminster Magistrates' Court, 4 January 2021.

only rely on the passage of time since the date of conviction.[47] See below at paras 5.40–5.42 and 5.48 regarding the differences.

5.38 To rely on this bar, it is not enough to show a long delay – it is also necessary to show either injustice or oppression occasioned by the time that has passed. This bar replicates provisions in earlier legislation, and a significant body of pre-2003 case-law on passage of time still applies.

Fugitives and 'unlawfully at large'

5.39 Perhaps the most important point that can be derived from the case-law is that delay brought about by the accused placing themselves beyond the reach of legal process[48] will prevent that person from relying on the passage of time in all but the most exceptional circumstances. In *Kakis v Government of the Republic of Cyprus*[49] Lord Diplock said:

> Delay in the commencement or conduct of extradition proceedings which is brought about by the accused himself by *fleeing the country*, *concealing his whereabouts* or *evading arrest* cannot, in my view, be relied upon as a ground for holding it to be either unjust or oppressive to return him [emphasis added].

5.40 This principle was refined in *Gomes and Goodyer v Trinidad and Tobago*[50] and subsequent authorities in two important ways. First, if a defendant deliberately flees, they cannot then rely on the passage of time, even if the requesting state has significantly contributed to the delay.[51] Second, the burden is on the requesting state to prove beyond all reasonable doubt that the requested person has deliberately and knowingly placed themselves beyond the reach of the relevant legal process.[52] The test is therefore subjective.[53]

47 *Konecny v District Court in Brno-Venkov, Czech Republic* [2019] UKSC 8 at para 53.

48 See *Pillar-Neumann v Public Prosecutor's Office of Klagenfurt, Austria* [2017] EWHC 3371 (Admin) in which the Divisional Court said at para 64 that: 'The essential question is ... whether the Requested Person has knowingly placed himself beyond the reach of legal process. Fleeing the country, concealing whereabouts or evading arrest are examples of so doing.'

49 [1978] 1 WLR 779, HL.

50 [2009] UKHL 21.

51 In *Gomes*, the requesting state had lost the file.

52 *De Zorzi v Attorney General Appeal Court of Paris, France* [2019] EWHC 2062 (Admin) at para 48.

53 At para 48.

5.41 In *Wisniewski v Poland*,[54] the court held that a person subject to a suspended sentence will be a fugitive if they know it is liable to be activated because of their breach of the terms of the suspension; it is not necessary that they know that it has been activated.

5.42 The test for whether a person is 'unlawfully at large' under subsection (b) of sections 14/82 is an objective one, unaffected by the requested person's state of knowledge.[55] A person is unlawfully at large if the person is at large in contravention of a lawful and immediate sentence of imprisonment under the applicable legal system.[56]

Injustice or oppression

5.43 The burden of proof is on the requested person to establish on the balance of probabilities that it would be unjust or oppressive to extradite them.

5.44 In *Kakis*, Lord Diplock set out a definition of 'injustice or oppression'. He stated that:

> 'Unjust' I regard as directed primarily to the risk of prejudice to the accused in the conduct of the trial itself, 'oppressive' as directed to hardship to the accused resulting from changes in his circumstances that have occurred during the period to be taken into consideration; but there is room for overlapping, and between them they would cover all cases where to return him would not be fair.[57]

5.45 In *Eason v Government of the United States of America*[58] the Divisional Court summarised the following points arising from the authorities regarding 'injustice':

a) if, because of the passage of time, a fair trial is now impossible, it would clearly be unjust to order extradition;
b) a court should, however, be very slow to come to such a conclusion where the state making the request is one that is shown to have, or may be presumed to have, appropriate safeguards to protect the defendant against unfairness resulting from the passage of time in the trial process;
c) the possibility or otherwise of a fair trial is not the only relevant consideration, as the question is not whether it would be unjust or oppressive to try the accused but whether it would be unjust or oppressive to extradite them.

54 [2016] EWHC 386 (Admin) at para 60.

55 *Wisniewski v Poland* [2016] EWHC 386 (Admin) at para 54.

56 *De Zorzi v France*, at para 46.

57 *Kakis v Government of the Republic of Cyprus* [1978] 1 WLR 779, HL at para 782.

58 [2020] EWHC 604 (Admin).

The judgment emphasises the strong public interest in honouring extradition arrangements.

5.46 On the meaning of 'oppression', the Divisional Court in *Eason* said (at para 28):

> As regards oppression in the form of hardship, it is clear that the test goes beyond mere or ordinary hardship, which is a comparatively common consequence of an order for extradition, and will not easily be satisfied: see *Gomes* at para 31. Where there has been culpable delay on the part of the requesting state, that is a relevant factor and may tip the balance in a case where the requested person is not himself to blame: see *Gomes* at paras 23 –27; and *La Torre v Italy* [2007] EWHC 1370 (Admin) at para 16 (per Laws LJ). Other relevant factors may include matters such as the seriousness of the offence, and the impact of extradition on other family members. Ultimately, an overall judgment on the merits is required and it is important to stay focused on the words of the statute itself: see *La Torre v Italy* at para 37; and *USA v Tollman & Tollman* at para 49.

5.47 To show oppression, a detailed proof of evidence from the requested person will be required, alongside evidence from family members and, in some cases, expert witnesses such as social workers or psychologists who can comment on the impact that extradition will have on dependent family members.

Passage of time and Article 8

5.48 There will often be an overlap between passage of time and ECHR Article 8 and they are often relied on by requested persons in tandem (see para 6.54). Where a person has been convicted in absence but has not deliberately absented themselves, a potential injustice arises from the drafting of EA 2003 ss14/82 which treats such a person as 'unlawfully at large' under subsection (b) and therefore precludes that person from raising injustice that may arise at a retrial, and restricts the passage of time consideration to the date of conviction, rather than the date of the commission of the offence under subsection (a). The Supreme Court in *Konecny v District Court in Brno-Venkov, Czech Republic*[59] recommended that this be amended by parliament, but indicated that until that time, Article 8 provides an appropriate and effective means of addressing passage of time in cases where the requested person has been convicted in absence.[60]

59 [2019] UKSC 8.

60 At para 57.

Cases where passage of time has barred extradition

5.49 The passage of time bar will always be fact-specific, but practitioners may find it helpful to consider examples of cases where passage of time has been successfully raised by requested persons, such as *Eason v United States of America*;[61] *Pillar-Neumann v Public Prosecutor's Office of Klagenfurt, Austria*;[62] *De Zorzi v Attorney General Appeal Court of Paris, France*;[63] *Purcell v Public Prosecutor of Antwerp, Belgium*;[64] *La Torre v Italy*;[65] *Kovac v Central Court in Prague, Czech Republic*;[66] and *Koc v Turkey*.[67]

Person's age – section 15

5.50 EA 2003 s15 provides that a person's extradition is barred by reason of their age if it would be conclusively presumed that they could not be guilty of the extradition offence because of their age. The judge will be required to assess whether extradition is barred on the assumptions that the conduct would amount to an offence in the UK, had it taken place in the UK and that the person had carried out the conduct.

5.51 In short, given that the age of criminal responsibility in this country is ten, if a person is said to have committed an offence when they were younger than ten, extradition will be barred. This bar only applies in Part 1 cases. Practitioners may have difficulty imagining circumstances in which a warrant for a child younger than ten would be issued, particularly given that there is now no EU country with a lower age of criminal responsibility than England and Wales. Indeed, the authors are not aware of a single case in which reliance has been placed on this bar to extradition under the EA 2003 and, in practice, it is redundant.

Hostage-taking considerations – section 83

5.52 EA 2003 s83 sets out another highly unusual bar to extradition which does not apply to Part 1 cases. It only applies where:

61 [2020] EWHC 604 (Admin).
62 [2017] EWHC 3371 (Admin).
63 [2019] EWHC 2062 (Admin).
64 [2017] EWHC 1328 (Admin).
65 [2007] EWHC 1370 (Admin).
66 [2009] EWHC 3528 (Admin).
67 [2021] EWHC 1234 (Admin).

- the conduct set out in the request would constitute an offence under section 1 of the Taking of Hostages Act 1982 or an attempt to commit such an offence;[68] and
- the requesting country is a party to the Hostage Taking Convention.

5.53 If both of these conditions apply, the court will have to examine whether the requested person might be prejudiced at trial because communications between them and the appropriate authorities (ie consular authorities) would not be possible.[69] Again, the authors are not aware of this bar to extradition being raised under the EA 2003.

Specialty – sections 17/95

5.54 The principle of specialty[70] provides that, where a person is extradited, the person will be prosecuted or proceeded against only for the offences in respect of which they are extradited, that is, those set out in the warrant or extradition request.

5.55 In respect of EA 2003 Part 1 cases, section 17 is a bar to extradition to be considered by the appropriate judge at the extradition hearing. For Part 2 cases, it falls to be considered by the Secretary of State for the Home Department (SSHD) after the extradition hearing.

5.56 To rely on the specialty bar, a requested person must show that appropriate specialty arrangements are not in place in the requesting state.[71] A specialty arrangement may exist because the law of the requesting state meets the requirements of sections 17/95 or through treaty provision.[72] There must be practical and effective

68 Taking of Hostages Act 1982 s1 states that:

(1) A person, whatever his nationality, who, in the United Kingdom or elsewhere–

(a) detains any other person ('the hostage'), and

(b) in order to compel a State, international governmental organisation or person to do or abstain from doing any act, threatens to kill, injure or continue to detain the hostage, commits an offence.

The Taking of Hostages Act 1982 was enacted to implement the International Convention against the Taking of Hostages.

69 The Convention carries a clause which modifies extradition arrangements between state signatories and indeed allows extensive extradition which goes beyond that provided for in EA 2003.

70 Specialty is also sometimes referred to as 'speciality' (and is referred to as such in the legislation).

71 *Enasoaie v Court of Bacau, Romania* [2021] EWHC 69 (Admin) at para 50.

72 *Welsh v Secretary of State for the Home Department* [2006] EWHC 156 (Admin) at para 28.

arrangements to ensure that the requested person will only be tried for the offence for which they have been extradited or others disclosed by the same facts.[73] In Part 1 cases under the EAW scheme, a strong presumption that European Union (EU) countries would act in accordance with their international obligations in respect of speciality applied.[74] The TCA retains specialty protection at Article 625,[75] and it appears likely that the courts will find that this presumption still applies.

5.57 The issue of specialty may arise in cases where sentences have been merged, and extradition is ordered for one but not all offences: see for example *Brodziak v Poland;*[76] and *Enasoaie v Court of Bacau, Romania.*[77]

Earlier extradition – sections 18, 19, 19A/96, 96A

5.58 EA 2003 ss18, 19 and 96 offer some (limited) protection to a person who has been extradited *to* the UK and subsequently faces a new warrant or request to be extradited from the UK.[78]

5.59 If the country that originally extradited the requested person to the UK is required to give consent to onward extradition and does not do so, that will act as a bar to extradition. As with the specialty bar, this is considered by the judge at the extradition hearing for Part 1 cases and by the secretary of state where the requesting state is a Part 2 territory.

Forum – sections 19B–F/83A–E[79]

5.60 Criminal conduct is increasingly cross-jurisdictional, meaning that there will often be more than one country in which a prosecution may take place. 'Forum non conveniens' is a civil law doctrine that gives courts power to refuse to hear a case where there is a more appropriate jurisdiction. In an extradition context, the forum bar

73 *Hilali v Spain* [2006] EWHC 1239 (Admin) at para 46.

74 *Brodziak v Poland* [2013] EWHC 3394 (Admin) at para 49.

75 Note TCA Article 625(1) allows a notification to be given by the UK or EU member states that consent is presumed to have been given to deal with a person for an offence other than that for which they were surrendered.

76 [2013] EWHC 3394 (Admin).

77 [2021] EWHC 69 (Admin).

78 There is a similar provision in EA 2003 s19A which applies when a person has been transferred to a country by the International Criminal Court.

79 As inserted by Crime and Courts Act 2013 Sch 20.

operates by way of EA 2003 ss19B–F (for Part 1 cases) and 83A–E (for Part 2 cases). These sections prevent extradition 'by reason of forum' if the extradition would not be in the interests of justice, although the matters relevant to an evaluation of 'the interests of justice' are limited by the legislation and 'do not leave to the court the task of some broad evaluation of what is just'.[80] The bar only applies in accusation cases.[81]

Gateway

5.61 EA 2003 ss19B/83A (as subsection (2)) state that extradition will not be in the interests of justice if the judge:

(a) decides that a substantial measure of D's relevant activity was performed in the United Kingdom; and
(b) decides, having regard to the specified matters relating to the interests of justice (and only those matters), that the extradition should not take place.

(Where 'D' is a person.)

5.62 The first condition, described as a 'gateway' in the case-law,[82] is that a substantial measure of the activity must have been performed in the UK. Relevant activity is defined as activity 'material to the commission of the extradition offence' and which is alleged to have been performed by the requested person. It is described as a gateway as, if the judge is not satisfied as to this, it will not be necessary to go on to consider the specified matters relating to the interests of justice.

Specified matters

5.63 The second condition imposes limits on the judge's discretion in looking at the interests of justice and allows the judge to 'have regard' only to the seven matters which are specified in the provisions, and to no other matters. The specified matters are as follows (at subsection (3)):

80 *Love v Government of the United States of America* [2018] EWHC 172 (Admin) at para 22.

81 The fact that a person is requested under a conviction warrant means that they cannot rely on the forum bar, even if that person is entitled to a re-trial having been convicted 'in absentia' – see *Bagri (Paramjit) v Public Prosecutor Bordeaux Court of First Instance, France* [2014] EWHC 4066 (Admin); and *Douglas Belbin v Regional Court of Lille, France* [2015] EWHC 149 (Admin).

82 *Pham v United States of America* [2014] EWHC 4167 (Admin) at para 85; *Atraskevic v Prosecutor General's Office, Republic of Lithuania* [2015] EWHC 131 (Admin) at para 16.

(a) the place where most of the loss or harm resulting from the extradition offence occurred or was intended to occur;
(b) the interests of any victims of the extradition offence;
(c) any belief of a prosecutor that the United Kingdom, or a particular part of the United Kingdom, is not the most appropriate jurisdiction in which to prosecute D in respect of the conduct constituting the extradition offence;
(d) were D to be prosecuted in a part of the United Kingdom for an offence that corresponds to the extradition offence, whether evidence necessary to prove the offence is or could be made available in the United Kingdom;
(e) any delay that might result from proceeding in one jurisdiction rather than another;
(f) the desirability and practicability of all prosecutions relating to the extradition offence taking place in one jurisdiction, having regard (in particular) to–
   (i) the jurisdictions in which witnesses, co-defendants and other suspects are located; and
   (ii) the practicability of the evidence of such persons being given in the United Kingdom or in jurisdictions outside the United Kingdom;
(g) D's connections with the United Kingdom.

5.64 'Having regard' means bearing in mind each of the specified matters, although in the particular case being considered one factor may be irrelevant, or not present, or of little weight, or of great importance.[83] Nonetheless, the judge must have regard to each of the specified matters individually.[84] In *United States of America v McDaid*,[85] the Divisional Court said that 'that evaluation is necessarily fact-specific, because the importance of each of the matters specified in subsection (3), and the weight to be given to each of them, will vary according to the circumstances of the case'.[86] It is not, however, a 'balancing exercise'.[87]

Place – sections 19B(3)(a)/83A(3)(a)

5.65 The first specified matter listed is place: the judge will have regard to the place where most of the loss or harm occurred or was intended to

83 *Shaw v Government of the United States of America* [2014] EWHC 4654 (Admin) at para 40.
84 *Shaw* at para 40.
85 [2020] EWHC 1527 (Admin).
86 At para 43.
87 At para 44.

occur. This would cover offences such as those where a person in the UK uses the internet to commit an offence in another jurisdiction, without leaving this one. This will usually be 'a very weighty factor'.[88]

Interests of the victims – sections 19B(3)(b)/83A(3)(b)

5.66 In looking at this specified matter, the judge will consider the views of the alleged victims as to where the trial should take place, but they are also required to have regard to where the interests of the alleged victim would best be served by having a trial.[89] As indicated in *Scott v United States of America*,[90] approving *Love*:

> ... victims of crime may have an interest in having the case tried according to their own local laws and procedures, and in any sentence being imposed following conviction reflecting the values of their own legal system, 'but their interest in having a trial at all is the more important.' ... If the choice is between a trial in one jurisdiction and no trial in the other jurisdiction, the interests of victims are likely to favour trial in the jurisdiction where a trial will take place.[91]

Prosecutor's belief – sections 19B(3)(c)/83A(3)(c)

5.67 EA 2003 defines 'a prosecutor' in these sections as a person who has responsibility for prosecuting offences in any part of the UK, whether or not the person also has other responsibilities.[92] This will exclude a prosecutor from the CPS Extradition Unit.[93]

5.68 The court has provided some guidance as to the exercise it must carry out in looking at the factor in sections 19B(3)(c)/83A(3)(c) under which the judge must take into account any belief of a prosecutor that the UK is not the most appropriate jurisdiction. In *Dibden v Tribunal de Grande Instance de Lille, France*, Simon J set out the limited basis upon which the court should review a prosecutor's belief saying: 'In my judgment, section 19B(3)(c) was not intended to invite a review of the prosecutor's belief as to the more appropriate jurisdiction on grounds short of irrationality. It was certainly not intended to invite a debate with demands for documents justifying the belief.'[94] He went on to say that the prosecutor's belief can be set out in a letter or statement but should be in writing, akin to a decision

88 *Love v United States* at para 28.

89 *Shaw* at para 61.

90 [2018] EWHC 2021 (Admin).

91 At para 43.

92 EA 2003 s19F.

93 *Shaw* at para 48.

94 [2014] EWHC 3074 (Admin) at para 35.

letter in immigration proceedings, and setting out the reasons for the prosecutor's belief.

5.69 Further principles regarding the 'prosecutor's belief' are set out in *Shaw v United States of America*:[95]

> 48. In my view, the correct construction of section 83A(3)(c) is, for present purposes, as follows: first, it is important to note the word 'any' at the start of the paragraph. There may or may not be a belief that is stated to the court in some form or another. It is only if there is one that this factor is going to be relevant.[96] The judge has to ask whether there is a belief; but if there is not, then he cannot have any further 'regard' to this factor. [Second], the key-word is 'belief'. It is not 'decision' or some similar word. A 'belief' in this context is more akin to a point of view or a conclusion based upon certain facts and other considerations. [Third], for these purposes, 'a prosecutor' must mean a domestic prosecutor within the United Kingdom: see the definition in section 83E(2). In England and Wales this means someone within the domestic branch of the CPS, rather than the separate and independent branch of the CPS, called the CPS Extradition Unit, which deals with extradition matters.
> 49. [Fourth], the 'belief' has to be a firm one in the sense that the prosecutor has to have concluded that the United Kingdom is 'not the most appropriate jurisdiction in which to prosecute' the person whose extradition is sought. Note the words 'the most appropriate'; therefore, it might be an appropriate jurisdiction but not necessarily 'the most appropriate'. [Fifth], it is important to note what precisely is the subject of the prosecution 'belief'. It is that the prosecution of the requested person for an offence (or offences) 'in respect of the conduct constituting the extradition offence' is not the most appropriate in the United Kingdom. In other words, the prosecutor has to consider the conduct that founds the alleged extradition offence itself, not other offences or other conduct that might be involved.

5.70 Further guidance relating to the prosecutors belief was provided in *Atraskevic v Prosecutor General's Office, Lithuania*:[97]

> The third general point concerns the construction of the statutory wording of factor *(c)*: viz. 'any belief' of a prosecutor that the UK or a particular part of it, is not the most appropriate jurisdiction in which to prosecute the requested person for the extradition offence. In our view, the use of the words 'any belief of a prosecutor' is important.

95 [2014] EWHC 4654 (Admin) at paras 48-49.

96 Note that, while in *Love v United States of America* [2018] EWHC 172 (Admin), Lord Burnett stated that the absence of a prosecutor's belief was a factor which modestly favoured the appellant, he came to the opposite conclusion in *Scott v United States of America* [2018] EWHC 2021 (Admin) at paras 28–32 having reviewed *Shaw* and *Atraskevic*.

97 [2015] EWHC 131 (Admin) at para 37.

The 'prosecutor' in question here is a domestic prosecutor, that is someone in the domestic CPS. Such a prosecutor may or may not have formed any such belief at the time of the extradition hearing. If none has been formed or expressed, the statutory wording does not require that any party or the court should demand that a prosecutor must then take steps to create a 'belief' on the part of the prosecutor. The initiative to declare 'a belief' or not lies with the domestic CPS. There is no statutory mechanism that enables the court to compel further investigation by the CPS so as to put it in a position to have a 'belief'. That view of the construction of this factor is consistent with the rule, applicable in extradition cases, that a decision by domestic authorities not to investigate whether there should be a criminal prosecution in the UK is not susceptible to judicial review except in wholly exceptional circumstances such as bad faith: *R (Bermingham) v DPP* [2007] QB 207 at [64]; *R (McKinnon) v Secretary of State for Home Affairs* [2009] EWHC 2021 at [53].

5.71 Practitioners should also note that under sections 19B(5)/83A(5) a prosecutor can apply to be made a party to the proceedings. If it appears to the judge that the prosecutor has considered the offences for which the requested person could be prosecuted in the UK in respect of the conduct constituting the extradition offence, the judge must make the prosecutor a party to the proceedings if an application is made by the prosecutor.

Availability of evidence – sections 19B(3)(d)/83A(3)(d)

5.72 The judge must also consider whether evidence necessary to prove the offence could be made available in the UK for an offence which corresponds to the extradition offence. This is not the same as all the evidence that might be available in the requesting state, and the assessment under this heading requires a comparison between the availability of evidence in this country and the requesting state.[98]

Delay – sections 19B(3)(e)/83A(3)(e)

5.73 Another consideration for the judge under sections 19B(3)/83A(3) will be the delay that might result in proceeding in one jurisdiction.

Trials in same jurisdiction – sections 19B(3)(f)/83A(3)(f)

5.74 The legislation requires the judge to look at where witnesses and other co-defendants are located and how practicable it would be for their evidence to be given in the UK. It is desirable when practicable for prosecution to take place in a single trial, where there is more

98 *Shaw at* at paras 49–50.

than one defendant, however, the position is less weighty where separate trials are inevitable, even if they were to take place in the same jurisdiction.[99] Judges are entitled to consider cost under the heading of practicability.[100]

Requested person's connections – sections 19B(3)(g)/83A(3)(g)

5.75 The judge is also required to have regard to the defendant's connections with the UK. 'Connection' is not a narrow concept, and while the court in *Love* did not provide an exhaustive definition, it was said that 'connection' would cover family ties, their nature and strength, employment and studies, property, duration and status of residence, and nationality.[101]

5.76 While bearing in mind that there is no predetermined hierarchy among the specified matters under sections 19B(3)/83A(3) (see para 5.64 above), practitioners should note that in the three cases in which the forum bar has been successfully invoked at the time of writing (*Love, Scott* and *McDaid*), the place where most of the loss or the harm took place and the requested person's connections to the UK appeared to be particularly important factors in the decision-making.

5.77 Under a separate subsection (ss19B(4)/83A(4)) that follows, the judge must also have regard to the desirability of not requiring the disclosure of material which is subject to restrictions on disclosure in the requesting state.

Prosecutor's certificate

5.78 Further complexity is added to the forum provisions by sections 19C/83B which allow the prosecutor to prevent an argument on forum by issuing a certificate. If the prosecutor does so, the only mechanism for challenge will be on appeal on judicial review principles. The certificate must certify particular matters, which are set out in sections 19D/83C (see below).

5.79 It will be evident that the legislation allows prosecutors a great deal of latitude. Sections 19C/83B also enable prosecutors to obtain adjournments to consider whether to issue a certificate. If an application is made, the judge must grant the adjournment application and

99 *Scott v United States of America* [2018] EWHC 2021 (Admin) at para 55.

100 *Piotrowicz v Regional Court in Gdansk, Poland* [2014] EWHC 3884 (Admin) at para 30.

101 *Love v Government of the United States of America* [2018] EWHC 172 (Admin) at para 40.

continue to adjourn for as long as appears reasonable. In addition, a prosecutor cannot be required to give a prosecutor's certificate.

5.80 Under sections 19D/83C, the certificate must certify both matter A and Matter B and either Matter C or Matter D – as follows.

Matter A

The responsible prosecutor has considered the offences for which D could be prosecuted in the UK.

AND

Matter B

The responsible prosecutor has decided that there are one or more such offences that correspond to the extradition offence.

5.81 It is mandatory for the prosecutor to certify that they have considered the offences and that they are extradition offences. In practice, this is unlikely to be contentious.

5.82 The prosecutor must also certify either Matter C or Matter D.

Matter C

The responsible prosecutor has made a formal decision that D should not be prosecuted for the corresponding offences, and the reason for that decision is a belief that –

(i) there would be insufficient admissible evidence for the prosecution; or

(ii) the prosecution would not be in the public interest

OR

Matter D

The responsible prosecutor believes that D should not be prosecuted because there are concerns about the disclosure of sensitive material in–

(a) the prosecution of D for the corresponding offences, or

(b) any other proceedings.

5.83 With regard to Matter C, the prosecutor must have taken a formal decision not to charge. The test here is effectively the same as the test for a charging decision under the Code for Crown Prosecutors. The formal decision is defined as referring to a decision made after complying with any relevant code of practice that the requested person should or should not be prosecuted. In most cases this will be the Full Code test.[102]

5.84 With regard to Matter D the prosecutor will need to certify that there are concerns about the disclosure of sensitive material. As with section 19B(4), the information which the prosecutor will have which will enable him or her to make the decision about the disclosure of sensitive material is unclear.

5.85 Although the prosecutor's certificate may appear to be a powerful tool, in reality, it is unlikely to be frequently deployed. This is because, once a certificate is issued, it allows decisions taken by the prosecutor to be subjected to scrutiny by the court, albeit only on appeal on judicial review principles.

CPS guidance

5.86 Practitioners dealing with a case engaging the forum bar should have regard to both the CPS Internal Process for dealing with Forum Bar cases (see appendix J) along with the guidance issued by the DPP on the handling of cases where the jurisdiction to prosecute is shared with prosecuting authorities overseas.[103]

Death penalty – section 94

5.87 The death penalty bar prevents the secretary of state from ordering a person's extradition to a Part 2 country if they could be, will be or have been sentenced to death. If, however, the secretary of state receives a written assurance that the death penalty will not apply to the requested person or will not be carried out (and they consider that assurance adequate), the requested person will not be able to rely on this bar. In a case where an assurance has been provided that the death penalty will not be carried out if imposed, consideration

102 The Code for Crown Prosecutors. Available at: www.cps.gov.uk/publication/code-crown-prosecutors.

103 See 'Director's Guidance on the handling of cases where the jurisdiction to prosecute is shared with prosecuting authorities overseas' (CPS, 2013), available at: www.cps.gov.uk/publications/directors_guidance/director_s_guidance_on_concurrent_jurisdiction.html. See also 'Attorney-General's Domestic Guidance for handling criminal cases affecting both England, Wales or Northern Ireland and the United States of America' (2007), at: www.publications.parliament.uk/pa/ld200607/ldlwa/70125ws1.pdf.

should be given as to whether remaining on death row in 'limbo' amounts to a violation of ECHR Article 3 (prohibition of torture and ill-treatment).[104]

Conviction in absence – sections 20/85

5.88 This bar prevents the extradition of persons convicted in their absence where they will not have a right to a retrial or review amounting to a retrial. There is, however, an important caveat: if the requested person deliberately absented themselves from their trial, they will not be able to rely on EA 2003 ss20/85 to prevent extradition. The intent of sections 20/85 is to give proper protection to the requested person's ECHR Article 6 rights (right to a fair trial).[105]

5.89 The steps that the judge must follow in deciding this question are prescribed by sections 20/85. In the extradition hearing, the judge must first decide whether the person was convicted in their absence (sections 20(1)/85(1)), and if so, whether they were deliberately absent (sections 20(3)/85(3)). This is a question of fact, and it is the judicial authority that bears the burden of proving, to the criminal standard, that a person was deliberately absent from their trial.[106] In any conviction case, it is imperative for the requested person's representative to ascertain whether the person was present when convicted, and if not, whether that person was deliberately absent from the trial.[107]

Deliberate absence from trial

5.90 There have been numerous authorities that have looked at the construction of 'deliberate absence' from trial. The Divisional Court's judgment in *Cretu v Romania*[108] is an authoritative statement of the principles to be followed. This case set out the way in which section 20 should be interpreted when applying the principle of conforming interpretation to read it in light of Article 4a of the Framework Decision on the European Arrest Warrant (EAW FD) (as

104 *Ghana v Gambrah* [2014] EWHC 1569 (Admin).

105 *Szatkowski v Regional Court in Opole, Poland* [2019] EWHC 883 (Admin) at para 33.

106 *Murtati v Albania* [2008] EWHC 2856 (Admin); *Benko v Hungary* [2009] EWHC 3530 (Admin); *Mitoi v Romania* [2006] EWHC 1977 (Admin).

107 *Emil Kis v District Court In Sokolov, Czech Republic* [2012] EWHC 938 (Admin).

108 [2016] EWHC 353 (Admin).

amended). While the principle of conforming interpretation no longer applies (and nor does the EAW FD), the terms of TCA Article 601(1)(i) replicate those of Article 4a, and it appears likely therefore that the court will continue to follow the principles set out by Burnett LJ (as he then was) in *Cretu*, as below:

i) 'Trial' in section 20(3) of the 2003 Act must be read as meaning 'trial which resulted in the decision' in conformity with article 4a paragraph 1.(a)(i). That suggests an event with a 'scheduled date and place' and is not referring to a general prosecution process, Mitting J was right to foreshadow this in *Bicioc*.[109]
ii) An accused must be taken to be deliberately absent from his trial if he has been summoned as envisaged by article 4a paragraph 1.(a)(i) in a manner which, even though he may have been unaware of the scheduled date and place, does not violate article 6 ECHR;
iii) An accused who has instructed ('mandated') a lawyer to represent him in the trial is not, for the purposes of section 20, absent from his trial, however he may have become aware of it ... [See below at para 5.96 for iv) and v).][110]

5.91 On further information, Burnett LJ went on to say that it would not be appropriate for requesting judicial authorities to be pressed for such information relating to the statements made in an EAW pursuant to FD Article 4a save in cases of ambiguity, confusion or possibly in connection with an argument that the warrant is an abuse of process. He emphasised that the EAW system was based on mutual trust and confidence.[111]

5.92 Relying on relevant CJEU case-law on FD Article 4a, the Divisional Court in *Foster Taylor v Italy*[112] looked at the meaning of 'trial which resulted in the decision' in the context of successive appeals, holding that this was the instance which led to the last decision:

> ... provided that the court at issue made a final ruling on the guilt of the person concerned and imposed a penalty on him, such as a custodial sentence, following an assessment, in fact and in law, of the incriminating and exculpatory evidence, including, where appropriate, the taking account of the individual situation of the person concerned.[113]

109 [2014] EWHC 628 (Admin), [2014] ACD 91.
110 At para 34.
111 At para 35.
112 [2019] EWHC 2938 (Admin).
113 At para 26 quoting *Criminal proceedings against Tupikas* (Case C-270/17PPU) para 81.

5.93 Providing further explanation on 'deliberate absence', the Divisional Court in *JK v District Court of Lublin, Poland*[114] stated that: 'what is required is ultimately an answer to the question whether the requested person has knowingly waived his right to a trial. Questions of manifest lack of diligence, for example, can be taken into account, but are evidential matters which go to answering that ultimate question'.[115] In *Dziel v Poland,*[116] Ouseley J said that breaching a duty to notify the court of a change of address is an example of a person deliberately putting themselves beyond the power of the prosecutor or court to notify him or her of the date and place of the proceedings, and in these circumstances, a person will be taken to have been deliberately absent.[117]

'Entitled' to a re-trial'

5.94 If the judge finds that the person was convicted in absence without having deliberately absented themselves, the judge must then go on to look at whether the person would be entitled to a retrial, or (on appeal) a review amounting to a retrial (EA 2003 ss20(5)/85(5)).[118]

5.95 A number of cases have examined the meaning of 'entitled', looking at whether a person can be said to be entitled where the entitlement to a retrial is subject to a court's discretion. The judgment of Rafferty LJ in *Nastase v Office of the State Prosecutor, Italy*[119] stated:

> The existence of procedural steps does not remove the entitlement to a retrial. Rather, the Italian authorities must be [permitted] to regulate their own proceedings by imposition of their own rules. Section 20 may create entitlements, but procedural rules set parameters within which such rights are exercisable.

114 [2018] EWHC 197 (Admin).

115 At para 49.

116 [2019] EWHC 351 (Admin) at para 28.

117 Practitioners should be aware of some uncertainty regarding propositions on deliberate absence set out by Hickinbottom J in *Stryjecki v. District Court in Lublin, Poland* [2016] EWHC 3309 (Admin) but subsequently subject to debate: see *Przemyslaw Bialkowski v Regional Court in Kielsce, Poland* [2019] EWHC 1253 (Admin) at paras 21–27.

118 See *Szatkowski v Regional Court in Opole, Poland* [2019] EWHC 883 (Admin) in which the Divisional Court stated that section 20(5) can be taken by implication to read 'whether the person *was* or would be entitled to a retrial' at para 34.

119 [2012] EWHC 3671 (Admin) at para 45. See also *Rexha v Officer of the Prosecutor, Court of Rome, Italy* [2012] EWHC 3397 (Admin) in which extradition was ordered where the judicial authority stated that whilst an absolute assurance that the requested person would be entitled to a retrial, it was 'highly probable' (para 43).

5.96 In *Cretu*,[120] continuing from those principles set out above at para 5.90 in relation to deliberate absence from trial, Burnett LJ stated that:[121]

> iv) The question whether an accused is entitled to a retrial or a review amounting to a retrial for the purposes of section 20(5), is to be determined by reference to [FD] article 4a paragraph 1(d).[122]
>
> v) Whilst, by virtue of section 206 of the 2003 Act, it remains for the requesting state to satisfy the court conducting the extradition hearing in the United Kingdom to the criminal standard that one (or more) of the four exceptions found in article 4a applies, the burden of proof will be discharged to the requisite standard if the information required by article 4a is set out in the EAW.[123]

5.97 Sections 20(8)/85(8) provides that the judge must not decide that a person would be entitled to a retrial under sections 20(5)/85(5) unless:

> ... in any proceedings that it is alleged would constitute a retrial or a review amounting to a retrial, the person would have these rights–
>
> (a) the right to defend himself in person or through legal assistance of his own choosing or, if he had not sufficient means to pay for legal assistance, to be given it free when the interests of justice so required;
>
> (b) the right to examine or have examined witnesses against him and to obtain the attendance and examination of witnesses on his behalf under the same conditions as witnesses against him.

5.98 While in Part 1 cases, it seems likely that the wording of FD Article 4a(1)(d) will be of continued relevance in light of its retention in the TCA (see para 5.90 above), in Part 2 cases, the position is different. In *Barci v The Government of Albania*[124] the Divisional Court stated (albeit obiter) that 'the "fair trial" rights relevant to the determination of [the question under section 85(5)] are those specified (and in my judgment, only those specified) in section 85(8) of the 2003 Act'.[125]

120 [2016] EWHC 353 (Admin).

121 At para 34.

122 FD EWA Article 4a(1)(d)(i) describes such proceedings as 'a re-trial, or an appeal, in which the person has the right to participate and which allows the merits of the case, including fresh evidence, to be re-examined, and which may lead to the original decision being reversed'. Article 4a(1)(d)(ii) requires that the person will be informed of the time frame within which they must request such a re-trial or an appeal.

123 As with the question of deliberate absence from trial, Burnett LJ's comments warning against pressing judicial authorities for further information save in particular circumstances (see para 5.91) follow iv) and v) and are therefore equally applicable.

124 [2017] EWHC 369 (Admin).

125 At para 33.

5.99 A warrant or extradition request may sometimes contain information on the right to a retrial, or it may be addressed by the requesting authority through the provision of further information provided to the court should there be a 'gap' that needs to be filled (see para 3.35). Practitioners should, however, bear in mind the warning at para 35 of *Cretu* (summarised at para 5.91 above) when dealing with Part 1 cases.

5.100 While defence expert evidence on the right to a re-trial used to be relatively common, following *Cretu* and *Pucieviciene*[126] such evidence is now discouraged: in *Kotsev v Sofia District Public Prosecutor's Office, Bulgaria* Knowles J summarised the position as follows:

> ... a clear statement from the issuing judicial authority that a defendant convicted in his absence will receive a re-trial/review and will have the rights specified in s20(8) should be accepted and should not be impugned by defence expert evidence save where bad faith etc is alleged.[127]

Physical or mental health – sections 25/91

5.101 If, during the extradition hearing, it appears to the judge that it would be unjust or oppressive to extradite the person by virtue of the person's physical or mental condition, the judge must either order the person's discharge,[128] or adjourn the hearing[129] until it appears to the judge that the person's physical or mental condition is such that it would no longer be unjust or oppressive to extradite them.[130] It is important to note that the mere fact that a person suffers from an illness is not enough to prevent extradition – it must be shown that, because of the illness or complaint, it would be unjust or oppressive to extradite the requested person. The words 'unjust and oppressive' have the same meaning here as in EA 2003 ss14/82.[131]

5.102 In order to satisfy a finding of 'oppression', a high threshold must be reached. The Administrative Court has said that: 'The term "unjust or oppressive" requires regard to be had to all the relevant

126 [2016] EWHC 1862 (Admin).

127 [2018] EWHC 3087 (Admin) at para 51.

128 EA 2003 s25(3)(a).

129 EA 2003 s25(3)(b).

130 See paras 5.43–5.47 for more detail on injustice or oppression: the Administrative Court in *Government of the Republic of South Africa v Dewani* [2012] EWHC 842 (Admin) confirmed that the words are 'to be read in the sense used in cases such as *Kakis*' (para 74).

131 *Government of the Republic of South Africa v Dewani* [2012] EWHC 842 (Admin) at para 74.

circumstances, including the fact that extradition is ordinarily likely to cause stress and hardship; neither of those is sufficient.'[132]

5.103 The practitioner acting for any requested persons with physical or mental health conditions will need to obtain medical evidence to demonstrate to the court why their complaint will lead to injustice or oppression. The practitioner should also carefully consider whether there are any other facts that lend support to a finding of oppression, for example: family circumstances; delay or a significant change in circumstance.

5.104 There is a rebuttable presumption that medical issues will be appropriately treated in the requesting state.[133] There are, however, some circumstances in which the complexity of the medical condition may make it necessary to seek further information or assurances as to the treatment that will be specifically available.[134] The requested person must put forward clear evidence of sufficient weight and cogency that it demands a specific response.[135]

Where a requesting state is asked to respond to a person's legitimate health concerns, it must provide, so far as is reasonably practicable, a response which meets the concerns of that specific individual.[136]

5.105 The court may consider that the standard of care will be less satisfactory for a requesting person in the requesting state; the test is whether or not the difference in treatment would mean that extradition would be oppressive.[137]

5.106 There is a significant body of case-law that looks, in particular, at those requested persons who are at risk of suicide.[138] In *Richen Turner v*

132 *Government of the Republic of South Africa v Dewani* [2012] EWHC 842 (Admin) at para 73.

133 *W v A Spanish Judicial Authority* [2020] EWHC 2278 (Admin) at para 59. Note that this decision cited the principle of mutual trust in support of this statement, nonetheless, it also cited the ECHR which applies post-Brexit and it appears likely that the court will continue to approach such cases on the basis of this presumption.

134 At para 59.

135 At para 64.

136 At para 34.

137 See *R (Mikolajczyk) v Wroclaw District Court, Poland* [2010] EWHC 3503 (Admin) at para 17: 'It is of course possible that treatment will be less satisfactory in Poland than in the United Kingdom, but the question is whether the difference in treatment would mean that extradition was oppressive. It is for the appellant to demonstrate that that is so.'

138 See, for example: *Jansons v Latvian Judicial Authority* [2009] EWHC 1845 (Admin); *Rot v District Court of Lublin, Poland* [2010] EWHC 1820 (Admin); *R (Prosser) v Secretary of State for the Home Department* [2010] EWHC 845 (Admin); *Wrobel v Poland* [2011] EWHC 374 (Admin); *R (Griffin) v City of London Magistrates' Court* [2011] EWHC 943 (Admin).

Government of the United States of America,[139] Aikens LJ summarised the following propositions from the case-law:

> (1) The court has to form an overall judgment on the facts of the particular case ... (2) A high threshold has to be reached in order to satisfy the court that a requested person's physical or mental condition is such that it would be unjust or oppressive to extradite him ... (3) The court must assess the mental condition of the person threatened with extradition and determine if it is linked to a risk of a suicide attempt if the extradition order were to be made. There has to be a 'substantial risk that [the appellant] will commit suicide'. The question is whether, on the evidence[,] the risk of the appellant succeeding in committing suicide, whatever steps are taken[,] is sufficiently great to result in a finding of oppression ... (4) The mental condition of the person must be such that it removes his capacity to resist the impulse to commit suicide, otherwise it will not be his mental condition but his own voluntary act which puts him at risk of dying and if that is the case there is no oppression in ordering extradition ... (5) On the evidence, is the risk that the person will succeed in committing suicide, whatever steps are taken, sufficiently great to result in a finding of oppression[?] ... (6) Are there appropriate arrangements in place in the prison system of the country to which extradition is sought [such] that those authorities can cope properly with the person's mental condition and the risk of suicide[?] ... (7) There is a public interest in giving effect to treaty obligations and this is an important factor to have in mind ...

5.107 Approving the above propositions in *Polish Judicial Authority v Wolkowicz (alias Del Ponti)*,[140] the President of the Queen's Bench Division stated that the key issue in almost every case will 'be the measures that are in place to prevent any attempt at suicide by a requested person with a mental illness being successful'. These should be examined in three stages:

1) The position while the requested person is being held in custody in the UK.
2) Arrangements that will be in place when the person is being transferred to ensure there are proper arrangements in place to prevent suicide. Medical records should be sent to those who will have custody during transfer.
3) It is to be presumed (in the absence of strong evidence to the contrary) that the receiving state within the EU will discharge its responsibilities to prevent the person committing suicide. It

139 [2012] EWHC 2426 (Admin) at para 28.
140 [2013] EWHC 102 (Admin) at para 10.

should not be necessary to require any assurances from requesting states within the EU.

5.108 In *Farookh v Judge of the Saarbrücken Regional Court, Germany*,[141] Fordham J condensed the *Turner* principles into a single 'compendious' question that was endorsed by the Divisional Court in *Fletcher v Government of India*[142] as being a 'correct statement of the test' to be applied:

> ... whether, on the evidence, whatever steps are taken – and even if the Court is satisfied that appropriate arrangements are in place in the prison system of the country to which extradition is sought so that those authorities will discharge their responsibilities to prevent the requested person committing suicide – the risk of the requested person succeeding in committing suicide, by reason of a mental condition removing the capacity to resist the impulse to commit suicide, is sufficiently great to result in a finding of oppression.[143]

5.109 It is possible that this test will be revisited on appeal in *Government of the USA v Assange* however this case is yet to be heard at the time of writing. In *Wolkowicz* the court emphasised it is 'only in a very rare case that a requested person will be likely to establish that measures to prevent a substantial risk of suicide will not be effective'.[144]

Abuse of process

5.110 Although the EA 2003 does not state that an abuse of the court's process will bar extradition, the courts have found that in certain circumstances it may.

5.111 Abuse of process arguments can only be deployed if all other bars to extradition have failed, ie it is a residual jurisdiction.[145] It is a free-

141 [2020] EWHC 3143 (Admin) at para 7.

142 [2021] EWHC 610 (Admin) at para 39.

143 [2020] EWHC 3143 (Admin) at para 9.

144 [2013] EWHC 102 (Admin) at para 10. On the difference between the test in relation to oppression and ECHR Article 3, see *Pesut v Republic of Croatia* [2015] EWHC 46 (Admin) at para 38: 'I accept that the concept of "oppression" in ss82 and 91 must imply a standard that is less demanding than that of Article 3. Were it otherwise, those provisions would be redundant since an extradition in breach of Article 3 would necessarily be barred by s87. Nonetheless, as this Court said in *Richen Turner*, "a high threshold has to be reached to satisfy the court that a requested person's physical or mental condition is such that it would be unjust or oppressive to extradite him".'

145 *Loncar v County Court in Vukovar, Croatia* [2015] EWHC 548 (Admin) at para 22.

standing ground of challenge which is separate from the other ways in which extradition may be barred and should be dealt with as such.[146] The underlying purpose of the abuse jurisdiction in extradition cases 'is to protect the integrity of the statutory scheme of the 2003 Act and the integrity of the EAW system, as well as to protect a requested person from oppression and unfair prejudice'.[147]

5.112 The implied jurisdiction of the court to consider abuse of process in the context of extradition proceedings was decided in relation to the EA 2003 in *R (Bermingham) v Director of the Serious Fraud Office*.[148] The court will start from the assumption that a requesting state is acting in good faith, which may be displaced by evidence.[149]

5.113 Procedural guidance from the case of *United States of America v Tollman*[150] is succinctly set out in *Haynes v Malta*:[151]

> To sustain an allegation of abuse of process in relation to proceedings under the Act, it is necessary, first, to identify with specificity what is alleged to constitute the abuse; secondly, to satisfy the court that the matter complained of is capable [of] amounting to an abuse; and thirdly, to satisfy the court that there are reasonable grounds for believing that such conduct has occurred. If the matter gets that far, then the court should require the judicial authority to provide an explanation. The court should not order extradition unless satisfied that no such abuse has taken place ...

5.114 As stated above, the requested person bears the burden of satisfying the judge (on the balance of probabilities) that, not only is the issue raised capable of amounting to an abuse, but also that there are reasonable grounds for believing that the abuse has occurred. It will be essential therefore for the requested person to bring cogent evidence of the abuse in order to satisfy the court that the conduct has occurred.

146 *Wawrzyczek v District Court in Bielsko-Biala, Poland* [2021] EWHC 64 (Admin) at para 86.

147 *Auzins v Prosecutor General's Office of Latvia* [2016] EWHC 802 (Admin) at para 44.

148 [2006] EWHC 200 (Admin).

149 *Ahmad and Aswat v The Government of the United States of America* [2006] EWHC 2927 (Admin), at para 101.

150 [2008] EWHC 184 (Admin).

151 [2009] EWHC 880 (Admin) at para 6.

5.115 The circumstances in which abuse of process may be argued are very limited. In *Giese v Government of the United States of America*[152] the Divisional Court stated that: 'There are likely to be few instances where a requested person fails to substantiate a bar but can succeed in an abuse argument.'[153] In *Belbin v Regional Court of Lille, France*[154] the Divisional Court set out the boundaries of the jurisdiction, emphasising its residual nature and saying that it would 'only exercise the jurisdiction if it is satisfied, on cogent evidence, that the Judicial Authority concerned has acted in such a way as to "usurp" the statutory regime of the EA [2003] or its integrity has been impugned'.[155] The court must also be satisfied that requested person will suffer prejudice, either in the extradition process in this country, or in the requesting state if they are surrendered.[156]

5.116 The court has drawn a distinction between an abuse of the extradition process by the prosecuting authority and an abuse resulting from the misconduct or bad faith of the police of the requesting state in the investigation of the case or the preparation of evidence for trial. Abuse arising from misconduct or bad faith by the police is a matter to be resolved by the requesting state and will not be capable of preventing a person's extradition.[157] Where the requesting state seeks the 'extradition of someone for a collateral purpose, or when they know that the trial cannot succeed',[158] this will fall into the former category and may be capable of amounting to an abuse of the court's process.

5.117 Various categories of abuse of process that the courts have examined in the context of extradition proceedings include: re-issue

152 [2018] EWHC 1480 (Admin).

153 At para 33.

154 [2015] EWHC 149 (Admin).

155 At para 59. Continuing in this paragraph, Aikens LJ said that cogent evidence was required because, under the EAW scheme, the starting point was mutual trust. It is likely that the courts will continue to require cogent evidence under the TCA arrangements; and see also *Ahmad and Aswat v The Government of the United States of America* [2006] EWHC 2927 (Admin) at para 101 regarding the assumption that the requesting state is acting in good faith.

156 At para 59.

157 *Symeou v Public Prosecutor's Officer, Patras, Greece* [2009] EWHC 897 (Admin) at para 34.

158 At para 33.

of an extradition request;[159] collateral motive;[160] disclosure;[161] and incorrect particulars.[162]

Immigration status

5.118 If a requested person has made a claim for asylum, they cannot be extradited while the asylum claim is pending.[163]

5.119 The question of whether extradition proceedings should be adjourned pending the outcome of the asylum claim is currently moot: in *R (Chichvarkin) v Secretary of State for the Home Department*[164] the Court of Appeal stated that, in circumstances where an asylum claim is being actively considered by the SSHD and the extradition court is considering whether extradition would lead to a breach of a person's human rights, this would 'weigh heavily in favour of an adjournment of the extradition proceedings'.[165] See also, however, *Kozlowski v District Court of Torun, Poland*,[166] in which Ouseley J (in the face of the then growing number of Polish appellants seeking to adjourn proceedings to await the outcome of asylum claims) warned against drawing a general point of principle from *Chichvarkin* and said that 'in cases involving Council of Europe and EU countries there ought to be a very firm approach not to grant adjournments'.[167] Nonetheless, *Chichvarkin* is a Court of Appeal decision, and where a requested person has made a realistic claim for asylum and the country of origin is within the Council of Europe but not an EU member state, careful consideration should be given to whether evidence given in the extradition hearings could adversely impact on the person or any family members that remain in the requesting state. If

159 *Auzins v Prosecutor General's Office of Latvia* [2016] EWHC 802 (Admin); *Camaras v Baia Local Court, Romania* [2016] EWHC 1766 (Admin); *Giese v Government of the United States of America* [2018] EWHC 1480 (Admin); *Wawrzyczek v District Court in Bielsko-Biala, Poland* [2021] EWHC 64 (Admin).

160 *Republic of Serbia v Ejup Ganic* [2011] EWHC 878 (Admin); *R (Lotfi Raissi) v Secretary of State for the Home Department* [2008] EWCA Civ 72.

161 *Government of Ukraine v Kononko* [2014] EWHC 1420 (Admin).

162 *Zakrzewski v Regional Court in Lodz, Poland* [2013] UKSC 2. See chapter 3, para 3.36.

163 EA 2003 ss39 and 121.

164 [2010] EWCA Civ 91.

165 At para 61.

166 [2012] EWHC 1706 (Admin).

167 At para 20.

there is such a risk, an adjournment could well be in the person's best interests.

5.120 The Refugee Convention prohibits the return of refugees to their home country.[168] While this is not explicitly covered in the EA 2003, it has been resolved by the Divisional Court in *District Court in Ostroleka v Dytlow*[169] in which the court approved the application of the abuse of process jurisdiction to the case of a requested person granted asylum. If the requested person is a refugee whose extradition is sought by the country of origin, or where a requested person sought by their country of origin has been granted leave to remain in the UK as a person with humanitarian protection they should be discharged.[170] It will be important to obtain the decision letter from the Home Office to satisfy the court that the person is indeed a refugee or has been granted humanitarian protection. The EA 2003 also provides that if a person is granted leave to remain or enter on the grounds that it would be a breach of the Human Rights Convention to remove the person to the territory to which extradition would be requested, the SSHD may order the person's discharge.[171]

5.121 Requested persons who have been granted asylum and then obtain British citizenship will not be given the protection afforded by the EA 2003 as they will no longer be a refugee and as a British citizen will have other protections.[172]

Grounds for refusal to extradite under the TCA

5.122 The TCA, like the EAW FD, contains mandatory and non-mandatory grounds for non-execution of AWs.

5.123 These grounds are not reproduced as such in the EA 2003, and in some cases they extend beyond the bars to extradition set out in the UK legislation (see in particular para 6.64ff regarding proportionality and paras 5.34–5.36 regarding political offences). The impact that this will have is unclear at this time: the effect of the surrender provi-

168 This is known as the principle of 'non-refoulement'.

169 *District Court in Ostroleka, Second Criminal Division (A Polish Judicial Authority) v Dytlow* [2009] EWHC 1009 (Admin).

170 At para 11. Regarding humanitarian protection, see *Government of Ukraine v Polishchuk*, Westminster Magistrates' Court, 5 September 2014.

171 EA 2003 s93(6A) as amended by Anti-social Behaviour, Crime and Policing Act 2014 s162(3).

172 *Turkey v Ozbek* [2014] EWHC 3469 (Admin).

sions of the TCA is not currently settled. The duty of conforming interpretation as set out in *Criminal proceedings against Pupino*[173] no longer applies, however, interpretative questions arise from European Union (Future Relationship) Act 2020 s29, which provides that existing domestic law has effect with such modifications as are required for the purposes of implementing the TCA, so far as the agreement concerned is not otherwise so implemented. At the time of writing, it is not clear whether the courts will regard the surrender provisions of the TCA as having been implemented through the EA 2003 or not. It is therefore unclear whether the courts will consider it necessary to 'modify' the EA 2003 for the purpose of implementing the TCA, or whether the ordinary construction that applies to international agreements will be used, ie that the court must have regard to international law and the UK's treaty obligations.

5.124 Mandatory grounds for non-execution of AWs are set out at TCA Article 600, as follows:

a) where the offence is covered by an amnesty in the executing state, where the executing state had jurisdiction to prosecute that offence;
b) double jeopardy;
c) a person's age.

5.125 In relation to the first, given the very limited use of amnesties in the UK, it appears unlikely that a challenge to extradition on this ground would arise, however, if it were to do so existing grounds of challenge under forum, ECHR Article 8 or abuse of process would provide a means to implement this mandatory bar to extradition. In respect of double jeopardy and a person's age, see paras 5.5 and 5.50 above.

5.126 Discretionary grounds are set out at TCA Article 601. In addition, the TCA includes a potential bar to extradition for political offences at Article 602, and a potential nationality bar (preventing extradition where the requested person is a national of a state that has invoked fundamental constitutional principles barring the extradition of its own nationals) at Article 603.

5.127 In respect of the nationality bar, this requires the following in order to take effect:

a) a notification to be made by the UK to the Specialised Committee on Law Enforcement and Judicial Cooperation; and
b) amendment of the EA 2003.

173 (Case C-105/03) [2006] QB 83.

5.128 At the time of writing, neither a notification nor an amendment to the EA 2003 has been made or appears likely to be made in the future. This bar is therefore relevant only to import extradition and is not covered in this book.

5.129 The political offence provision operates differently. Article 602 allows a state to provide a notification to the Specialised Committee on Law Enforcement and Judicial Cooperation that would, in summary, allow a state to disapply the general rule against refusal on the grounds that an offence is political[174] for offences other than terrorist offences (as defined in the TCA).

5.130 As at 5 March 2021, the following 12 countries had made a notification: Belgium, Czechia, Denmark, France, Croatia, Italy, Cyprus, Poland, Portugal, Slovakia, Finland and Sweden.[175] TCA Article 602(3) provides that where a notification has been made, the executing state may apply reciprocity. Although the UK has not made a notification, therefore, where a request is made by a country that has done so, it will be theoretically open to the UK as the executing state to refuse to extradite for a political offence, other than the defined terrorist offences.

5.131 At the time of writing, it is unclear how the courts will interpret Article 602, which covers different ground from the extraneous considerations bar (see paras 5.23–5.37), albeit there are some respects in which they are coextensive. As drafted, the effect of the article, along with the notifications in this jurisdiction, would seem to be that a discretionary ground of refusal for political offences (other than terrorist offences as defined) exists only in respect of the countries listed above which have given a notification. The EA 2003 has not, however been amended to reflect this, and the uncertainty

174 TCA Article 602(1) provides: 'The execution of an arrest warrant may not be refused on the grounds that the offence may be regarded by the executing State as a political offence, as an offence connected with a political offence or as an offence inspired by political motives.'

175 Letter from Kevin Foster MP, Minister for Future Borders and Immigration, to Lord Ricketts, Chair of the EU Security and Justice Sub-Committee, House of Lords, dated 5 March 2021.

set out at para 5.123 is therefore particularly pertinent here. Given that the definition of a political offence has historically been limited in scope,[176] and the finite number of relevant states, it may be that cases in which this issue may be raised are rare, and the uncertainty remains unresolved for some time.

176 The concept of a political offence was part of the corpus of extradition law pre-2003. An offence of a political character was defined by Viscount Radcliffe in *R v Governor of Brixton Prison, ex p Schtraks* [1964] AC 556, HL at p591 as follows:

> In my opinion the idea that lies behind the phrase 'offence of a political character' is that the fugitive is at odds with the state that applies for his extradition on some issue connected with the political control or government of the country. The analogy of 'political' in this context is with 'political' in such phrases as 'political refugee,' 'political asylum' or 'political prisoner.' It does indicate, I think, that the requesting state is after him for reasons other than the enforcement of the criminal law in its ordinary, what I may call its common or international, aspect.

CHAPTER 6

Human rights and proportionality

continued

Introduction

6.1 In dealing with both Extradition Act (EA) 2003 Part 1 and Part 2 cases, the judge will be required to consider whether extradition would be compatible with a person's rights under the European Convention on Human Rights (ECHR or 'the Convention') within the meaning of the Human Rights Act (HRA) 1998. If the judge decides the question in the negative, they must order the person's discharge.[1]

6.2 The court must apply different tests in respect of particular ECHR rights, in deciding whether extradition would result in a violation of those rights. Where a requested person challenges extradition on the grounds of a prospective violation, a requesting state will frequently offer assurances which seek to show that the risk of that prospective violation can or has been negated. Such assurances are most frequently provided in relation to ECHR Article 3 (prohibition of torture and inhuman and degrading treatment) and Article 6 (right to a fair trial) challenges (see para 6.57ff below).

6.3 An additional consideration applies in respect of Part 1 cases where the arrest warrant (AW) is an accusation warrant. In these cases, the judge must decide whether the extradition would be disproportionate.[2] There is no equivalent provision for Part 2 cases.

Fundamental rights under the Trade and Cooperation Agreement

6.4 EA 2003 ss21 and 21A were not amended following the Trade and Cooperation Agreement (TCA).[3] It therefore remains the case that, for Part 1 cases, a judge must decide whether the person's extradition would be compatible with their ECHR rights. In relation to Part 1 countries, TCA Article 604(c) provides that, 'if there are substantial grounds for believing that there is a real risk to the protection of the fundamental rights of the requested person, the executing judicial authority may require, as appropriate, additional guarantees as to the

1 EA 2003 ss21 and 21A for Part 1; and s87 for Part 2.

2 EA 2003 s21A.

3 As at the time of writing. Trade and Cooperation Agreement between the European Union and the European Atomic Energy Community, of the one part, and the United Kingdom of Great Britain and Northern Ireland, of the other part, Document 22021A0430(01), 30 April 2021, https://eur-lex.europa.eu/legal-content/EN/TXT/?uri=uriserv:OJ.L_.2021.149.01.0010.01.ENG.

treatment of the requested person after the person's surrender before it decides whether to execute the arrest warrant'.[4]

Presumption of compliance

Overview

6.5 All Council of Europe (CoE) countries are signatories to the ECHR. There is therefore a presumption that such countries will be capable of offering adequate protection of a requested person's human rights,[5] although see below for circumstances in which this presumption may be rebutted. In relation to EU member states, it seems likely that the presumption of compliance will continue to be particularly strong, given that TCA Article 524(1) states that cooperation 'is based on the ... long-standing respect for democracy, the rule of law and the protection of fundamental rights and freedoms of individuals'.

6.6 Even for countries that have not signed the ECHR, there will often be a presumption of compliance with international human rights norms. For many years, the courts have asserted that there are 'fundamental assumptions that the requesting state is acting in good faith and that the fugitive will receive a fair trial in the courts of the requesting state'.[6] Although this presumption can be rebutted by evidence, it will be all the more difficult to displace 'where the requesting state is one in which the United Kingdom has for many years reposed the confidence not only of general good relations, but also of successive bilateral treaties consistently honoured'.[7] Examples of such countries are the states which are not CoE members which have been specified as those in respect of which a provisional arrest

4 Although it is tempting to conflate this provision with the test under Article 3, given the identical language, the TCA provision is a discretionary mechanism which allows guarantees to be sought in relation to any fundamental right. The test under Article 3 is, in effect, a mandatory ground for refusal in those cases where there are substantial grounds for believing that there is a real risk of inhuman or degrading treatment or torture.

5 See *Gomes and Goodyer v Trinidad and Tobago* [2009] UKHL 21 at para 35: 'Council of Europe countries in our view present no problem. All are subject to article 6 of the Convention and should readily be assumed capable of protecting an accused against an unjust trial – whether by an abuse of process jurisdiction like ours or in some other way.'

6 *Serbeh v Governor of HMP Brixton* [2002] EWHC 2356 (QB) at para 31.

7 *Ahmad v Government of the United States of America* [2006] EWHC 2927 (Admin) at para 101.

may be carried out without a warrant on the basis of an INTERPOL (International Criminal Police Organization) Red Notice or Diffusion (see para 8.13). The specification of these countries was made on the basis of the UK having a high level of confidence in them 'as extradition partners, in their criminal justice systems and in their use of extradition'.[8]

Displacing the presumption of compliance

6.7 The presumption of compliance with ECHR rights may be displaced in certain circumstances.

Evidence required

6.8 In relation to Part 1 countries, under the European Arrest Warrant (EAW) scheme in place pre-Brexit, the approach of the administrative court had been that the presumption of compliance was 'capable of being rebutted by clear and cogent evidence, which establishes that ... extradition would not be compatible with the defendant's Convention rights'.[9] In *Krolik v Poland*,[10] Sir John Thomas P, as he then was, stated that ' as to the type of evidence required ... something approaching an international consensus is required, if the presumption is to be rebutted'.

6.9 The evidence needed to assess the existence of a risk of a breach of fundamental rights was later examined in the Court of Justice of the European Union (CJEU) decision of *Aranyosi and Căldăraru*[11] in relation to Article 3. That case set out the approach to be taken where there was 'objective, reliable, specific and properly updated' information demonstrating that there were systemic or generalised deficiencies in detention conditions prevailing in a requesting state.[12] The court stated that where this material demonstrates a real risk of inhuman or degrading treatment by virtue of the prison conditions in a requesting state, the executing state must request supplementary information on the specific conditions in which the person concerned will be detained, in order to discount the existence of this

8 Extradition (Provisional Arrest) Bill Explanatory Notes, para 7, https://publications.parliament.uk/pa/bills/cbill/58-01/0138/en/200138en.pdf.

9 *Agius v Court of Magistrates, Malta* [2011] EWHC 759 (Admin) at para 18.

10 [2012] EWHC 2357 (Admin) at para 7.

11 *Pál Aranyosi and Robert Căldăraru v Generalstaatsanwaltschaft Bremen* (joined cases C-404/15 and C-659/15 PPU).

12 *Aranyosi and Căldăraru*, para 104.

risk. If the existence of the risk cannot be discounted within a reasonable time, the court must decide whether to refuse extradition.[13] The same approach to the basis of the assessment was subsequently confirmed by the CJEU in relation to Article 6 in *Minister for Justice and Equality v LM*.[14] See also para 6.35.

6.10 It is likely that the courts will continue to use the same approach to the displacement of the presumption post-Brexit.[15] It is of note that, in some instances, the administrative court has adopted the 'objective, reliable, specific and properly updated' wording in relation to Part 2 countries: see *Yilmaz and Yilmaz v Turkey*[16] and *Government of Ecuador v Larco*;[17] although see also *Sanchez v Government of the United States of America* in which the court stated that the crucial point in *Yilmaz* was that 'there was a body of evidence powerfully indicating that there might well be a real risk of Art.3 mistreatment if the Yilmazes were extradited to Turkey'.[18] The 'international consensus' test has also recently been applied in Part 2 cases: see *Kaderli v Turkey*[19] (although introduced here because the defence expert concluded there was an international consensus on corruption in Turkey); and *Sekrieru v Azerbaijan*[20] where the decision of the District Judge applying that test was upheld on appeal.

6.11 In practice, a court's willingness to find that the presumption of compliance has been displaced will differ according to a number of factors, including the country's record of previous compliance. When seeking to persuade a court that a person should be discharged under EA 2003 ss21, 21A or 87, it is of the utmost importance to put before the court a persuasive body of evidence of a lack of compliance with human rights obligations.

Pilot judgments

6.12 The pilot judgment procedure of the European Court of Human Rights (ECtHR) aims to deal with systemic or structural human rights violations in CoE. A pilot judgment will displace the presumption

13 *Aranyosi and Căldăraru*, para 104.

14 (C-216/18) PPU.

15 While Art 609 (c) allows a court to seek guarantees if it finds substantial grounds for believing a real risk to a requested person's fundamental rights, it is silent on the approach to be taken in making this assessment.

16 [2019] EWHC 272 (Admin) at para 18.

17 [2020] EWHC 1797 (Admin) at para 44.

18 [2020] EWHC 508 (Admin) at para 70.

19 [2021] EWHC 1096 (Admin).

20 [2021] EWHC 735 (Admin).

that a CoE country will honour its obligations under the ECHR.[21] The ECtHR has handed down pilot judgments that point to structural problems in the detention systems of the countries concerned which cause a violation of the Article 3 rights of prisoners; there are also a number of pilot judgments in relation to systemic violations of Article 6: see the ECtHR website for a list of pilot judgments.[22] The requesting state may respond to such a challenge by either adducing evidence to show that the systemic problems have been dealt with, or by giving assurances (see para 6.57ff below regarding assurances).

ECHR Article 2 (right to life) and Article 3 (prohibition of torture and inhuman and degrading treatment)

Overview

6.13 ECHR Article 2 states that everyone's right to life shall be protected by law.

6.14 Challenges under Article 2 have been brought where it is alleged that a person will be killed by other prison inmates (*Dewani*);[23] by gang members (*McLean*)[24] by the state (*Bah*);[25] or where a person's extradition is sought by a country that applies the death penalty.[26]

6.15 Article 3 provides that no one shall be subjected to torture or to inhuman or degrading treatment or punishment.[27] Requested persons have argued that their Article 3 rights will be violated by, for example, inter-prisoner violence arising from being targeted as a result of ethnicity (*Konuksever*);[28] prison conditions in a particular country (*Krolik*);[29] or life imprisonment without parole (*Harkins*

21 *Shmatko v The Russian Federation* [2018] EWHC 3534 (Admin) at para 36.

22 See: www.echr.coe.int/Documents/FS_Pilot_judgments_ENG.pdf.

23 *Government of South Africa v Dewani* [2010] EWHC 3398 (Admin).

24 *McLean v High Court of Dublin, Ireland* [2008] EWHC 547 (Admin).

25 *The Government of the Republic of Gambia v Bah* Westminster Magistrates' Court (3 February 2012).

26 Although see *Soering v UK* (1989) 11 EHRR 439 where, in relation to a death penalty case, extradition was refused on the grounds of Article 3 rather than Article 2.

27 Where Article 2 is argued, Article 3 will frequently be argued alongside it, given that inhuman or degrading treatment will often be a corollary of a threat to life.

28 *Konuksever v Government of Turkey* [2012] EWHC 2166 (Admin).

29 *Krolik v Several Judicial Authorities of Poland* [2012] EWHC 2357 (Admin).

and Edwards).[30] As these examples show, the risk may be from the state itself, or may arise from threats by non-state actors. It can also relate to grossly disproportionate sentences or inadequate medical treatment.

The test

6.16 In seeking to persuade a court that a requested person should not be extradited under ECHR Article 2 or Article 3, the burden will be on the requested person to show that there are substantial grounds for believing that the person, if extradited, faces a real risk of either being killed[31] or being subjected to torture or to inhuman or degrading treatment.[32] The court must examine the 'foreseeable consequences of sending the applicant to the receiving country, bearing in mind the general situation there and his personal circumstances'.[33] As stated above, assurances are frequently provided by requesting states in response to challenges on Article 3 grounds (see para 6.57ff).

6.17 Given the heavy burden on the requested person, it will not be enough to rely simply on the requested person's own evidence.[34] Witnesses of fact who can support the requested person's account may be appropriate, along with expert witnesses who can speak to the specific risk faced by the requested person. Case-law from the ECtHR can be used, along with reports from governmental and non-governmental organisations (NGOs), such as the US State Department and the Council of Europe Committee for the Prevention of Torture, to bolster the evidence of expert witnesses. Country guidance issued in the context of an asylum case should be treated as an authoritative starting point.[35]

30 *Harkins and Edwards v UK* (2012) 55 EHRR 19.

31 Although, as Lord Bingham points out in *R (Ullah) v Special Adjudicator* [2004] UKHL 26, the test that the court applied in *Dehwari v Netherlands* (2000) 29 EHRR CD 74 was 'near certainty' rather than real risk: at para 24. See also *Georgiev v Bulgaria* [2012] EWHC 3979 (Admin).

32 *Soering v UK* (1989) 11 EHRR 439 at para 91.

33 *Saadi v Italy* (2009) 49 EHRR 30 at para 130. See also *Soering v UK* (1989) 11 EHRR 439 at para 90.

34 *G v District Court of Czestochowa, Poland* [2011] EWHC 1597 (Admin).

35 *Lutsyuk v Government of Ukraine* [2013] EWHC 189 (Admin) at paras 15–16.

Non-state actors

6.18 Where the risk of a violation is from a non-state actor, it will be necessary to show that the state will fail to provide reasonable protection against such a risk.[36] If protective measures are proposed by the requesting state, it will also be necessary to look at whether the protective measures the state would be required to put in place would themselves risk a breach of Article 3.[37]

Prison conditions

6.19 The question of whether the conditions within a prison will give rise to a violation of a requested person's Convention rights is frequently raised. The most frequent challenge arises from overcrowding (see para 6.21 below), but in all cases where prison conditions are in issue, it will be necessary to look at the conditions as a whole (see para 6.22), including but not limited to: healthcare; sanitary conditions and facilities; the length of time a person is required to spend in their cell; inter-prisoner violence; the provision of appropriate food and drink; bedding; daylight, air, ventilation; room temperature; the means of transportation; staff-to-inmate ratio; the provision of activities / outdoor exercise and any other issues as relevant to the requested person. The presumption of compliance with the Convention applies to prison conditions as it does in relation to all Convention rights: see paras 6.5–6.12 regarding the evidence needed to displace the presumption, and pilot judgments.

6.20 Challenges brought on grounds that are specific to the requested person or the location in which it is proposed that they will be held are more likely to be successful than generalised assertions of a prospective violation. Unless the place of incarceration is specified in the extradition request, if prison conditions are likely to be in issue, supplemental information about where the requested person will be held, both pre- and post-trial if applicable, should be requested. An expert report dealing with the conditions in a specific prison may

36 *R (Bagdanavicius) v Secretary of State for the Home Department* [2005] UKHL 38, [2005] 2 AC 668.

37 *Lord Advocate v Zain Taj Dean* [2017] UKSC 44. In that case, the Taiwanese authorities offered assurances setting out protective measures that would be put in place for the requested person, who argued that those measures amounted to a form of solitary confinement which risked a breach of his Article 3 rights. See also *Tabuncic v Government of Moldova* [2021] EWHC 1269 (Admin) regarding the Article 3 risk arising from the use of solitary confinement as a means of protecting a prisoner at paras 27 and 39.

assist a requested person in establishing a risk of a prospective violation (see para 9.37 regarding expert reports).

Overcrowding

6.21 Overcrowding is a problem facing prison systems across the world. The ECtHR looked at the principles relevant to ECHR Article 3 challenges on the grounds of overcrowding in the case of *Muršić v Croatia*.[38] The applicable principles were summarised by the High Court in *Shumba v France*[39] as below:

> In the context of prison overcrowding, there will be a strong presumption of a breach of Article 3 if any of the following criteria are absent:
> (1) a private sleeping place within a prison cell;
> (2) at least 3m² of floor space per prisoner; and
> (3) an overall surface area of the cell which is such as to allow the detainees to move freely between the furniture items.

6.22 Where a detainee is allocated between 3m² and 4m² of personal space, a violation of Article 3 will be found if there are other aspects of inappropriate physical conditions: in particular, regard will be had to access to outdoor exercise; natural light or air; availability of ventilation; adequacy of room temperature; access to private toilet facilities; and compliance with basic sanitary and hygiene requirements.[40]

6.23 The presumption of a violation is capable of being rebutted. The relevant factors are set out in *Muršić v Croatia*[41] as follows, and must be cumulatively met:

> (1) the reductions in the required minimum personal space of 3 sq. m are short, occasional and minor ...;
> (2) such reductions are accompanied by sufficient freedom of movement outside the cell and adequate out-of-cell activities ...;
> (3) the applicant is confined in what is, when viewed generally, an appropriate detention facility, and there are no other aggravating aspects of the conditions of his or her detention ...

Assurances

6.24 See para 6.57ff regarding assurances.

38 (2017) 65 EHRR 1.
39 [2018] EWHC 1762 (Admin) at para 39.
40 *Shumba* at paras 39–40.
41 (2017) 65 EHRR 1 at para 138.

ECHR Article 4 (prohibition of slavery and forced labour)

6.25 ECHR Article 4 – which prohibits slavery, servitude and forced labour – imposes a positive obligation on state authorities to take operational measures to protect victims, or potential victims, of trafficking where they are aware, or ought to have been aware, of circumstances giving rise to a credible suspicion that an identified individual had been, or was at real and immediate risk of being, trafficked or exploited.[42] In the UK, the National Referral Mechanism (NRM) provides a framework for the authorities to identify victims of human trafficking. The Court of Appeal has made it clear that defence lawyers must make enquiries if there is credible material that they have a client who might have been the victim of trafficking in relation to criminal proceedings.[43] It is the authors' view that this should apply equally in extradition cases.

6.26 In *Polish Judicial Authorities v Celinski and others*[44] the Divisional Court considered the position of an appellant who had referred herself to the UK Human Trafficking Centre (UKHTC). The Court provided guidance as to how the appropriate judge is to approach such a referral:

> A District Judge, having heard the evidence, must therefore himself determine the issue as to whether the requested person has been trafficked, having been assisted by the CPS and the UKHTC by provision of the relevant evidence in their possession, subject to principles of public interest immunity from disclosure. Judges should not normally adjourn hearings for a referral to the UK Competent Authority, nor defer the effect of their extradition decisions pending a decision on a referral by the UK Competent Authority.[45]

6.27 Where a person has been identified by the competent authority as a victim of trafficking, the question of whether a risk of a breach of their Article 4 rights upon extradition arises. See *IM v Regional Prosecutor's Office of Ruse, Bulgaria*[46] and *C v Latvia*[47] for a discussion of the relevant issues.

42 *Rantsev v Cyprus and Russia* (2010) 51 EHRR 1 at para 286.

43 See, for example, *R v O* [2008] EWCA Crim 2835. See also the Law Society's practice note on 'Criminal prosecutions of victims of trafficking, 2 December 2019, www.lawsociety.org.uk/en/topics/criminal-justice/criminal-prosecutions-of-victims-of-trafficking.

44 [2015] EWHC 1274 (Admin).

45 At para 52.

46 [2019] EWHC 602 (Admin).

47 [2016] EWHC 2211 (Admin).

ECHR Article 5 (right to liberty and security) and Article 6 (right to a fair trial)

Overview

6.28 Under ECHR Article 5, everyone has the right to liberty and security of person. This is not an absolute right, and the provision specifies the circumstances in which a person may be deprived of their liberty and the procedural protections.

6.29 ECHR Article 6 safeguards the right to a fair trial. It provides that a person is entitled to a fair and public hearing within a reasonable time by an independent and impartial tribunal in the determination of their civil rights or of any criminal charge. It also sets out the basic rights of those charged with a criminal offence. There is often an overlap between challenges made under this article and the abuse of process jurisdiction.

6.30 Article 5 challenges will frequently arise in tandem with those under Article 6, where, for example, it is suggested that, if a person is returned to the requesting state, they will be held in pre- trial detention for lengthy periods.[48]

The test

6.31 In relation to both Articles 5 and 6, the burden of proof will be on the requested person to show to the standard of probability, that there are substantial grounds for believing that there is a real risk of a flagrant denial of the right in question. In *R (Ullah) v Special Adjudicator*,[49] the House of Lords stated that 'where reliance is placed on Article 6 it must be shown that a person has suffered or risks suffering a

48 The application of Article 5 to those held in detention pending extradition, i.e. in the requested state, was examined in *Lukaszewski v The District Court in Torun, Poland* [2012] UKSC 20, where it was argued that the Article 5 rights of requested persons should operate to extend the period in which an appeal against an order for extradition could be served on the prosecution beyond that set out in the Civil Procedure Rules. The court held, following the decision in *MT (Algeria) v Secretary of State for Home Department* [2009] UKHL 10, that Article 5 did not apply to the proceedings as they were not challenging detention per se, but challenging the underlying decision to extradite the appellants. Nevertheless, as that case also points out, Article 5 rights were relied on in *R (Kashamu) v Governor of Brixton Prison (No 2)* [2001] EWHC Admin 980, [2002] QB 887 to hold that the district judge should consider whether there had been an abuse of process rendering the detention unlawful under Article 5(4).

49 [2004] UKHL 26.

flagrant denial of a fair trial in the receiving state ... Successful reliance on Article 5 would have to meet no less exacting a test'.[50] If the requested person raises an objection of substance to extradition, the burden moves to the requesting state to counter the objection.[51]

6.32 Further guidance on this test can be found in case-law. First, real risk 'means a risk which is substantial and not merely fanciful; and it may be established by something less than proof of a 51% probability'.[52] It is a high bar, but the height is not derived from the standard of proof, or the establishment of a real risk, but from the degree of denial of a fair trial if the risk eventuates.[53] The meaning of 'flagrant' was elaborated on by Lord Bingham in *EM (Lebanon) v Secretary of State for the Home Department*,[54] quoting from a ECtHR case that stated that 'the use of the adjective is clearly intended to impose a stringent test of unfairness going beyond mere irregularities or lack of safeguards in the trial procedures such as might result in a breach of Article 6 if occurring within the Contracting State itself'.[55] In *Ahorugeze v Sweden*, the ECtHR said that: 'The term "flagrant denial of justice" has been considered synonymous with a trial which is manifestly contrary to the provisions of Article 6 or the principles embodied therein.'[56]

6.33 Where the requested person has been able to show a real risk of a breach of Articles 5 or 6, the requesting state may seek to respond by offering assurances (as with Article 3). In such cases, the *Othman* principles regarding assurances set out below (at para 6.58) will apply.[57]

6.34 There have been few successful challenges to extradition under these articles. Some US extradition requests have been refused where a person has faced possible detention under a 'civil commitment order'. It has been held that in certain circumstances, this form

50 At para 24. Although that was an asylum case, the test nevertheless also applies in extradition cases. See para 24 of *Janovic v Prosecutor General's Office, Lithuania* [2011] EWHC 710 (Admin).

51 *Rwanda v Ntezirayo* [2017] EWHC 1912 (Admin) at para 91.

52 *Brown v Government of Rwanda* [2009] EWHC 770 at para 34.

53 *Rwanda v Ntezirayo* [2017] EWHC 1912 (Admin) at para 92.

54 [2008] UKHL 64.

55 At para 34, quoting *Mamatkulov and Askarov v Turkey* (2005) 41 EHRR 25, 537 para OIII 14.

56 (2012) 55 EHRR 2 at para 114.

57 *Othman (Abu Qatada) v United Kingdom* (2012) 55 EHRR 1. See *Ravi Shankaran v Government of the State of India and another* [2014] EWHC 957 (Admin) which applied the *Othman* principles in respect of an Article 5 challenge.

of indeterminate confinement for a person deemed mentally ill and dangerous poses a real risk of a flagrant denial of a person's Article 5(1) rights.[58]

6.35 Recent challenges in relation to Article 6 have looked at the independence of the judiciary in Poland. The CJEU case of *Minister of Justice and Equality v LM*[59] stated that a two-step approach in relation to Article 6 should be taken, as follows:

1) The executing judicial authority must, as a first step, assess, whether there is a real risk, on account of systemic or generalised deficiencies in the requesting state, of the fundamental right to a fair trial being breached. This assessment must be made on the basis of material that is objective, reliable, specific and properly updated.[60]
2) That authority must, as a second step, assess specifically and precisely whether, in the particular circumstances of the case, there are substantial grounds for believing that, following their surrender to the issuing member state, the requested person will run that risk.[61]

6.36 This approach was followed in *Lis (No 2)*[62] where the court rejected the requested person's challenge on Article 6 grounds.

6.37 A successful challenge on Article 6 grounds was made by alleged Rwandan génocidaires in 2017.[63] The Divisional Court refused extradition on the grounds that there was a real risk that the requested persons would suffer a flagrant breach of their Article 6 rights if extradited. While a number of potential violations of Article 6 were raised by the requested persons, it was the inadequacy of defence representation viewed in the context of other weaknesses within the criminal justice system that was critical.[64]

6.38 In *Popoviciu v Romania*[65] in the context of a trial which had already taken place in which the requested person had adduced credible evidence of improper, corrupt and criminal conduct on the part of the trial judge, the Divisional Court found that there was a real risk that the requested person had suffered an extreme example of a lack of

58 *Sullivan v United States* [2012] EWHC 1680 (Admin) and *Giese v United States* [2015] EWHC 2733 (Admin), although see also *Giese v United States* [2018] EWHC 1480 (Admin) in which assurances that the requested person would not be subject to civil commitment were found to be adequate.

59 (C-216/18) PPU.

60 *Minister of Justice and Equality v LM*, para 61.

61 *Minister of Justice and Equality v LM*, para 68.

62 *Lis v Regional Court in Warsaw, Poland* [2019] EWHC 674 (Admin).

63 *Rwanda v Nteziryayo* [2017] EWHC 1912 (Admin).

64 *Rwanda v Nteziryayo* [2017] EWHC 1912 (Admin) at para 377.

65 [2021] EWHC 1584 (Admin).

judicial impartiality, such that there was no question as to the consequences for the fairness of the trial.[66] Alongside a breach of Article 6, the court also found a real risk that the requested person would suffer a complete denial of his Article 5 rights, as his imprisonment would be arbitrary.[67]

6.39 Other examples of successful challenges on Article 6 grounds can be found in a series of first instance decisions in respect of requests from the UAE.[68]

6.40 In *Othman (Abu Qatada)*,[69] an ECtHR decision on deportation, the court held the admission of torture evidence:[70]

> ... is manifestly contrary, not just to the provisions of Article 6, but to the most basic international standards of a fair trial. It would make the whole trial not only immoral and illegal, but also entirely unreliable in its outcome. It would, therefore, be a flagrant denial of justice if such evidence were admitted in a criminal trial.

6.41 Expert evidence, such as a report or witness statement from an appropriately qualified lawyer, academic or NGO with knowledge of the justice system in the requesting state will almost always be required. Any other evidence of, for example, ways in which the requesting state has breached the requested person's Article 5 or 6 rights in the past, will of course also be of assistance.

ECHR Article 7 (no punishment without law)

Overview

6.42 ECHR Article 7 prohibits the retrospective application of the criminal law and requires an offence to be clearly defined in the law, while allowing for an inevitable element of foreseeable judicial

66 At para 164.

67 At para 167.

68 See *UAE v Saujani*, Westminster Magistrates' Court, 5 August 2015; *UAE v Halliday*, Westminster Magistrates' Court, 22 December 2015; and *UAE v Cowe*, Westminster Magistrates' Court, 15 October 2015.

69 *Othman (Abu Qatada) v UK* (2012) 55 EHRR 1.

70 At para 267. See also para 259 of that judgment for examples of cases where it has been accepted that certain forms of unfairness could amount to a flagrant denial of justice.

interpretation.[71] Challenges on this ground do not arise frequently in extradition cases and there are few authorities on point.[72]

The test

6.43 The test referred to by Lord Steyn in the Supreme Court case of *R (Ullah) v Special Adjudicator*[73] was said to be the 'real risk of a flagrant violation' test applicable in Article 6 challenges. A question was raised over whether the Article 3 test of substantial grounds for believing that there is a real risk was more appropriate by Sir John Thomas in *Arranz v Spanish Judicial Authority*[74] who noted that it would be for the Supreme Court to determine whether it should reconsider the issue.

Note that this was referred to in the magistrates' court decision of *Government of USA v Assange*[75] which is (at the time of writing) subject to appeal.

ECHR Article 8 (right to respect for private and family life)

Overview

6.44 ECHR Article 8 provides that everyone has a right to respect for their private and family life, their home and their correspondence. It goes on, however, to qualify that right, saying that:

> There shall be no interference by a public authority with the exercise of this right except such as is in accordance with the law and is necessary in a democratic society in the interests of national security, public safety or the economic wellbeing of the country, for the prevention of disorder or crime, for the protection of health or morals, or for the protection of the rights and freedoms of others.

6.45 It is, therefore heavily qualified and a number of cases have emphasised that there is a strong public interest in honouring extradition treaties to justify the inevitable interference caused by an order for extradition.

71 *SW v UK* (1996) 21 EHRR 363 at para 36.

72 See *Osieniecki v Regional Court in Radom, Poland,* [2012] EWHC 1096 (Admin).

73 [2004] UKHL 26 at para 45.

74 [2013] EWHC 1662 (Admin).

75 Westminster Magistrates' Court 4, January 2021 (www.judiciary.uk/wp-content/uploads/2021/01/USA-v-Assange-judgment-040121.pdf).

6.46 Article 8 is raised as a challenge to extradition on behalf of the requested persons in the majority of contested Part 1 cases, although succeeds in a small proportion of them. Practitioners must therefore ensure that clients are given realistic advice about their likelihood of success if they do seek to raise it as a challenge to extradition.

The test

6.47 In deciding whether a person's extradition would be compatible with their Article 8 rights, the question is always 'whether the interference with the private and family lives of the extraditee and other members of his family is outweighed by the public interest in extradition'.[76] The court will look for hardship which is out of the ordinary: '[F]amilial distress inherent in enforced separation and financial hardship by removal of a breadwinner are almost inevitable in all cases of extradition and are generally ... not enough in themselves to be sufficient.'[77] In assessing the proportionality of the interference, the court will take into account a number of considerations, among which are the gravity of the offence;[78] time to be served (and how much time has been served in this country);[79] any health considerations; the requested person's circumstances; delay;[80] and the effect of extradition on innocent members of an extraditee's family. The Supreme Court judgment in *HH v Deputy Prosecutor of the Italian Republic, Genoa*[81] cautioned against the assumption that there is an

76 As stated by Baroness Hale giving the leading judgment in *HH v Deputy Prosecutor of the Italian Republic, Genoa* [2012] UKSC 25 at para 8.

77 *Debiec v District Court of Piotrkow Tybunalski, Poland* [2017] EWHC 2653 (Admin) at para 35.

78 See para 132 of *HH*: 'we must exercise caution not to impose our views about the seriousness of the offence or offences under consideration or the level of sentences or the arrangements for prisoner release which we are informed are likely to operate in the country seeking extradition. It certainly does not follow that extradition should be refused just because the sentencing court in this country would not order an immediate custodial sentence: however it would become relevant to the decision if the interests of a child or children might tip the sentencing scale here so as to reduce what would otherwise be an immediate custodial sentence in favour of a non-custodial sentence (including a suspended sentence).'

79 *Wysocki v Polish Judicial Authority* [2010] EWHC 3430 (Admin).

80 See, for example, *Dabrowski v Regional Court in Radom Poland* [2017] EWHC 179 (Admin); and *Siwak v Circuit Court of Tarnobrzeg, Poland* [2020] EWHC 1776 (Admin) where the culpable delay on the part of the authorities led to a diminution of the weight to be attached to the public interest.

81 [2012] UKSC 25.

'exceptionality test', while stating, however, that given the constant and weighty public interest in extradition, the cases in which extradition is held to be a disproportionate interference with a person's Article 8 rights are likely to be exceptional.

6.48 In *HH* Lady Hale discussed the information that the court requires in assessing a child's interests in the light of Article 8. She stated:

> If the children's interests are to be properly taken into account by the extraditing court, it will need to have some information about them. There is a good analogy with domestic sentencing practice, although in the first instance the information is likely to come from the parties, as there will be no pre-sentence report. The court will need to know whether there are dependent children, whether the parent's removal will be harmful to their interests and what steps can be taken to mitigate this. This should alert the court to whether any further information is needed. In the more usual case, where the person whose extradition is sought is not the sole or primary carer for the children, the court will have to consider whether there are any special features requiring further investigation of the children's interests, but in most cases it should be able to proceed with what it has.[82]

Lady Hale went on to say that:

> The important thing is that everyone, the parties and their representatives, but also the courts, is alive to the need to obtain the information necessary in order to have regard to the best interests of the children as a primary consideration, and to take steps accordingly.[83]

6.49 In cases where the requested person is the sole carer of a child or where the extradition of both parents is sought, it is imperative that evidence be put before the court as to the consequences for the child of a separation from their parents and evidence from a child psychologist and/or social worker should be obtained. Guidance on the areas which such experts should cover can be found at paras 82–86 of the *HH* judgment.

6.50 In *Polish Judicial Authorities v Celinski and others*,[84] the Divisional Court reiterated the principles laid down in *Norris* and *HH* and stated that it should rarely be necessary to cite any other decisions made in Article 8 cases.[85] The Lord Chief Justice (LCJ) also highlighted the following factors:

82 At para 82.

83 At para 86.

84 [2015] EWHC 1274 (Admin).

85 At para 14(iii).

- The public interest in ensuring that extradition arrangements are honoured is high as is the public interest in not creating a safe haven for fugitives in the UK.[86]
- Decisions of the judicial authority of an EU member state making a request for extradition should be afforded a proper degree of mutual confidence and respect.[87]
- Factors that mitigate the gravity of the offence or culpability in an accusation case are matters that will be considered by the court in the requesting state in the event of a conviction.[88]
- In a conviction case, it will rarely be appropriate for the appropriate judge to consider whether the sentence imposed significantly differs from what a UK court may impose because a) the appropriate judge will not have details of the person's previous offending behaviour, b) each member state is entitled to set its own sentencing regime and levels of sentence provided they are in accordance with the Convention.[89]

6.51 The LCJ stated that it was important that appropriate judges clearly set out an analysis of the facts as found at the extradition hearing and give 'sufficient and clear, adequate reasons' for the conclusion arrived at by balancing the relevant considerations. The LCJ proposed incorporating a 'balance sheet' into the decisions of the appropriate judge that sets out the 'pros' and 'cons' of extradition. Practitioners may therefore wish to incorporate the 'balance sheet approach' into their submissions.

6.52 Where there are concurrent family and extradition proceedings, no inflexible rule applies as to the order in which proceedings should be decided, however, 'the expectation is that extradition proceedings will progress swiftly with such information as is needed to determine an Article 8 issue touching the future of children gathered quickly and deployed before the District Judge'.[90]

6.53 There is an obvious overlap between the balancing exercise that is undertaken in Article 8 cases and the proportionality test at EA 2003 s21A. Given the provisions in the TCA which situate proportionality as a foundational principle in Part 1 cases, it is possible that there will be a greater convergence between these two means of challenge: see para 6.71 below.

86 At para 9.
87 At para 10.
88 At para 12.
89 At para 13.
90 *RT v Circuit Court in Tarnobrzeg, Poland* [2017] EWHC 1978 (Admin) at para 54.

6.54 Where a requested person is not a fugitive, the factors relevant to an Article 8 argument will very frequently be part of an assessment of oppression under EA 2003 ss14 and 25. Practitioners should take note of the comments of Lord Lloyd-Jones in *Konecny v Czech Republic*.[91] That case considered the unfairness which arises from the fact that the passage of time under section 14 starts to run from the date of conviction, rather than the date of the offence where a warrant is categorised as a conviction warrant, even where the requested person is unaware that a trial has taken place until they have been arrested on the extradition warrant (see para 5.48). Lord Lloyd-Jones stated that Article 8 provides an appropriate and effective means of addressing passage of time resulting in injustice or oppression in such cases, until the legislation can be amended.[92]

ECHR Article 10 (freedom of expression)

6.55 The right to freedom of expression under ECHR Article 10 is rarely invoked in extradition cases. For a discussion of the issues, see the magistrates' court judgment in *United States v Assange*[93] which is (at the time of writing) subject to appeal.

ECHR Article 18 (restriction of rights for illegitimate purposes)

6.56 Under ECHR Article 18, states are prohibited from restricting Convention rights for illegitimate purposes. This article therefore only applies where a Convention right has been restricted, most commonly under Article 5 or Article 6. The ECtHR case-law has found illegitimate restrictions in several cases in which rights have been restricted in order to impede a person from participating in political activism: see *Ilgar Mammadov v Azerbaijan (No 2)*[94] and *Merabishvili v Georgia*.[95]

91 [2019] UKSC 8.

92 At para 57.

93 Westminster Magistrates' Court, 4 January 2021 (www.judiciary.uk/wp-content/uploads/2021/01/USA-v-Assange-judgment-040121.pdf).

94 App No 919/15, 16 November 2017.

95 App No 72508/13, 28 November 2017.

Assurances

6.57 While the burden is initially on the requested person to establish a real risk of a violation (see above for the applicable tests), where such grounds have been met, the legal burden then shifts to the requesting state to show that there is no such risk.[96] Diplomatic assurances that extradition will not result in a violation of Convention rights may be given by a requested state in relation to any proposed breach, but are most commonly offered in Article 3 and Article 6 cases. See also the TCA at Article 604 which refers to 'guarantees' (para 6.4 above).

The *Othman* criteria

6.58 In *Othman (Abu Qatada) v UK*,[97] the ECtHR looked at whether assurances received from Jordan were sufficient to remove any real risk of ill-treatment. It set out the following principles in relation to Article 3 expulsion cases:

> 187. In any examination of whether an applicant faces a real risk of ill-treatment in the country to which he is to be removed, the Court will consider both the general human rights situation in that country and the particular characteristics of the applicant. In a case where assurances have been provided by the receiving State, those assurances constitute a further relevant factor which the Court will consider. However, assurances are not in themselves sufficient to ensure adequate protection against the risk of ill-treatment. There is an obligation to examine whether assurances provide, in their practical application, a sufficient guarantee that the applicant will be protected against the risk of ill-treatment. The weight to be given to assurances from the receiving State depends, in each case, on the circumstances prevailing at the material time ...
>
> 188. In assessing the practical application of assurances and determining what weight is to be given to them, the preliminary question is whether the general human rights situation in the receiving State excludes accepting any assurances whatsoever. However, it will only be in rare cases that the general situation in a country will mean that no weight at all can be given to assurances ...
>
> 189. More usually, the Court will assess first, the quality of assurances given and, second, whether, in light of the receiving State's practices they can be relied upon. In doing so, the Court will have regard, inter alia, to the following factors:

96 *Ion Sekrieru v Government of Azerbaijan* [2021] EWHC 735 (Admin).
97 (2012) 55 EHRR 1.

> (i) whether the terms of the assurances have been disclosed to the Court ...;
> (ii) whether the assurances are specific or are general and vague ...;
> (iii) who has given the assurances and whether that person can bind the receiving State ...;
> (iv) if the assurances have been issued by the central government of the receiving State, whether local authorities can be expected to abide by them ...;
> (v) whether the assurances concern treatment which is legal or illegal in the receiving State ...;
> (vi) whether they have been given by a Contracting State ...;
> (vii) the length and strength of bilateral relations between the sending and receiving States, including the receiving State's record in abiding by similar assurances ...;
> (viii) whether compliance with the assurances can be objectively verified through diplomatic or other monitoring mechanisms, including providing unfettered access to the applicant's lawyers ...;
> (ix) whether there is an effective system of protection against torture in the receiving State, including whether it is willing to cooperate with international monitoring mechanisms (including international human rights NGOs), and whether it is willing to investigate allegations of torture and to punish those responsible ...;
> (x) whether the applicant has previously been ill-treated in the receiving State ...; and
> (xi) whether the reliability of the assurances has been examined by the domestic courts of the sending/Contracting State ...

6.59 The use of this list in the context of extradition proceedings has been approved by the administrative court, which has warned, however, that the factors should not be treated as a 'tick-box' list and that the circumstances of each person's case should be examined carefully.[98]

6.60 In relation to Article 3 assurances, in the context of assurances given by Romania, the Divisional Court in *Zagrean*[99] approved the following factors for evaluating assurances:

(i) the terms of assurances must be such that, if they are fulfilled, the person returned will not be subjected to treatment contrary to Article 3;
(ii) the assurances must be given in good faith;
(iii) there must be a sound objective basis for believing that the assurances will be fulfilled;
(iv) fulfilment of the assurances must be capable of being verified.

98 *Ilia v Appeal Court in Athens, Greece* [2015] EWHC 547 (Admin) at para 39.

99 The court in *Mures and Bistrita-Nasuad Tribunal v Zagrean; Petru Sunca v Iasi Court of Law, Romania; Stelian Chihaia v Bacau Court of Law, Romania* [2016] EWHC 2786 (Admin) at paras 51–53.

6.61 There is no restriction as a matter of law as to who may or may not give assurances; each case will depend on its own facts.[100] Where an assurance is not given or endorsed by a judicial authority, the court must undertake a free evaluation of the assurance, examining and assessing all relevant evidence.[101] In the ECtHR case of *Bivolaru and Moldovan v France*[102] the Strasbourg court was not satisfied by assurances provided by Romania which contained stereotypical language. The Divisional Court in *Popoviciu v Romania*,[103] commenting on *Moldovan*, stated that:

> ... the caution against 'stereotypical assurances' should be regarded as an exhortation to focus on substance rather than form, and should not be taken as meaning that any use of a form of words which has also been used in another case must necessarily be regarded as inadequate to satisfy a court that art.3 obligations will be observed.[104]

Evidence of breach of assurances

6.62 In recent years, some requested persons have been able to obtain evidence of breaches of assurances given in respect of past extraditees. Evidence of past compliance or non-compliance with an earlier assurance will obviously be relevant in deciding whether an assurance can be relied upon.[105] In the Supreme Court judgment of *Zabolotnyi v Mateszalka District Court, Hungary*,[106] Lord Lloyd-Jones said that:

> A state's failure to fulfil assurances in the past may be a powerful reason to disbelieve that they will be fulfilled in the future.... The weight to be attached to a previous breach of assurance would be likely to vary from case to case depending on all the circumstances, including how specific the previous assurance was and whether the breach was deliberate or inadvertent ... The breach would, however, clearly be relevant ... In the same way, the absence of evidence that a

100 *Shankaran v Government of India* [2014] EWHC 957 (Admin) at para 59, approved in *Zabolotnyi v Mateszalka District Court, Hungary* [2021] UKSC 14.

101 *Zabolotnyi v Mateszalka District Court, Hungary* [2021] UKSC 14 at para 50. See *Snowden v Ghana* [2018] EWHC 198 (Admin) for a case in which the Divisional Court rejected the appellant's argument that assurances which were said to be equivocal and conditional gave rise to a real risk of a breach of his ECHR Article 3 rights, but looked to the context in which the assurances were given.

102 App Nos 40324/16 and 12623/17.

103 [2021] EWHC 1584 (Admin).

104 At para 174. See also *Cretu v Romania* [2021] EWHC 1693 (Admin).

105 *Zabolotnyi v Mateszalka District Court, Hungary* [2021] UKSC 14 at para 46.

106 [2021] UKSC 14 at para 46.

state has ever acted in breach or in disregard of an assurance of this nature would be relevant ...

6.63 There is no distinction between a breach of an assurance given to the UK and the breach of an assurance given to a third country, if established.[107]

Proportionality

Extradition Act 2003 s21A

6.64 In 2014, EA 2003 s21 was amended to include a new section 21A entitled 'Person not convicted: human rights and proportionality'. The amendment added a statutory consideration for judges at section 21A(1)(b), to be dealt with after having looked at whether extradition would be compatible with a person's Convention rights. In effect, it brought into force a new proportionality bar to extradition. Notably, it only applies to Part 1 cases (AWs) and to those that are accused.[108]

6.65 EA 2003 s21A states:

> **21A Person not convicted: human rights and proportionality**
> (1) If the judge is required to proceed under this section (by virtue of section 11) the judge must decide both of the following questions in respect of the person ('D')–
> (a) whether the extradition would be compatible with the Convention rights within the meaning of the Human Rights Act 1998;
> (b) whether the extradition would be disproportionate.
> (2) In deciding whether the extradition would be disproportionate, the judge must take into account the specified matters relating to proportionality (so far as the judge thinks it appropriate to do so); but the judge must not take any other matters into account.
> (3) These are the specified matters relating to proportionality–
> (a) the seriousness of the conduct alleged to constitute the extradition offence;
> (b) the likely penalty that would be imposed if D was found guilty of the extradition offence;
> (c) the possibility of the relevant foreign authorities taking measures that would be less coercive than the extradition of D.

107 At paras 45–50.

108 Hansard reveals that the justification for the distinction was the four month minimum sentence requirement in conviction cases, which was considered a sufficient proportionality safeguard (https://hansard.parliament.uk/lords/2013-12-11/debates/13121184000865/Anti-SocialBehaviourCrimeAndPolicingBill).

(4) The judge must order D's discharge if the judge makes one or both of these decisions–
   (a) that the extradition would not be compatible with the Convention rights;
   (b) that the extradition would be disproportionate.
(5) The judge must order D to be extradited to the category 1 territory in which the warrant was issued if the judge makes both of these decisions –
   (a) that the extradition would be compatible with the Convention rights;
   (b) that the extradition would not be disproportionate.

6.66 In determining whether extradition is disproportionate, the judge must have regard to only those specified matters set out in section 21A(3). The proportionality bar does, however, come as a secondary review of proportionality, given that the NCA should already have carried out a proportionality check at the certification stage and in doing so, should have applied the LCJ's guidance (see para 3.11 above). The Divisional Court has provided guidance as to how the appropriate judge should determine the issues in EA 2003 s21A(3): in *Miraszewski and others v District Court in Torun, Poland and others,*[109] Pitchford LJ set out the following principles:

Seriousness of the offence (EA 2003 s21A(3)(a))

6.67 a) The LCJ's guidance contained within the Criminal Practice Directions Amendment No 2 [2014] EWHC Crim 1569 provides a measure of assistance to the assessment of seriousness.[110]
b) The LCJ's guidance is appropriate for identifying a 'floor' rather than a ceiling for the assessment of seriousness.[111]
c) The LCJ's guidance is aimed at offences at the very bottom end of the scale of seriousness about which it is unlikely there could be any dispute.[112]
d) The guidance states that in the identified cases the triviality of the conduct alleged would alone require the judge to discharge the requested person.[113]
e) A judge making the proportionality decision is not limited by the categories identified within the guidance provided for by the LCJ. A judge may conclude that an offence is not serious even

109 [2014] EWHC 4261 (Admin).
110 At para 27.
111 At para 28.
112 At para 28.
113 At para 28.

though it does not fall within the categories listed in the guidance.[114]

f) Other offences may be assessed by the judge as being non-serious or trivial offences.[115]

g) The seriousness of conduct alleged to constitute the offences is to be judged, in the first instance, against domestic standards although, as in all cases of extradition, the court will respect the views of the requesting state if they are offered.[116]

h) The main components of the seriousness of the conduct are the nature and quality of the acts and the harm caused to the victim. The appropriate judge should not adjourn to seek the requesting state's views on the subject.[117]

Likely penalty that would be imposed if D was found guilty of the extradition offence (EA 2003 s21A(3)(b))

6.68 i) The principal focus is on the question of whether it would be proportionate to order the extradition of a person who is not likely to receive a custodial sentence in the requesting state.[118]

j) Appropriate respect for the sentencing regime of a member state is required, however, in the extremely rare case when a particular penalty would be offensive to a domestic court in the circumstances of the particular criminal conduct the judge may adjust the weight to be given to 'the likely penalty'.[119]

k) The broad terms of subsection (3)(b) permit the judge to make the assessment on the information provided and, when specific information from the requesting state is absent, the judge is entitled to draw inferences from the contents of the EAW and to apply domestic sentencing practice as a measure of likelihood.[120]

l) It does not follow that the likelihood of a non-custodial penalty precludes the judge from deciding that extradition would be proportionate.[121]

114 At para 28.
115 At para 28.
116 At para 36.
117 At para 36.
118 At para 37.
119 At para 38.
120 At para 38.
121 At para 39.

Possibility of the relevant foreign authorities taking measures that would be less coercive than the extradition of D (EA 2003 s21A(3)(c))

6.69 m) There is an evidential burden on the requested person to identify less coercive measures that would be appropriate in the circumstances.[122]

n) Where the requested person has left the requesting state with knowledge of their obligations to the requesting state's authorities, but in breach of them, it is unlikely that the appropriate judge will find less coercive methods appropriate. However, there may be occasions when the less coercive procedure is appropriate. If the requested person fails to respond to those alternative measures the issue of a further warrant and extradition could hardly be resisted.[123]

6.70 The specified matters in section 21A(3) are not listed in order of importance[124] and the appropriate judge will need to specifically address each of the subsection (3) issues and should give reasons for the weight he attaches to each factor.[125]

Proportionality under the Trade and Cooperation Agreement

6.71 Practitioners should note the complication that arises in EA 2003 Part 1 cases from the surrender provisions of the TCA which promote the consideration of proportionality from its previous status as an amendment to the EA 2003 to a foundational principle (see TCA Articles 597 and 613(1)). There are further questions raised by the TCA provisions which it will be necessary for the courts to grapple with, as follows:

- Article 597 does not distinguish between accusation and conviction warrants, although EA 2003 s21A is unamended and therefore still applies only to accusation warrants. At the time of writing, this has not been dealt with by the High Court.[126] See

122 At para 41.
123 At para 41.
124 At para 32.
125 At para 33.
126 See *Saptelei v Hunedoara Law Court of Romania* [2021] EWHC 506 (Admin) in which it was argued in a pre-existing EAW case that, given that the TCA does not distinguish between accusation and conviction cases, the court's approach to Article 8 should be modified. The argument was rejected by the Divisional Court following the case of *Polakowski v Westminster Magistrates' Court* [2021] EWHC 53 (Admin) in which the court observed that a pre-existing EAW case would be governed by the pre-existing legal framework.

para 5.123 regarding the interaction between the TCA and the domestic legislation.

- While Article 597 uses similar wording as that set out at EA 2003 s21A(3)(a)–(c), it adds an additional factor, that is, 'avoiding unnecessarily long periods of pre-trial detention'. While the EA 2003 includes provisions aimed at avoiding long periods of pre-trial detention (that is, ss12A and 21B), these do not fall within the limited proportionality assessment to be considered at s21A.
- Unlike EA 2003 s21A, the TCA does not explicitly state that other matters must not be taken into account in assessing proportionality.

CHAPTER 7

The initial hearing in arrest warrant cases

Introduction

7.1 This chapter covers the initial hearing that takes place following a requested person's arrest under Part 1 of the Extradition Act (EA) 2003, referred to as 'arrest warrant' (AW) cases. Initial hearings in Part 2 cases are considered in chapter 8.

7.2 This chapter will consider:

- procedural requirements;
- challenging production and service;
- identification issues;
- requested persons facing domestic proceedings/sentence;
- issues to be raised to challenge extradition;
- bail;
- proceeding to an uncontested extradition hearing;
- competing AW requests.

Certified or provisional arrest warrant?

7.3 The most common way for a person to be arrested under EA 2003 Part 1 is by way of a certified[1] AW. In such cases, the procedure as set out in para 7.9 below will be followed.

7.4 However, arrest under Part 1 can also be provisional. A provisional arrest takes place where a constable, customs officer or a service police officer has reasonable grounds for believing that a Part 1 warrant (AW) has been or will be issued by a category 1 territory.[2]

7.5 A person arrested under a provisional AW must be brought before the appropriate judge within 48 hours of arrest and must be given a copy of the warrant as soon as practicable after arrest. An AW and National Crime Agency (NCA) certificate must also be produced to the judge within 48 hours of arrest.

7.6 If the person is brought before the court within 48 hours but the AW and NCA certificate have not been so produced, the judge may extend the period by a further 48 hours if the judge decides (on the balance of probabilities) that production of the documents could not reasonably be complied with within the initial 48-hour period. If this

1 The NCA is responsible for certifying AWs.
2 EA 2003 s5.

time limit is not complied with, it is possible to apply for the requested person to be discharged.[3]

7.7 Provisional arrest is used where the NCA has yet to certify an issued AW and there is a need to arrest immediately.

The initial hearing

7.8 The initial hearing starts when the requested person is brought before the appropriate judge. The appropriate judge has the same powers (as near as may be) as a magistrates' court would have if the proceedings were the summary trial of information against the person[4] which includes the power to adjourn the initial hearing.[5]

7.9 The requested person who has been arrested under EA 2003 Part 1 will appear in custody.[6] As in all court proceedings, persons brought before the court will be asked to give their name and date of birth. The requested person will have an interpreter present with them to assist if required. Practitioners should try to retain the interpreter used to take instructions in the cells for continuity.

7.10 Once the requested person has been identified, the Crown Prosecution Service (CPS) representative acting on behalf of the judicial authority will introduce themselves and the person acting on behalf of the requested person.

7.11 The CPS representative will confirm that the court has a copy of the AW, Part 1 certificate and the arrest statement. They will then summarise the AW and provide the court with the circumstances of arrest. The court will be asked to find that the requested person has been served with a copy of the AW as soon as practicable after arrest[7] and produced before the appropriate judge as soon as practicable.[8]

3 See Criminal Procedure Rules (CrimPR) 50.16(2) for the procedure to be followed where the failure to comply with this time limit gives rise to an application to discharge the requested person. While this rule requires the defendant to make an application for discharge in writing unless the court directs otherwise, in practice such applications should be made orally at the first opportunity for requested persons who are remanded in custody, given that continued detention in such circumstances may be unlawful.

4 EA 2003 s7(6).

5 EA 2003 s7(9) and (10) and CrimPR 50.3.

6 A person may not be granted bail by the police when arrested on an AW. A person arrested under EA 2003 Part 2 may be granted bail (EA 2003 ss72(4)(a) and 74(4)(a)).

7 EA 2003 s4(2).

8 EA 2003 s4(3).

Service of the AW

7.12 EA 2003 s4(2) states that a copy of the warrant must be given to the person as soon as practicable after their arrest. If this section is not complied with and the person applies to the judge to be discharged, the judge *may* order the person's discharge.[9]

7.13 The arrest statement will usually say when the AW was served upon the requested person. It may be the case that the arresting officer merely gives the AW to the person upon arrest and then immediately takes it from that person and places it in their property bag while the requested person is in custody. Another source of information about service of the AW would be the custody record, but this would have to be requested from the police station that the requested person was detained at. The AW must be in the language of the state requesting the person's extradition. Furthermore, the NCA certificate should be attached. There is no requirement that the AW be in the native language of the requested person.

7.14 If the requested person has not been served with the AW then an application should be made to the judge for discharge. It should be noted, however, that although EA 2003 s4(4) gives the judge discretion as to whether to discharge, this is not normally exercised in favour of the requested person. Judges will look at what prejudice has actually been suffered by the AW not being served upon the requested person and will often seek to remedy the problem by ensuring that a copy of the AW is given to the requested person in the dock. The practitioner will also have had an opportunity to provide advice to the requested person on the content of the AW before going into court.

Production before the appropriate judge

7.15 EA 2003 s4(3) states that the requested person must be brought as soon as practicable before the appropriate judge. If this requirement is not complied with and the person applies to the judge to be discharged, the judge *must* order the person's discharge.[10] Unlike

9 EA 2003 s4(4). See CrimPR 50.16(2) for the procedure to be followed where the failure to comply with this time limit gives rise to an application to discharge the requested person. While this rule requires the defendant to make an application for discharge in writing unless the court directs otherwise, in practice such applications should be made orally at the first opportunity for requested persons who are remanded in custody, given that continued detention in such circumstances may be unlawful.

10 EA 2003 s4(5).

section 4(4), the judge has no discretion and must discharge if they find that the person has not been produced before the judge as soon as practicable.

7.16 What is deemed to be 'as soon as practicable' is a factual determination that will differ from case to case and from judge to judge. The leading authority on production is *R (Nikonovs) v Governor of Brixton Prison*.[11] The facts of that case were set out in para 4 of the judgment:

> At 5.45 on the morning of Saturday 17 September G S L Court Services, who were responsible for conveying Mr Nikonovs to court, telephoned the Boston Custody Suite to say that Mr Nikonovs would not be collected until Monday as Bow Street Magistrates Court was not open over the weekend. In fact this was an error, the court was open on Saturday. In the event Mr Nikonovs was not brought before a judge at Bow Street until 14:00 hours on Monday 19 September, which was nearly 66 hours after his arrest at Boston police station and some 74 hours after his arrest at his home.

7.17 The judge at the magistrates' court refused to discharge Nikonovs, who subsequently sought a writ of 'habeas corpus ad subjiciendum.' The High Court granted the writ of 'habeas corpus' and discharged Nikonovs. As part of their reasoning, the court stated that: 'the criterion is practicable rather than the more elastic reasonably practicable' and:[12]

> No one suggests it was not practicable to bring him to London that day. He could have been brought to Bow Street and the district judge was very unhappy that he was not. He was not, in the event, brought before District Judge Wickham at Bow Street until 14:00 hours on the Monday afternoon. In these circumstances I have no hesitation in concluding that the applicant was not brought before an appropriate judge as soon as practicable.

7.18 This approach appears to have been tempered by the High Court in *Huczko v Governor of HMP Wandsworth*.[13] This was also a case where a writ of 'habeas corpus ad subjiciendum' was sought following the refusal of the judge to order the requested person's discharge. In this case, the requested person was arrested and taken the following day to Hammersmith Magistrates' Court in West London. This was an error, as he should have been taken to Westminster Magistrates' Court (WMC) in order to be produced before an appropriate judge. The requested person was detained for four hours at Hammersmith

11 [2005] EWHC 2405 (Admin).

12 At para 21.

13 [2012] EWHC 4134 (Admin).

Magistrates' Court until it was appreciated that he should have been taken to WMC. He was transferred to the correct court where he arrived at about 1 pm. He was then brought before a judge just after 4 pm. The judge found that, despite the human error, he had been produced within 16 hours of his arrest and therefore as soon as practicable. The Divisional Court agreed. In considering whether there has been a breach of section 4(3), it is right for the court to have regard both to 'the cause and to the duration of the delay.'[14]

7.19 The current 'referral' time at WMC for receiving new cases is 3.30 pm.[15] After that time, a case can only be accepted if it is referred to an appropriate judge and the judge agrees to accept the late arrival. If it is unlikely that the initial hearing would be concluded by 4.30 pm, the judge will likely refuse to accept the arrival of the requested person and the requested person will be lodged overnight in a London police station to be produced the following day.

7.20 When deciding whether to argue that a requested person has not been brought before an appropriate judge as soon as practicable, it is important to consider the following:

- What time was the person arrested?
- Was the arrest a planned arrest or unexpected?
- What time did the person arrive at the police station and when was his detention authorised?
- When were arrangements made for the collection of the requested person to be taken to court?
- What time was the person transported from the police station to the court?
- How far was the distance between the police station and the court?
- Did anything occur during the transportation to the court that unexpectedly delayed the arrival?
- If the requested person was arrested the day before, was the case referred to an appropriate judge for a decision on whether to accept the requested person into custody?
- If so, what information was conveyed to the court about the estimated time of arrival and what was the response of the judge?

14 At para 18.

15 The referral time is court practice and practitioners should check from time to time that it remains 3.30 pm.

Only after considering these questions will the representative be in a position to realistically determine whether or not to challenge the requested person's late production.

7.21 As general guidance, if it has taken two working days to get to court, production should be challenged. If the person was produced before the appropriate judge on the day of arrest or even the following day, unless the distance to be travelled was short, an argument that the person was not produced as soon as practicable will usually be untenable.

7.22 After the CPS representative acting on behalf of the judicial authority has made the introductions the judge will ask the defence representative if there are any challenges to service and production. If there are, submissions should be made there and then.[16] If further time is sought to obtain evidence to make good the submissions, the initial hearing can be adjourned.

7.23 Once the case has moved beyond the initial hearing, these issues cannot be revisited.[17] If there are no challenges, then the judicial authority will ask the judge to move on to the issue of identity.

7.24 If the defence submissions on either service of the AW or production at court are successful, then the person is discharged from the extradition request. This does not mean that the person is immune from extradition, as the AW can be reissued.

Identity

7.25 The appropriate judge must next decide whether the person brought before them is the person who is referred to in the AW. Very often identity will not be in dispute – the requested person will have already given details of their identity on arrest and when asked by the court – but it may be challenged by the defence.

7.26 The appropriate judge must determine identity on the balance of probabilities.[18]

16 See CrimPR 50.16(2) for the procedure to be followed where the failure to comply with this time limit gives rise to an application to discharge the requested person. While this rule requires the defendant to make an application for discharge in writing unless the court directs otherwise, in practice such applications should be made orally at the first opportunity for requested persons who are remanded in custody, given that continued detention in such circumstances may be unlawful.

17 *Hilali v The National Court of Madrid, Spain* [2006] EWHC 1239 (Admin).

18 EA 2003 s7(3).

7.27 There are many sources from which the court can determine identity. As already mentioned above, the requested person will have given their details when asked by the court. The appropriate judge will also have recourse to the arrest statement and the details that were given to the police upon arrest. Furthermore, identity documents may have been seized. Finally, the Police National Computer (PNC) may determine their true identity if the requested person has been the subject of a livescan check.[19]

7.28 If identity is still in doubt, the judicial authority may seek a set of fingerprints from the requesting state in order to compare them with those taken upon arrest.

7.29 AWs also contain a section in box A that allows for the judicial authority to enter details about the requested person's 'distinctive marks' or to provide a description of the requested person. Many judicial authorities take advantage of this and provide a full description including known tattoos and scars.

7.30 AWs may be accompanied by a photograph of the person sought that could help the appropriate judge determine identity.

7.31 If the judge decides that the person before them is not the person in respect of whom the AW was issued, the judge must order discharge. If the judge concludes that it is the correct person, then the case must proceed to EA 2003 s8 and the issue of consent.

7.32 The requested person must be warned that if identity is unsuccessfully challenged, this may affect the weight to be attached to their evidence at the extradition hearing and may undoubtedly affect the outcome of any bail application.[20]

Appealing service, production and identity

7.33 Appeals under the EA 2003 in AW cases are brought under section 26 (for the requested person) and section 28 (for the issuing judicial authority). Sections 26 and 28 relate to appeals regarding decisions made at the extradition hearing. Sections 4–7 are considered to involve issues dealt with at the 'initial hearing' and are therefore not subject to the statutory appeal provisions of sections 26 or 28. Furthermore, such decisions cannot be re-opened under the

19 See *Prendi v Government of the Republic of Albania* [2015] EWHC 1809 (Admin) in which information from an INTERPOL Red Notice was held to be inadmissible.

20 *Adedeji v Public Prosecutor's Office, Germany* [2012] EWHC 3237 (Admin).

Magistrates' Courts Act 1980 s142, as would be the case in criminal proceedings.[21]

7.34 The only way of challenging an adverse decision under sections 4–7 is by way of a judicial review or, if the person is in custody, applying for a writ of 'habeas corpus ad subjiciendum.' This approach was approved by the High Court in *Nikonovs*.

Other issues before consent

7.35 If the person before the court is subject to a charge in the UK, then the extradition hearing *must* be adjourned prior to dealing with consent[22] until the charge is disposed of.[23] Consent will not be taken and the court will proceed to deal with bail.[24]

7.36 If the person before the court is subject to a sentence of imprisonment in the UK, then the judge *may* adjourn the extradition hearing until the sentence of imprisonment has been served. A judge can adjourn the hearing for up to six months before the matter has to be brought back before the court. Again, under EA 2003 s8B consent will not be taken if the appropriate judge exercises their decision to adjourn.

7.37 Sections 8A and 8B were introduced into the legislation in order to prevent a requested person escaping prosecution in the UK or escaping having to serve a sentence by consenting to extradition and being removed from the jurisdiction before being prosecuted or completing their sentence.[25] The CrimPR also require a court to adjourn if informed that a requested person has been charged with an offence in the UK.[26]

7.38 If a requested person is subject to a lengthy sentence of imprisonment, the CPS will obtain instructions from the judicial authority as to whether it wishes to seek the requested person's temporary extradition known as 'temporary surrender.' The requesting state will be required to provide an undertaking stating that the requested person will be kept in custody pending their trial and returned to the UK after proceedings have concluded in that state. If the court agrees to

21 *Klimeto v Westminster Magistrates' Court* [2013] 1 WLR 420 and *Nur v Public Prosecutor Van der Valk* [2005] EWHC 1874 (Admin).

22 EA 2003 s8A.

23 EA 2003 s8A(2)(a)–(d).

24 The required information about consent must be given: *Morozovs v Latvian Judicial Authority* [2013] EWHC 367 (Admin).

25 *R (Governor of Wandsworth Prison) v Kinderis* [2007] EWHC 998 (Admin).

26 CrimPR 50.3(5).

temporary surrender, the requested person will be returned to the UK to serve the remainder of the sentence.

Consent

7.39 Once the court has progressed through sections 4–7 of the Act the next issue to be dealt with at the initial hearing is that of consent.[27] The consent procedure was discussed in chapter 4. The clerk of the court will put the consent procedure to the requested person, who will be asked to indicate whether they wish to consent to their extradition. They will be reminded that once consent is given, it is irrevocable. If the requested person consents to their extradition, they will be asked to sign the consent form. The interpreter will translate this if required. It is advisable to ask the court for a copy of the signed consent order to keep on the requested person's file.

7.40 The effect of consent is that a person consenting to extradition will waive appeal rights, and will be extradited within ten days of having consented to extradition. This ten-day period can be extended upon an application from the judicial authority if it is not possible to effect removal within that time.

7.41 Where requested persons do not consent to their extradition they will be informed that they can change their mind at any time.

Opening proceedings

7.42 The permitted period within which the extradition hearing is to begin following the date of arrest is 21 days.[28] In the vast majority of cases this is not possible due to difficulties with listings. The judge will therefore 'formally open' proceedings but make no decisions. This satisfies the requirement that the hearing is to begin within 21 days of the date of arrest.

7.43 If proceedings have been adjourned under EA 2003 s8A or s8B, then the permitted period within which the extradition hearing is to begin is extended by the number of days for which the proceedings have been adjourned.[29]

27 EA 2003 s8(1)(c).

28 EA 2003 s8(4).

29 EA 2003 s8(4A) as inserted by Anti-social Behaviour, Crime and Policing Act 2014 s155.

Issues to be raised at extradition hearing to resist extradition

7.44 The court will next ask the advocate to indicate whether any issues will be raised or whether the matter can proceed to an uncontested hearing. If there are issues to raise these should be outlined by the advocate at the initial hearing. These issues may come under scrutiny from the judge and the advocate must be prepared to fully justify why the issue to be raised is tenable, why time is required to prepare the case and why it is in the interests of justice to adjourn.

7.45 The issues raised to challenge extradition may be one or more of the following:

- validity of the AW (EA 2003 s2);
- the offence(s) contained in the AW is/are not extradition offences (section 10);
- one (or more) of the bars to extradition (sections 11–19B);
- conviction in absence (section 20);
- extradition would be incompatible with Convention rights and/or disproportionate (accusation cases only) (sections 21/21A);
- physical/mental health of requested person (section 25);
- abuse of process.

Case management forms, date for hearing and directions

7.46 The defence advocate should complete a case management form for all cases where extradition is contested. The case management form can be found at appendix H. The form warns the requested person that 'the information you provide must be accurate as it may be checked, and it may be referred to at a later hearing.' The form must therefore be completed accurately.

7.47 Should issues arise later in the proceedings that were not included in the form, it is important to notify both the court and the CPS as soon as they arise so that all parties are on notice in advance of the extradition hearing.

7.48 Having identified the issues to be contested, the court will then proceed to fix a date for the extradition hearing to take place. The court will fix a date for a case management hearing to take place in complex cases where more than a few days court time are required for the extradition hearing and this will usually be listed one month before the extradition hearing. A judge may be allocated in complex cases to ensure judicial continuity in case management, although this may not happen until close to the extradition hearing date.

7.49 The advocate will need to provide a realistic time estimate in order to assist the court in finding a date for the hearing. By way of example, an EA 2003 s10 extradition offence argument could take as little as one hour, whereas a substantial issue where expert evidence is to be called could last days or even weeks.

7.50 Once a date is fixed the court will make directions. A signed directions form will be provided to the parties setting out the agreed directions with which they must comply.[30] These will include directions for:

- a statement of issues (if required);
- a proof of evidence;
- defence evidence (if any);
- response from judicial authority;
- service of skeleton arguments;
- joint bundle.

7.51 In extradition proceedings, where the requested person is to be called to give evidence, a signed proof of evidence has to be served in advance (see para 9.35). This allows the CPS acting on behalf of the judicial authority to seek instructions on issues raised within the statement. It can also then be adopted in evidence by the requested person, drastically reducing the amount of time required for examination in chief.

7.52 A skeleton argument will also be required in most, if not all, contested cases. The preparation of the skeleton argument and other documents for the extradition hearing will be explored in chapter 9. When agreeing to directions, it is important to remember that it may take at least a week for the requested person's legal aid application to be determined. Work is unlikely to start straight away on a case unless the requested person is paying privately and has put the representative in funds.

7.53 Further, if the requested person is remanded in custody, sufficient time needs to be allowed for legal visits to take place.

7.54 On occasions, the duty solicitor may have too many cases to deal with to allow time for the completion of the case management form for each case. The court makes allowance for this and the last question on the form asks: 'Have you had sufficient time to advise your

30 If a representative is unable to comply with a direction, an application to vary the direction should be made.

client on potential challenges? If not why not?' It is acceptable to indicate 'no' and state the reason: in these cases, the court will direct that the case management form be completed and submitted within seven days of the initial hearing or by the second hearing, whichever is sooner.

Bail

7.55 The final issue for the court to determine at the initial hearing is that of bail.[31] Bail applications in all proceedings, but especially in extradition proceedings, need to be structured. As discussed in chapter 4, there are enquiries specific to extradition proceedings which the court will make of the advocate if bail is to be granted. It is important to have a sufficient bail package of conditions in place and for that reason telephone calls will very often need to be made to family members in order to obtain a security or locate travel documents.

7.56 There is no presumption in favour of bail in conviction cases and, in reality (in both accusation and conviction cases) a requested person is unlikely to be granted bail without a security.

7.57 The conditions usually imposed in extradition cases include:

- security/surety or both (pre-release condition);
- surrender/retention of travel documents (pre-release condition);
- residence;
- not to apply for international travel documents;
- reporting to a police station;
- curfew;
- to provide the court with a mobile telephone number and for the phone to be kept on and charged at all times;
- geographical restriction.

The taking of securities and sureties

Securities

7.58 All securities need to be paid through WMC. Assistance is provided at the first floor helpdesk. Those offering securities do not need to attend court if they can deposit the funds via an electronic transfer.

31 EA 2003 s8(1)(d).

In this situation the proposed security contacts[32] the WMC bail department who will provide them with the bail security form, which will request the following information:

- full name;
- date of birth;
- telephone number;
- address;
- bank details:
  - bank name;
  - account number;
  - sort code;
- nationality;
- occupation.

7.59 The person paying the security will also need to provide proof of identity (passport/ID card/driver's licence) in addition to documents establishing address verification (bank statement/utility bill). This is in order to comply with Anti-Money Laundering Regulations. Where the depositor is able to provide a photo card driving licence (UK or European Economic Area (EEA)) or a full government issued passport it is not necessary to provide proof of address.

7.60 On receipt of the completed bail security form and proof of identity, the details of the HM Courts and Tribunals Service (HMCTS) bank account will be released along with the case number to quote as the reference for the payment.

7.61 The requested person cannot usually be released from custody until the court has received cleared funds into their central bail account. It is therefore imperative that the court reference number is recorded accurately as a mistake could lead to a delay on the payment being identified.

Sureties

7.62 Sureties can be taken at WMC (and it is preferable for a person providing a surety to attend for a bail hearing), but may also be taken at other magistrates' courts or police stations if the surety is unable to attend the bail hearing. Representatives should ensure that anyone standing surety is aware that, should the requested person fail to attend, they will stand to lose the funds promised.

32 Tel 020 3126 3020.

7.63 A surety will need to attend the court or police station with proof of identity and proof of the availability and liquidity of funds being offered.

7.64 If the surety is to be taken at a police station, the person standing surety will need to take the court extract of the bail hearing to the police station, and ask the police to complete a form 616. Whether the surety is taken at court or at the police station, the police will check whether the proposed surety has any previous convictions. When the surety is taken, the person acting as surety is likely to be asked about their relationship with the requested person and may be questioned about their ability to ensure that the requested person does not abscond. Practitioners should ensure that sureties are made continuous, that is, that the surety will extend to each and every hearing in the case, and not just to the next appearance. It is an offence under Bail Act 1976 s9 to indemnify a surety.

Place of detention

7.65 If a male requested person is remanded into custody, he will be taken to HMP Wandsworth or HMP Pentonville unless he is assessed on arrival at the prison to be a category A prisoner, in which case he will be transferred to HMP Belmarsh. Female requested persons remanded into custody will go to HMP Bronzefield.

Breach of bail

7.66 If the requested person subsequently breaches any bail condition, EA 2003 s198 allows the local court to deal with the breach.

Bail appeals

7.67 Where a magistrates' court withholds bail in extradition proceedings or imposes conditions in granting bail in extradition proceedings, the High Court may grant bail or vary the conditions.[33]

7.68 An appeal of a bail decision is made to the High Court by submitting form N161 to the Administrative Court Office together with the fee of £255. An appeal can also be made against the imposition of certain bail conditions.[34] The CPS will need to be put on notice of such an application and the Administrative Court will usually list the

33 Criminal Justice Act (CJA) 1967 s22(1A).

34 *Sarao v United States of America* [2015] EWHC 1570 (Admin).

hearing within 48 hours (excluding weekends and bank holidays). A fully completed CRM 14 to cover the High Court bail application will need to be submitted at the time the form EX244 is lodged to ensure a representation order is granted without delay.

7.69 If the requested person is granted bail by the appropriate judge the CPS can appeal the decision.[35] If they do so, they must give written notice within two hours of giving their notice of an intention to appeal the bail decision. The bail appeal will be heard at the High Court within 48 hours. The bail appeal proceeds by way of a re-hearing.[36]

Uncontested extradition hearings

7.70 If there are no issues to be raised on behalf of the requested person – or the person wishes to return to the requesting state but does not consent to their extradition – the matter will very often proceed to an uncontested extradition hearing there and then. It is therefore important for the advocate to be prepared for this as a possibility.

7.71 The court has to be satisfied of the following before ordering extradition:

- the extradition request is a valid request within the meaning of EA 2003 s2;
- the offences contained in the AW are extradition offences;
- there are no bars to extradition;
- there is no conviction in absence, or the requested person accepts deliberately absenting themselves (conviction cases only);
- the requested person does not have a physical or mental condition that would render extradition oppressive or unjust;
- extradition would be compatible with the requested person's rights under the European Convention on Human Rights (ECHR) within the meaning of the Human Rights Act 1998 (and in accusation cases, that extradition would not be disproportionate).

35 The prosecution's power to appeal a grant of bail made in the magistrates' court is found in Bail (Amendment) Act 1993 s1(1A). In 2003, section 1(1A) was amended by EA 2003 s200, which stated that the prosecution may appeal to a judge of the Crown Court against the granting of bail. In 2007, however, section 1(1A) was further amended by paragraph 28 of Part 2 of Schedule 13 to the Police and Justice Act 2006, which substituted 'High Court' for 'Crown Court'. Bail appeals are therefore heard by the High Court.

36 Bail Amendment Act 1993 s1(9).

7.72 At an uncontested extradition hearing, the prosecutor acting on behalf of the judicial authority will conduct most of the hearing, taking the judge through the warrant. The prosecutor will refer to EA 2003 s64 or s65 in establishing extradition offences and will submit that no bars to extradition are raised and that extradition would be compatible with the requested person's ECHR rights.

7.73 The judge will ask the advocate on behalf of the requested person if there are any representations to be made. Having received confirmation that there are none, the judge will make the extradition order pursuant to EA 2003 s21(3) if it is a conviction warrant or s21A(5) if it is an accusation warrant.

7.74 The judge should then inform the requested person that they have seven days to apply for permission to appeal the decision to order extradition (see chapter 11). If no application for permission to appeal is lodged, then arrangements are made for extradition within the ten days that follow the end of the seven-day period. The requested person will also be informed that due to the numbers awaiting extradition, this period can be – and very often is – extended on application to the court. If the requested person is not removed in the relevant period and there has been no extension of time application granted, then the court must order their discharge unless reasonable cause can be shown for the delay.[37]

7.75 The requested person – if remanded in custody – will be informed that every day spent in custody awaiting extradition will be deducted from any sentence imposed in the event of a conviction, or if convicted, the time will count against any sentence of imprisonment imposed. This information is transmitted to the requesting judicial authority by the NCA on surrender of the requested person.

Competing arrest warrant requests

7.76 On rare occasions an AW will be issued by two different category 1 territories. If during the relevant period[38] the judge is informed that there are competing AW requests, they may:

- order further proceedings on the warrant under consideration to be deferred until the other warrant has been disposed of, if the warrant under consideration has not been disposed of; or

37 EA 2003 s35(5). See chapter 11, para 11.190 for a discussion on what may amount to a reasonable cause for delay.

38 The relevant period starts when the person is brought before the appropriate judge and ends when the person is extradited or discharged: EA 2003 s44(2).

- order the person's extradition on the warrant under consideration to be deferred until the other warrant has been disposed of, if an order for extradition has been made on the warrant under consideration.

7.77 The appropriate judge when deciding the above must take account of:

- the relative seriousness of the offence concerned;
- the place where each offence was committed (or was alleged to have been committed);
- the date on which each warrant was issued;
- whether in the case of each offence, the person is accused or alleged to be unlawfully at large after conviction.[39]

39 EA 2003 s44(7).

CHAPTER 8

Extradition requests from outside the European Union (Extradition Act 2003 Part 2 requests)

continued

Introduction

8.1 Extradition requests from outside the European Union (EU) are governed by Part 2 of the Extradition Act (EA) 2003 and are often referred to as 'Part 2 requests.' The procedure for dealing with Part 2 requests is different from the procedure for dealing with requests under Part 1 of the EA 2003, known as 'arrest warrant (AW)' requests.

8.2 Part 2 requests can either be 'provisional' or 'full' requests for extradition and the procedure following arrest is different depending on which it is. In addition, and to further complicate matters, the Extradition (Provisional Arrest) Act (E(PA)A) 2020 amends the EA 2003 so as to allow for the provisional arrest without a warrant of a requested person wanted by specified countries for serious extradition offences.

8.3 This chapter will cover the following areas: category 2 countries; ad hoc arrangements for extradition; the validity of Part 2 requests; the issue and execution of a Part 2 request; the initial hearing for provisional arrests (with and without a warrant) and full requests; challenges at the extradition hearing; extradition offences; the requirement to show a prima facie case; and the role of the Secretary of State for the Home Department (SSHD) in Part 2 cases.

Category 2 countries

8.4 The following countries have all been designated as category 2 territories as they have bilateral or multilateral extradition treaties with the UK or are non-EU countries that are signatories to the European Convention on Extradition (ECE) or the London Scheme for Extradition within the Commonwealth:

> Albania, Algeria, Andorra, Anguilla, Antigua and Barbuda, Argentina, Armenia, Aruba, Australia, Azerbaijan, The Bahamas, Bangladesh, Barbados, Belize, Bermuda, Bolivia, Bonaire, Bosnia and Herzegovina, Botswana, Brazil, British Antarctic Territory, British Indian Ocean Territory, Brunei, Canada, Cayman Islands, Chile, Colombia, Cook Islands, Cuba, Curaçao, Dominica, Ecuador, El Salvador, Falkland Islands, Faroe Islands, Fiji, The Gambia, Georgia, Ghana, Greenland, Grenada, Guatemala, Guyana, Hong Kong Special Administrative Region, Haiti, Iceland, India, Iraq, Israel, Jamaica, Kenya, Kiribati, Kosovo, Kuwait, Lesotho, Liberia, Libya, Liechtenstein, Malawi, Malaysia, Maldives, Mauritius, Mexico, Moldova, Monaco, Montenegro, Montserrat, Morocco, Nauru, New Zealand, Nicaragua, Nigeria, North Macedonia, Norway, Panama, Papua New Guinea, Paraguay, Peru, Philippines, Pitcairn, Henderson, Ducie and Oeno Islands, Republic

of Korea, Russian Federation, Saba, Saint Christopher and Nevis, St Helena, Ascension and Tristan da Cunha, Saint Lucia, Saint Vincent and the Grenadines, San Marino, Serbia, Seychelles, Sierra Leone, Singapore, Sint Eustatius, Sint Maarten, Solomon Islands, South Africa, South Georgia and the South Sandwich Islands, The Sovereign Base Areas of Akrotiri and Dhekelia, Sri Lanka, Swaziland, Switzerland, Tanzania, Thailand, Tonga, Trinidad and Tobago, Turkey, Turks and Caicos Islands, Tuvalu, Uganda, Ukraine, United Arab Emirates, United States, Uruguay, Vanuatu, Virgin Islands, Western Samoa, Zambia, Zimbabwe.

Ad hoc arrangements

Reliance on international conventions

8.5 A country that has not been designated a category 2 territory but is a party to an international convention (to which the UK is also a party) can request the extradition of a person under EA 2003 s193 if the SSHD has designated that international convention and specifies conduct to which the convention applies.[1] The relevant conventions to which the UK is a party can be found in the Extradition Act 2003 (Parties to International Conventions) Order 2005 SI No 46.[2]

Memorandum of understanding

8.6 A country that is not an extradition treaty partner with the UK can also make extradition requests and be treated as if it were a category 2 territory. This can be achieved by the government of the UK and the government of the requesting state entering into an arrangement for the person's extradition (a 'memorandum of understanding' (MoU)) and by the SSHD recognising that the two countries have entered into a 'special extradition arrangement.' Once this is agreed, the SSHD will issue a certificate under EA 2003 s194 and the extradition proceedings will be as for those of a category 2 request under Part 2 of the Act.

1 Anti-social Behaviour, Crime and Policing Act 2014 s169 substituted a new EA 2003 s193.

2 www.legislation.gov.uk/uksi/2005/46/contents/made.

8.7 Since 2004, ad hoc arrangements have been made in relation to individuals sought by: Afghanistan,[3] Bahrain,[4] Kosovo, Kuwait, Morocco,[5] Rwanda, and Taiwan.[6]

Dealing with Part 2 extradition requests

8.8 The duty solicitor at Westminster Magistrates' Court (WMC) will from time to time have to deal with EA 2003 Part 2 requests. They are far less common than Part 1 (AW) requests. Between 2016 and 2020, there were 37 arrests made in the UK under Part 2 on the basis of extradition requests from Albania, Australia, Armenia, Canada, India, Kuwait, Mexico, Moldova, Montenegro, Norway, Switzerland, Thailand, Turkey, UAE, USA and Russia.[7]

8.9 On notification from the Crown Prosecution Service (CPS) extradition prosecutor or the court that a Part 2 extradition request is expected, the first question to ask will be whether it is a provisional arrest (with or without warrant) or full request for extradition. The answer to this question will determine how the case will proceed that day and how much time is likely to be required with the client:

- If it is a *full request,* then it will be necessary to consider possible bars to extradition and human rights considerations, and therefore more time may be required with the client. This is because the court will ask the representative to identify the issues in the case and will proceed to fix a date for the extradition hearing to take place unless the court agrees to adjourn the case to a case management hearing for the challenges to extradition to be identified and a date fixed for the extradition hearing.
- If it is a *provisional warrant* (with or without a warrant), only bail instructions will be required as, until the full request is received, it is likely to be premature to identify the possible challenges to extradition.

3 Ad hoc arrangements were made for individuals whose extradition were sought by the UK.

4 Ad hoc arrangements were made for individuals whose extradition were sought by the UK.

5 Ad hoc arrangements were made for individuals whose extradition were sought by the UK.

6 Kosovo, Kuwait and Morocco all made 'ad hoc' requests for extradition prior to becoming extradition treaty partners.

7 Freedom of information (FOI) reference 64046, 6 June 2021.

Provisional arrest (without a warrant)

8.10 The E(PA)A 2020 amended the EA 2003 and introduced a new form of arrest: arrest without a warrant. It applies to those whose extradition is sought by specified countries listed in EA 2003 Sch A1 'Specified category 2 territories' for serious extradition offences. The E(PA)A 2020 amended Part 2 of the EA 2003 by inserting ss74A–74E, and added Sch A1.[8]

8.11 Provisional arrest without a warrant can arise if an INTERPOL Red Notice[9] or Diffusion Notice issued by a country listed in EA 2003 Sch A1[10] has been certified by the National Crime Agency (NCA).

8.12 Certification by the NCA is a prerequisite before an arrest without warrant can occur, incorporating a form of safeguard into the system. There is however, no judicial oversight as there is in the issuance of a provisional warrant of arrest.

8.13 Specified countries listed in Schedule A1[11] are:

- Australia;
- Canada;
- Iceland;[12]
- Liechtenstein;
- New Zealand;
- Norway;[13]
- Switzerland;
- United States.

The list of specified countries can be amended by way of statutory instrument[14].

8 Brought into force by the Extradition (Provisional Arrest) Act 2020 (Commencement No 1) Regulations 2020.

9 INTERPOL (International Criminal Police Organization) Red Notices are the usual way in which police become aware that a person is wanted. However, the power in the E(PA)A 2020 is not limited to red notices and could apply in respect of any international request for arrest.

10 As introduced by E(PA)A 2020 Sch para 3. The countries that were included on Schedule A1 were selected as the UK has a high level of confidence in them as extradition partners, in their criminal justice systems and in their use of extradition – see Extradition (Provisional Arrest) Bill Explanatory Notes: https://publications.parliament.uk/pa/bills/cbill/58-01/0138/en/200138en.pdf.

11 As at the time of writing.

12 Added to Schedule A1 by virtue of Regulation 2(2) Extradition (Provisional Arrest) Act 2020 (Commencement No 1) Regulations 2020.

13 Added to Schedule A1 by virtue of Regulation 2(2) Extradition (Provisional Arrest) Act 2020 (Commencement No 1) Regulations 2020.

14 Additional countries in whose law enforcement systems the UK has a similar high level of confidence could therefore be specified in the future, where both Houses of Parliament approve the legislation.

NCA Certification

8.14 The NCA may issue a certificate if it:

a) receives a valid request,[15] made by an authority of a specified category 2 territory for a person's arrest;[16]
b) is satisfied that the request is made under arrangements which allow such a request to be made;[17]
c) has reasonable grounds for believing that the offence specified in the request is a serious[18] extradition offence;[19] and
d) is satisfied[20] that the seriousness of the conduct constituting the offence makes it appropriate to issue the certificate.[21]

8.15 The certificate issued by the NCA must certify the information contained within section 74B(2)(a)–(e). A requested person may challenge the certification by the NCA at the first hearing and the appropriate judge *must* order the person's discharge if satisfied that there were no reasonable grounds for the NCA to have issued a certificate.[22] Challenges are likely to arise as to whether the request was valid, whether the certificate contained the information required by section 74B(2), and whether the conduct constituting the offence was sufficiently serious to make it appropriate to issue a certificate. A certificate may be withdrawn and re-issued by the NCA, prior to the arrest of a requested person (for example, in order to fix defects in it), without the need for the request to be re-issued.

Procedure following arrest

8.16 A person arrested without a warrant must be given a copy of the NCA certificate as soon as practicable after their arrest[23] and must be brought before the appropriate judge as soon as practicable.[24] If the NCA certificate is not provided to the requested person as soon as

15 EA 2003 s74C sets out what is meant by 'valid requests for arrest.'
16 EA 2003 s74B(1)(a).
17 EA 2003 s74B(1)(b).
18 A serious extradition offence is defined in EA 2003 s74B(10) as an offence that is punishable in the UK with a sentence of imprisonment of three years or more (as opposed to 12 months).
19 EA 2003 s74B(1)(c).
20 The explanatory note to the E(PA)A 2020, at para 45, gives the example of a low level theft as not being appropriate for certification, despite it being a 'serious extradition offence' (theft carrying s a maximum sentence of seven years) – see: https://publications.parliament.uk/pa/bills/lbill/2019-2019/0028/20028en.pdf.
21 EA 2003 s74B(1)(d).
22 EA 2003 s74D(1)(b)(i).
23 EA 2003 s74A(2).
24 EA 2003 s74A(3).

practicable after arrest or if it did not comply with section 74B(2) and they apply to the judge to be discharged, the judge *may* order their discharge.[25] If the person is not brought to court as soon as practicable after arrest and an application for discharge is made, the judge *must* order their discharge.[26] If the Judge discharges on the basis that the certificate did not conform to section 74B(2), a fresh request will need to be made before it can be certified.

Issuing a provisional warrant of arrest

8.17 A provisional warrant of arrest can be issued if an appropriate judge is satisfied (on information in writing or on oath) that a person is accused of an offence in a category 2 territory or is alleged to be unlawfully at large after conviction[27] and that the person is believed to be in the UK or the person is on their way to the UK or is believed to be on their way to the UK.[28]

8.18 The appropriate judge may issue a warrant for a person's arrest if they have reasonable grounds for believing that:[29]

- the offence for which the person is accused of/convicted of is an extradition offence and;
- there is written evidence/information[30] about this.

8.19 The evidence/information is that which would justify the issuance of a warrant for the arrest of a person accused of the offence within the judge's jurisdiction (if accused of an offence) or would justify the issue of a warrant for the arrest of a person unlawfully at large after conviction.[31]

8.20 The defence is not involved in the issuing of a provisional warrant of arrest. Applications are often made 'in camera' and the first a person will know about a Part 2 arrest warrant is when it is executed.

8.21 Provisional warrants tend to be used in cases where it is perceived that there is some urgency. An example of where a provisional warrant may be used is where a person is in transit in the UK, en route to another country via a connecting flight, and the person has

25 EA 2003 s74D(10)(a)(i)–(ii)
26 EA 2003 s74D(10)(b)(ii).
27 EA 2003 s73(2).
28 EA 2003 s73(1).
29 EA 2003 s73(3).
30 Evidence is required for those countries required to demonstrate a prima facie case, otherwise it is information only.
31 EA 2003 s73(4).

been identified as being wanted in another country (possibly by the existence of an INTERPOL Red Notice or diffusion notice). In those circumstances, a full request may not have been sent to the Home Office because the requesting state is not aware of the presence of the requested person in the UK. The relevant embassy of the jurisdiction concerned may be contacted to ascertain whether they seek the provisional arrest of the person and if so to provide information in support of their request to place before an appropriate judge.

Arrest following the issuing of a provisional warrant

8.22 Once a provisional warrant of arrest has been issued, any police officer or customs officer can execute it, even if neither the warrant nor a copy of it is in the possession of the person executing it.[32]

8.23 A person arrested under a provisional warrant must be given a copy of it as soon as practicable after arrest.[33] The person will be cautioned in the following terms: 'You do not have to say anything. Anything you do say may be given in evidence.' This is the pre-1995 caution[34] and does not contain the reference to failing to mention facts that are later relied upon in court.

8.24 Following arrest, the requested person will be taken to the local police station where they will be booked into custody and have their detention authorised. Like all of those arrested and taken to a police station, those arrested under a provisional warrant will be entitled to speak to a solicitor. This will very often be the duty solicitor. There will be no interview and the sole purpose of detention is to secure the requested person's attendance at WMC as soon as practicable.[35] Production as soon as practicable is not required if the person is granted bail by a constable following his arrest or the SSHD decides that the request for the person's extradition is not to be proceeded with because a competing extradition request exists.

8.25 The International Jurisdiction Office (IJO) at WMC will be notified of the person's arrest and arrangements will be made for production at the court. If the arrest is after the court 'referral time' for accepting prisoners (currently 3.30 pm), then the person will be kept

32 EA 2003 s73(6)(b).

33 EA 2003 s74(2).

34 The law contained in the Criminal Justice and Public Order Act (CJPOA) 1994 in relation to inferences from silence came into force in April 1995, as did new codes of practice made under the Police and Criminal Evidence Act 1984 (PACE) that amended the caution to be given to those arrested.

35 EA 2003 s74(3).

at the police station for production the following day unless the judge agrees to accept the person into the cells after 3.30 pm.[36]

Extradition request and certificate (full request)

8.26 If the SSHD receives a valid request for extradition, they must issue a certificate pursuant to EA 2003 s70(1).[37] A valid request for extradition from a category 2 territory must be made in the approved way and also contain the statement referred to in section 70(4) or 70(4A).

8.27 In relation to section 70(4), the statement is one that:

- the person is accused in the category 2 territory of the commission of an offence specified in the request; and
- the request is made with a view to their arrest and extradition to the category 2 territory for the purpose of being prosecuted for the offence.

8.28 In relation to section 70(4A), the statement is one that:

- the person has been convicted of an offence specified in the request by a court in the category 2 territory; and
- the request is made with a view to their arrest and extradition to the category 2 territory for the purpose of being sentenced for the offence or of serving a sentence of imprisonment or another form of detention imposed in respect of the offence.

8.29 A request for extradition is made in the approved way if it is made by an authority of the territory that the SSHD believes has the function of making requests for extradition in that territory,[38] or by a person recognised by the SSHD as a diplomatic or consular representative of the territory.[39]

8.30 The SSHD *may* refuse to issue a certificate if the person whose extradition is requested has been recorded as a refugee within the meaning of the Refugee Convention[40] or has been granted leave to enter or remain in the UK on the basis that it would be a breach of

36 The court will only accept an arrested requested person after 3.30 pm if the case is likely to conclude by 4.30 pm. In the vast majority of cases, this will not be achievable and so the court will not accept the arrested requested person.

37 This is subject to section 70(2), which contains circumstances in which the SSHD may refuse to issue a certificate.

38 EA 2003 s70(7)(a).

39 EA 2003 s70(7)(b).

40 EA 2003 s70(2)(b).

Article 2 or 3 of the European Convention on Human Rights[41] (ECHR) to remove that person to the territory who is requesting extradition.

8.31 Once a full request for extradition has been certified, the request and certificate must be sent to the appropriate judge[42] at WMC for an arrest warrant to be issued.

8.32 The judge may issue a warrant for the arrest of the requested person if they have reasonable grounds for believing that:

a) the offence in respect of which extradition is requested is an extradition offence;[43] and
b) there is evidence that would either:
   i) justify the issue of a warrant for the arrest of a person accused of the offence within the judge's jurisdiction, if the person whose extradition is requested is accused of the commission of the offence;[44]
   ii) justify the issue of a warrant for the arrest of a person unlawfully at large after conviction of the offence within the judge's jurisdiction, if the person whose extradition is requested is alleged to be unlawfully at large after conviction of the offence.[45]

Arrest on a full request

8.33 A person arrested under a 'full request' must be given a copy of the extradition request as soon as practicable after their arrest[46] and must be brought as soon as practicable before the appropriate judge.[47] If the warrant is not provided to the requested person as soon as practicable and they apply to the judge to be discharged, the judge *may* order their discharge. If the person is not brought to court as soon as practicable after arrest and an application for discharge is made, the judge *must* order their discharge.

41 EA 2003 s70(2)(c).
42 EA 2003 s70(9).
43 EA 2003 s71(2)(a).
44 EA 2003 s71(3)(a).
45 EA 2003 s71(3)(b). If the category 2 territory has been designated by the SSHD as not having to provide evidence to demonstrate a prima facie case, the word 'evidence' in EA 2003 s71 (2) and (3) is to be read as 'information'.
46 EA 2003 s72(2).
47 EA 2003 s72(3).

8.34 The person need not be brought before the appropriate judge if they are granted bail by a constable following their arrest[48] or the SSHD decides that the request for the person's extradition is not to be proceeded with because there is a competing extradition request in existence (see EA 2003 s126 and para 8.98 below).

Production at Westminster Magistrates' Court

8.35 There are often difficulties in getting a person to WMC as soon as practicable after arrest, and practitioners must consider the reasons for any delay very carefully: it can sometimes result in the proceedings quickly coming to an end if the authorities have not managed to secure the attendance of the person at court as soon as practicable.

8.36 An arrest can take place anywhere in England and Wales. Unless it is a planned arrest, this can itself cause difficulties, as it may be the first time an officer has made an arrest under the EA 2003. The officer may not be familiar with the EA 2003 and may overlook the need to get the person to WMC as soon as practicable. The arrest may have taken place over 200 miles from London and transport will need to be arranged by police.

8.37 Further complications can arise when a person has been arrested and charged with an offence in England and Wales and is then arrested under EA 2003 on a Part 2 request. If the person is denied bail on the domestic matter and taken to the local magistrates' court before being taken to WMC to be dealt with under the EA 2003, it may not be deemed to have been 'as soon as practicable.' A more detailed assessment of what is deemed to be 'as soon as practicable' can be found in chapter 7 at paras 7.15–7.21.

First hearing – arrest without a warrant

8.38 When a person is arrested without a warrant, they must be produced before an appropriate judge as soon as practicable. Failure to comply must result in the person's discharge.

8.39 On being produced, the appropriate judge must determine whether a provisional arrest warrant would have been issued (had the person not already been under arrest) on the basis of any evidence or

48 While EA 2003 s72(4)(a) refers to a person being granted bail following arrest, the authors are not aware of a case where this has occurred.

information before the court.[49] In so determining, the appropriate judge will consider the criteria as set out above at paras 8.17–8.19.

8.40 If the judge determines that a provisional warrant of arrest would not have been issued, the requested person will be discharged.[50] However, the judge may adjourn determination of the issue to allow for further evidence or information to be produced,[51] provided that: a) an application for an adjournment is made in accordance with the rules of court,[52] and b) the judge is satisfied on the balance of probabilities that evidence or information could not reasonably have been produced in time to avoid the need for the adjournment.[53] More than one adjournment may be granted; however, the total period of an adjournment cannot exceed 72 hours[54] (not including bank holidays and weekends).

8.41 If an adjournment is granted, the judge will either remand the requested person in custody or grant bail.

8.42 If it is determined that a provisional warrant of arrest *would* have been issued, the appropriate judge is required to proceed under EA 2003 s74E which replicates the procedure as set out below commencing at para 8.49.[55] In effect, this puts the requested person in the same position as a person arrested pursuant to a provisional warrant of arrest.

First hearing – provisional arrest

8.43 At the first hearing, the requested person will be produced from custody and, as in all court hearings, will be asked for their name and date of birth. Note that identity is not to be determined at the initial hearing, although the person will be identified in the dock.

8.44 The appropriate judge must inform the person that they are either accused of the commission of an offence in a category 2 territory or that they are alleged to be unlawfully at large after conviction.[56] The required information about consent must then be given[57] unless the appropriate judge is informed that the person is charged with an offence in the UK or serving a sentence of imprisonment (see below).

49 EA 2003 s74D(1).
50 EA 2003 s74D(2).
51 EA 2003 s74D(4).
52 EA 2003 s74D(4)(a).
53 EA 2003 s74D(4)(b).
54 EA 2003 s74D(7).
55 EA 2003 s74E closely mirrors EA 2003 ss74(7)–(11).
56 EA 2003 s74(7)(a).
57 EA 2003 s74(7)(b).

The consent procedure is the same as that discussed in AW cases (see chapter 7, paras 7.39–7.41).

Person charged with an offence in the UK or serving a sentence of imprisonment

8.45 If the person before the court is subject to a charge in the UK then the extradition hearing *must* be adjourned at this point pursuant to EA 2003 s76A until the charge is either disposed of, withdrawn, proceedings are discontinued or an order is made for the charge to lie on file. Consent will not be taken (although the requested person should be given the required information about consent)[58] and the court will proceed to deal with bail.

8.46 If the person before the court is subject to a sentence of imprisonment in the UK then the judge *may* adjourn the extradition hearing until the sentence of imprisonment has been served. A judge can adjourn the hearing for up to six months before the matter has to be brought back before the court. Again, under section 76B, consent will not be taken.

8.47 Sections 76A and 76B were introduced into legislation in order to prevent a requested person escaping prosecution or from having to serve a sentence in the UK by consenting to extradition and being removed from the UK before domestic proceedings are concluded.

8.48 If a requested person is subject to a lengthy sentence of imprisonment, the CPS will ordinarily obtain instructions from the requesting state as to whether it wishes to seek the requested person's temporary extradition: this is known as 'temporary surrender.' If temporary surrender is sought, the requesting state will be required to provide an undertaking stating that the requested person will be kept in custody pending their trial and returned to the UK after proceedings have concluded in that state. If the court agrees to temporary surrender, the requested person will be returned to the UK to serve the remainder of the sentence.

Date for service of the full extradition request

8.49 On a provisional arrest (either with or without a warrant), neither the requested person nor the court will have the papers referred to in EA 2003 s70(9) (certificate issued by the SSHD and the extradition

58 *Morozovs v Latvian Judicial Authority* [2013] EWHC 367 (Admin).

request). The judge must therefore set a date by which they must have received the documents referred to in section 70(9).

8.50 The required period for service of the papers is 45 days, starting with the date of arrest. Certain countries are designated by the SSHD[59] for the purposes of section 74(11)(b) with a longer period for service of papers. Those countries and the relevant periods are:

- Argentina – 65 days
- Bolivia – 65 days
- Bosnia and Herzegovina – 65 days
- Brazil – 65 days
- Chile – 65 days
- Colombia – 65 days
- Cuba – 65 days
- El Salvador – 65 days
- Guatemala – 95 days
- Haiti – 65 days
- Hong Kong Special Administrative Region – 65 days
- India – 65 days
- Iraq – 65 days
- Kuwait – 65 days
- Liberia – 95 days
- Libya – 65 days
- Mexico – 65 days
- Morocco – 65 days
- Nicaragua – 65 days
- Panama – 65 days
- Paraguay – 65 days
- Peru – 95 days
- Saint Helena, Ascension and Tristan da Cunha – 65 days
- Thailand – 65 days
- United Arab Emirates – 65 days
- United States – 65 days.

8.51 The court will fix a date for the service of the papers and list the case for a review hearing a few days before the papers are due to be served. If the papers referred to in section 70(9) are not received by the judge by the date for service, the requested person must be discharged from the request upon their application.

59 Extradition Act 2003 (Designation of Part 2 Territories) Order 2003 SI No 3334 amended by SIs 2004/1898, 2005/365, 2005/2036, 2006/3451, 2007/2238, 2008/1589, 2010/861, 2013/1583, 2015/992 and section 43(1) of the Police and Justice Act 2006.

8.52 The final matter for the court to determine at the first hearing after a person has been arrested under a provisional arrest warrant is the issue of bail (see chapter 7 paras 7.55–7.66).

Service of the full extradition request

8.53 A request for extradition is only valid if it contains a certificate issued by the SSHD that the extradition request has been made in the approved way and identifying the order by which the territory requesting extradition is designated as a category 2 territory. If a certificate has been issued by the SSHD, the request and certificate must be sent to the appropriate judge.[60]

8.54 The documents sent to the appropriate judge should include:

- certificate issued by the SSHD;
- particulars of the person whose extradition is requested;[61]
- particulars of the offence specified in the request;[62]
- in an accusation case, a warrant for the person's arrest that has been issued in the category 2 territory;[63]
- in a conviction case, a certificate of the conviction issued in the category 2 territory and (if the person has been sentenced) of the sentence imposed.[64]

8.55 Once the papers are received, the judge must then proceed to fix a date within which the extradition hearing must begin (see para 8.58 below).

First hearing – full request

8.56 As with the first hearing under a provisional arrest, the judge must inform the person that they are either accused of the commission of an offence in a category 2 territory or that they are alleged to be unlawfully at large after conviction.[65] The required information[66] regarding consent must then be given[67] (unless the requested person is subject to a charge in the UK or is serving a sentence of imprisonment – see

60 EA 2003 s70(9).
61 EA 2003 s78(2)(b).
62 EA 2003 s78(2)(c).
63 EA 2003 s78(2)(d).
64 EA 2003 s78(2)(e).
65 EA 2003 s72(7)(a).
66 EA 2003 s72(8)(a)–(c).
67 EA 2003 s72(7)(b).

above) and then the judge must either remand the person in custody or on bail (see chapter 7, paras 7.55–7.66).[68]

8.57 The judge will ask the defence advocate to identify the challenges to extradition to be raised at the extradition hearing. It may be that there has been insufficient time to identify the issues. If this is the case, more time should either be sought that day or the court should be invited to adjourn the case so that the full request for extradition can be considered and challenges identified at a case management hearing. This may be the most appropriate way to deal with large and complex cases where the papers contained in the full request for extradition can be voluminous. If the case is so adjourned, the defence will be expected to serve a statement of issues in advance of the next hearing identifying the challenges to extradition. The case management hearing will be heard by the judge that will have conduct of the extradition proceedings and preside over the extradition hearing, thus providing judicial continuity.

Opening the extradition hearing

8.58 Although the extradition hearing has to be fixed for a date within two months of the requested person first appearing before the court, in reality the court will fix a date for the full extradition hearing beyond the two-month deadline. In order to do this, the extradition hearing will be 'formally opened' and then adjourned with no decisions made. Opening or starting the extradition hearing and adjourning it in this way means that the two-month period set down in the EA 2003 has been complied with. There is no timeframe within which the extradition hearing must be concluded. However, if the court does not 'formally open' the extradition hearing and the extradition hearing does not subsequently commence within two months from the date the requested person first appeared before the court, and an application is made to the court for discharge, the appropriate judge must order the person's discharge.[69] For that reason, appropriate judges will often formally open the extradition hearing at the initial hearing on a full request or the first hearing after papers have been served.

8.59 The judge can fix a later date for the extradition hearing if they believe it is in the interests of justice to do so.

68 EA 2003 s72(7)(c).
69 EA 2003 s75(4).

Time spent in custody awaiting extradition

8.60 Unlike in AW cases, time spent remanded in custody in extradition proceedings may not necessarily be taken into account in all Part 2 countries[70] – it will be necessary to look at the specific extradition arrangements with a Part 2 country to determine whether time spent on remand will count towards any sentence. The final matter for the court to determine at the first hearing after a person has been arrested on a full request is the issue of bail (see chapter 7, paras 7.55–7.66).

Initial stages of the extradition hearing in Part 2 cases

8.61 At the outset of the extradition hearing, the appropriate judge must decide whether the documents sent by the SSHD include the information that is set out in para 8.54 above. The requesting state will often be directed to serve an opening note that outlines compliance with EA 2003 s78.

8.62 If any of the documents referred to above are not before the appropriate judge, they *must* order the person's discharge. If they are all present, the appropriate judge must then consider whether:

- the person appearing or brought before them is the person whose extradition is requested;[71]
- the offence specified in the request is an extradition offence;[72]
- copies of the documents sent to the appropriate judge by the SSHD have been served upon the person whose extradition is sought.[73]

8.63 The requested person may seek to resist extradition on the basis that the conduct alleged would not amount to an extradition offence had the conduct occurred in England and Wales and that the request for extradition is not valid because it does not contain the papers referred to in section 70(9).

70 The Privy Council in *Gomes v The State (Trinidad and Tobago)* [2015] UKPC 8 held that the judge presiding over Mr Gomes' trial in Trinidad had been entitled not to credit him for the 45 months spent in custody in the UK while fighting his extradition.

71 EA 2003 s78(4)(a).

72 EA 2003 s78(4)(b).

73 EA 2003 s78(4)(c).

8.64 Identity – as in AW cases – is to be determined by the appropriate judge on the balance of probabilities.[74]

8.65 If the judge decides any of the questions in para 8.62 in the negative, they must order the person's discharge.[75]

8.66 Once the preliminary stages of the extradition hearing have been conducted and the questions answered in the affirmative, the appropriate judge must then proceed under section 79 and consider whether any of the statutory bars to extradition apply.

Challenges to extradition

8.67 Challenges to extradition are dealt with in chapter 5. In short, the following can be raised to resist extradition:

- rule against double jeopardy (EA 2003 s80);
- extraneous considerations (section 81);
- passage of time (section 82);
- hostage-taking considerations (section 83);
- forum (section 83A);
- prima facie case (sections 84 and 86);
- conviction in person's absence (section 85);
- physical or mental condition (section 91).

8.68 A challenge can also be brought on the basis that the warrant does not contain sufficient particulars of the offence. Although the wording in section 78(2)(c) is narrower than in section 2(4)(c) (for Part 1 cases) it was held in *Dudko v The Government of the Russian Federation*[76] by Thomas LJ that: 'the provision in s78(4)(c) [sic] should be interpreted to the same effect as that in s2(4)(c) using solely, as Dyson LJ suggested, the plain and ordinary meaning of that section without any gloss.'

8.69 The requested person also has the protection of the Human Rights Act 1998 and in accordance with EA 2003 s87 the appropriate judge must consider whether the person's extradition would be compatible with ECHR rights (EA 2003 s87): see chapter 6. Finally, the court has the power to stay proceedings as an abuse of process (see chapter 5, para 5.110).

74 EA 2003 s78(5).
75 EA 2003 s78(6).
76 [2010] EWHC 1125 (Admin) at para 16.

Extradition offences

8.70 If the conduct alleged in the extradition request does not meet the requirements of 'dual criminality' then the judge must order the person's discharge. See chapter 3, para 3.61 for further detail regarding dual criminality and the transposition exercise. EA 2003 s137 deals with accusation cases and s138 with conviction cases. The most common conduct that constitutes an extradition offence can be found in sections 137(3) and 138(3), although the representative should also be aware of the other subsections in sections 137 and 138.

8.71 Conduct constitutes an extradition offence in relation to the category 2 territory if these conditions are satisfied (section 137(3)):

(a) the conduct occurs in the category 2 territory;
(b) the conduct would constitute an offence under the law of the relevant part of the United Kingdom punishable with imprisonment or another form of detention for a term of 12 months or a greater punishment if it occurred in that part of the United Kingdom;
(c) the conduct is so punishable under the law of the category 2 territory.

8.72 The requirement in (b) is different from that which is required under Part 1 (AW cases). The conduct not only has to be an offence in the relevant part of the UK had it occurred there, it must also punishable with a sentence of at least 12 months' imprisonment in the UK.

8.73 The provisions for those convicted and sentenced impose a similar requirement that the conduct is punishable with a sentence of 12 months or greater in the UK. The actual sentence passed in the category 2 territory must be for a term of four months or greater (section 138(3)):

(a) the conduct occurs in the category 2 territory;
(b) the conduct would constitute an offence under the law of the relevant part of the United Kingdom punishable with imprisonment or another form of detention for a term of 12 months or a greater punishment if it occurred in that part of the United Kingdom;
(c) a sentence of imprisonment or another form of detention for a term of 4 months or a greater punishment has been imposed in the category 2 territory in respect of the conduct.

8.74 Conduct that occurs *outside* of the category 2 territory may also be an extradition offence if it would constitute an extraterritorial offence under the relevant part of the UK.[77]

77 EA 2003 ss137(4) and 138(4).

8.75 Finally, conduct can amount to an extradition offence if it occurred outside the category 2 territory and no part of it occurred in the UK, is punishable under the law of the category 2 territory with 12 months' imprisonment (in accusation cases) or at least four months' imprisonment has been imposed (in conviction cases) and the conduct constitutes, or if committed in the UK would constitute, an offence as set out in sections 137(6) and 138(6).[78]

8.76 Practitioners should be aware of the rule in *Osunta v The Public Prosecutor's Office in Dusseldorf, Germany*[79] which allows for excision of conduct that would not amount to an extradition offence.

Prima facie case

8.77 One of the main differences between extradition requests from Part 1 and Part 2 is the requirement for the requesting state to establish a prima facie case. Part 2 cases are split into two categories: Type A and Type B.

8.78 **Type A** cases relate to Part 2 countries that have been designated by the SSHD as not having to establish a prima facie case. Signatories to the ECE, as well as Australia, Canada, New Zealand and the USA,[80] have all been designated and are not required to establish a prima facie case. For those designated countries, they need only provide 'information' about the accusation or conviction. This requirement is often satisfied in an affidavit from the investigating police officer or the prosecutor.

8.79 The following countries have been designated as **Type A** countries:

> Albania, Andorra, Armenia, Aruba, Australia, Azerbaijan, Bonaire, Bosnia and Herzegovina, Canada, Curaçao, Faroe Islands, Georgia, Greenland, Hong Kong SAR, Iceland, Israel, Liechtenstein, Moldova, Monaco, Montenegro, New Zealand, North Macedonia, Norway, Republic of Korea, Russian Federation, Saba, San Marino, Serbia, Sint Eustatius, Sint Maarten, South Africa, Switzerland, Turkey, Ukraine and the United States.

8.80 For extradition requests from **Type B** countries, the court must consider whether the requesting state can establish a prima facie case.

78 EA 2003 ss137(5) and 138(5).

79 [2007] EWHC 1562 (Admin) at para 29.

80 Australia, Canada, New Zealand and the USA are not signatories to the ECE but the prima facie requirement was removed on the basis they are democratic states and trusted extradition partners.

If they cannot, the judge must discharge.[81] Section 84 deals with cases where the requested person has not been convicted and section 86 where a person has been convicted. If a requested person was either convicted in their presence or deliberately absented themselves from their trial, the judge is not required to consider section 86 and must proceed to section 87'. Sections 84 and 86 are in identical terms:

(1) If the judge is required to proceed under this section he must decide whether there is evidence which would be sufficient to make a case requiring an answer by the person if the proceedings were the summary trial of an information against him.
(2) In deciding the question in subsection (1) the judge may treat a statement made by a person in a document as admissible evidence of a fact if–
    (a) the statement is made by the person to a police officer or another person charged with the duty of investigating offences or charging offenders, and
    (b) direct oral evidence by the person of the fact would be admissible.
(3) In deciding whether to treat a statement made by a person in a document as admissible evidence of a fact, the judge must in particular have regard–
    (a) to the nature and source of the document;
    (b) to whether or not, having regard to the nature and source of the document and to any other circumstances that appear to the judge to be relevant, it is likely that the document is authentic;
    (c) to the extent to which the statement appears to supply evidence which would not be readily available if the statement were not treated as being admissible evidence of the fact;
    (d) to the relevance of the evidence that the statement appears to supply to any issue likely to have to be determined by the judge in deciding the question in subsection (1);
    (e) to any risk that the admission or exclusion of the statement will result in unfairness to the person whose extradition is sought, having regard in particular to whether it is likely to be possible to controvert the statement if the person making it does not attend to give oral evidence in the proceedings.
(4) A summary in a document of a statement made by a person must be treated as a statement made by the person in the document for the purposes of subsection (2).
(5) If the judge decides the question in subsection (1) in the negative he must order the person's discharge.
(6) If the judge decides that question in the affirmative he must proceed under section 87.

81 EA 2003 ss84(5) and 86(5).

(7) If the judge is required to proceed under this section and the category 2 territory to which extradition is requested is designated for the purposes of this section by order made by the Secretary of State–
(a) the judge must not decide under subsection (1), and
(b) he must proceed under section 87.[82]

8.81 The relevant principles when considering EA 2003 s84(1) and s86(1) were set out by the Divisional Court in *Devani v Kenya*[83] which stated that a three-stage process is involved:

1) The first stage, following the decision of the House of Lords in *Norris v Government of the United States of America*, is to identify, for the relevant charge, the 'essence of the conduct' which is alleged by the requesting state.[84]
2) The appropriate judge must then determine, upon the assumption that the relevant conduct had occurred in the UK, whether that conduct would be an offence under UK law.[85]
3) The appropriate judge must finally then determine whether the requesting state has proved, on the basis of all admissible evidence (taking account of the admissibility rules set out in EA 2003 ss84(2)–(4), 202 and 205), whether there is sufficient evidence to substantiate the conduct alleged.

8.82 The issue for the judge in extradition proceedings is whether there *is* a case to answer.[86] The judge must determine whether, on one possible view of the material before the court, they are satisfied that there is evidence upon which the requested person could be convicted at a summary trial.[87]

8.83 The judge must apply the two-stage test from *Galbraith*,[88] and should consider all the evidence before the court, including evidence called by the requesting person.[89] If the judge determines there is no evidence which would be sufficient to make a case requiring an answer by the person if the proceedings were the summary trial of an information against them, then the judge *must* order the requested person's discharge.

82 Subsections (8)–(9) omitted.

83 [2015] EWHC 3535 (Admin), as approved in *Mallya v Government of India*.

84 *Devani v Kenya* [2015] EWHC 3535 (Admin) para 47.

85 *Devani v Kenya* [2015] EWHC 3535 (Admin) at para 47.

86 As opposed to in a criminal trial context in which the judge is required to determine whether there is 'no case to answer'.

87 *Devani v Kenya* [2015] EWHC 3535 (Admin) at para 48.

88 *R v Galbraith* [1981] WLR 1039

89 *Shankaran v Government of the State of India and The Secretary of State for the Home Department* [2014] EWHC 957 (Admin).

Admissibility of evidence

8.84 Questions of admissibility in extradition proceedings are governed by English law.

8.85 EA 2003 s84 (and the equivalent provision in s86) permits the court to admit hearsay evidence.[90] Section 84(2) permits a judge to 'treat a statement made by a person in a document as admissible evidence of a fact if – (a) the statement is made by the person to a police officer or another person charged with the duty of investigating offences or charging offenders, and (b) direct oral evidence by the person of the fact would be admissible'. Section 84(3) directs the court to have regard to the discrete factors set out within that provision.

8.86 EA 2003 s202(3) states that a document issued in a category 2 territory may be received in evidence if it is duly authenticated.[91] However, EA 2003 s202(5) states that s202(3) does not prevent a document that is not duly authenticated from being received in evidence.

Role of the Secretary of State for the Home Department

8.87 In AW cases it is the appropriate judge that orders a person's extradition. In Part 2 cases, the SSHD performs this function.

8.88 Once a case is sent by the appropriate judge to the SSHD, they have two months to make an order for extradition. The two-month period starts on the day on which the case is sent to the SSHD. Thus, if a case is sent to the SSHD on, for example, 17 May, they must order extradition by midnight on 16 July.[92] If they do not, the requested person *must* be discharged.[93] That time period can be extended on application by the SSHD to the appropriate judge and can be extended more than once.[94]

90 Multiple hearsay is not admissible.

91 EA 2003 s202(4) defines 'duly authenticated' as a) a document that purports to be signed by a judge, magistrate or officer of the territory, aa) a document that purports to be certified, whether by seal otherwise, by the Ministry or Department of the territory responsible for justice or foreign affairs, or b) a document that purports to be authenticated by oath or affirmation of a witness.

92 Unless the end date happens to fall on a weekend or bank holiday in which case it will be the next working day.

93 *Zaporozhchenko v Westminster Magistrates' Court* [2011] EWHC 34 (Admin).

94 EA 2003 s99(4).

Person charged with an offence/sentenced to imprisonment in the UK

8.89 If a person is charged with an offence in the UK while the case is pending before the SSHD then the SSHD *must not* make a decision with regard to the person's extradition until the charge is disposed of; the charge is withdrawn; proceedings are discontinued or an order is made for the charge to lie on file.[95]

8.90 If a sentence of imprisonment has been imposed in respect of the offences charged, then the SSHD *may* defer making a decision with regard to the person's extradition until the person is released from detention.[96]

8.91 If the case is sent to the SSHD by the appropriate judge and the person is serving a sentence of imprisonment, the SSHD may also defer making a decision with regards to the person's extradition until the person is released from detention (whether on licence or otherwise).[97]

Representations to the SSHD

8.92 During the first four weeks following the case being sent to the SSHD, the SSHD cannot make an order for extradition. This is to allow for representations to be made by the requested person. If representations are not received in the four weeks following the case being sent, then the SSHD need not consider them.[98] The SSHD need not delay the making of a decision during the first four weeks if the person has consented to extradition.[99]

8.93 The SSHD has a limited remit when considering representations. Representations can be made regarding:

- the death penalty;
- specialty;
- earlier extradition to the United Kingdom from another territory;
- earlier transfer to the United Kingdom by the International Criminal Court.[100]

95 EA 2003 s97(2).
96 EA 2003 s97(3).
97 EA 2003 s98(2).
98 EA 2003 s93(5).
99 EA 2003 s93(7)(a).
100 EA 2003 s93(2)(a)–(d).

8.94 The SSHD is required to consider the above issues whether or not representations are received. If no issues are found, the SSHD will order extradition. If representations are received and rejected by the SSHD then an extradition order will be signed (unless the exceptions in section 93(4) apply). An order for extradition (or discharge) must be made under the hand of one of the following:[101]

- the SSHD;
- a minister of state;
- a Parliamentary under-secretary of state;
- a senior official.[102]

8.95 If the representations are rejected, the requested person and their legal representatives will receive a response from the SSHD to the representations together with the order for extradition. If the representations are accepted, the SSHD will order the person's discharge from the extradition request.

8.96 Once the extradition order is received, the requested person has 14 days in which to lodge and serve an application for permission to appeal, from the date on which the SSHD informs the requested person (or his legal representatives) that an order for extradition has been made.[103] If no application for permission to appeal is lodged the person must be extradited to the category 2 territory within 28 days of the decision of the SSHD. This period can be extended on an application to the court.

8.97 If the requested person is not removed within the relevant period, an application should be made to the appropriate judge at WMC for discharge (see chapter 11, para 11.181).[104] Discharge must follow unless reasonable cause can be shown for the delay in removal.[105]

Competing extradition requests

8.98 There may be very rare occasions where two different category 2 territories make extradition requests for the same person. Under EA 2003 s126, if the SSHD receives a valid request for extradition, the person

101 EA 2003 s101.

102 A senior official is defined as a member of the senior civil service (grade 7 or above) or a member of the senior management structure of Her Majesty's Diplomatic Service.

103 EA 2003 s103(9).

104 EA 2003 s117(3).

105 *R (Tajik) v City of Westminster Magistrates' Court* [2012] EWHC 3347 (Admin).

is in the UK and before the person is extradited the SSHD receives another valid request for the person's extradition, the SSHD may:

- order proceedings on one of the requests to be deferred until the other one has been disposed of, if neither of the requests has been disposed of;[106] or
- order the person's extradition to be deferred until the other request has been disposed of, if an order for extradition has already been made.[107]

8.99 The SSHD must take into account the following factors when applying section 126(2):

- the relative seriousness of the offences concerned;
- the place where each offence was committed (or alleged to have been committed);
- the date when each request was received;
- whether, in the case of each offence, the person is accused or unlawfully at large after conviction.[108]

Competing AW and Part 2 requests for extradition

8.100 In even rarer scenarios there may be a situation where there exists an AW and a Part 2 extradition request for the same person. Where there is a valid AW and a valid Part 2 request in existence, and the person has not been extradited on either, the SSHD may:[109]

- order proceedings on either the AW or the Part 2 request to be deferred until the other one has been disposed of; or
- order the person's extradition in pursuance of the AW to be deferred until the Part 2 request has been disposed of, if an order for extradition has been made on the AW; or
- order the person's extradition on the Part 2 request to be deferred until the AW has been disposed of, if an order for extradition on the Part 2 request has been made.

8.101 The factors to be taken into consideration by the SSHD are:[110]

- the relative seriousness of the offences concerned;
- the place where each offence was committed (or alleged to have been committed);

106 EA 2003 s126(2)(a).
107 EA 2003 s126(2)(b).
108 EA 2003 s126(3)(a)–(d).
109 EA 2003 s179.
110 EA 2003 s179(3)(a)–(d).

- the date when the AW was issued and the date when the Part 2 request was received;
- whether the person is accused or alleged to be unlawfully at large.

8.102 The SSHD is under no obligation to inform a requested person of a competing request, and as a matter of policy the Home Office will not inform a requested person of the existence of a request until the person has been arrested.

Asylum claims

8.103 EA 2003[111] s121 prevents the extradition of a person who has claimed asylum (whether before or after the issue of the warrant), until the final determination of that claim. In order to prevent a removal, the SSHD should be provided with the date an asylum claim was made and the reference number. The SSHD will not disclose the fact that an asylum claim has been made to the requesting state. See chapter 5, para 5.119 for circumstances where an application is made to adjourn extradition proceedings pending the outcome of an asylum claim.

111 As amended by Anti-social Behaviour, Crime and Policing Act 2014 s162.

CHAPTER 9

Preparing for the contested hearing

continued

Introduction

9.1 Preparing even the most straightforward case for a contested hearing is likely to take some hours, particularly when time is factored in to allow for interpreters and travel to prisons to take instructions from those remanded in custody. It is important to consider these factors when setting a timetable for a contested hearing in court. This chapter will look at the casework that may need to be undertaken prior to any hearing.

Visiting the client in custody

9.2 It will often take time for a prison visit to be arranged (it can take a week or more for a slot to become available), and the booking of a visit should therefore be prioritised. It is also possible to see clients remotely, by video-link, and sometimes a slot for a remote visit can be arranged sooner than an in-person visit.

9.3 When visiting in person, it can take over half an hour to gain entry to the visiting area, so it is always worth arriving at the prison well before the visit is due to start. The use of an interpreter will necessarily reduce the time available for the exchange of information, and a 'double visit' may be required.

9.4 While the relevant law and procedure will have been explained to the requested person at the first hearing, it will often be worth running through this again, in order to ensure the requested person has a proper understanding. In addition, lawyers will find that there are a large number of prisoners on remand at HMP Wandsworth in extradition cases, many of whom have developed considerable knowledge about extradition.

Use of interpreters

9.5 Criminal defence practitioners should be familiar with the Law Society practice note 'Use of interpreters in criminal cases',[1] which applies equally to extradition as to other types of criminal proceedings. The quality of interpreters provided by the court can vary greatly, and those representing requested persons will be aware of

1 At: www.lawsociety.org.uk/en/topics/criminal-justice/use-of-interpreters-in-criminal-cases (10 December 2019).

the need to ensure, as far as is possible, that the interpreter is competent.

9.6 Some requested persons may be confident in everyday speech, but not at a hearing that involves complicated legal concepts and terminology. It may be that they did not have an interpreter at the first hearing, but feel that one would be necessary for the extradition hearing. The court is familiar with such requests being made.

9.7 When seeing requested persons (or defence witnesses) outside court, the interpreter will need to be arranged by the solicitor. If the client is legally aided, the Legal Aid Agency (LAA) will pay a maximum of £25 per hour for an interpreter (or £28 per hour outside London).[2] If the interpreter's fees fall within this rate, there will be no need to apply for prior authority, unless it is anticipated that the time spent by the interpreter will exceed around four hours. If, however, it proves impossible to find an interpreter who will work at this rate (in the case, for example, of a rare language), an application for prior authority should be made, demonstrating that the case is exceptional and setting out the steps taken to find an interpreter.

Case management and court directions

9.8 In most contested cases, the following documents will need to be prepared for service on the court and the prosecution:

- statement of issues;
- proof of evidence;
- witness statements;
- expert reports;
- objective evidence;
- skeleton argument.

9.9 This chapter will look at the preparation of each of these in turn. Prior to the extradition hearing, all documents in the case should be put together into a joint hearing bundle to be served on the court.

9.10 At the initial hearing, directions will be set for the service of the above documents, although in more complex cases (and in Extradition Act (EA) 2003 Part 2 cases) these directions may be made at a subsequent hearing. If the case is not straightforward (and most cases where there is an arguable point will not be) there may be one or indeed several case management hearings. A review hearing may be listed at the initial

2 Criminal Legal Aid (Remuneration) Regulations 2013 SI No 435 Sch 5.

hearing, or more commonly the matter will be listed for review at the request of one of the parties prior to the extradition hearing.

9.11 If there are difficulties in complying with the directions, it is essential to make a written application to the court to extend time for service. Ignoring such directions may lead the court to exclude material served late or to consider wasted costs. Although it is possible to make applications administratively in criminal proceedings, the practice of the International Jurisdiction Office (IJO) is to list all such applications (including applications to vary bail) in court. Where the application is agreed by the other side or is not contentious, it is possible to request that attendance be excused; but where the application is opposed, attendance at court will obviously be preferable.

9.12 Two weeks before the extradition hearing, the court should send a case readiness form which should be completed and returned to the court.

Taking instructions

9.13 Some basic instructions should already have been taken at the initial hearing, covering the areas set out in the checklists in the appendices. The requested person should be asked whether they have, or can get hold of, any documentary evidence (for example, papers from the court in the requesting state). People often retain important documents and may not realise their significance. Those in custody will sometimes have friends or family who can assist in obtaining any documentation. Full background instructions should be taken when preparing for the contested hearing, covering:

- family background and current circumstances;
- education;
- employment;
- health;
- immigration history;
- reason for coming to the UK;
- reason for leaving the requesting state;
- previous convictions in this or any other jurisdiction;
- concerns regarding extradition to the requesting state.

9.14 As with any client, the areas that will be covered will be led, to some extent, by the particular circumstances of that client. It is, of course, always important to foster a relationship with the client that encourages them to raise any issues that they think relevant, and it is good practice to ask the requested person whether there is anything that they can think of that has not been covered.

9.15 It may be necessary to take instructions directed towards the particular bar that the requested person wishes to raise. Clearly, there are some areas where a client's instructions will be of less importance. For example, if a person is arguing that prison conditions in a particular country will result in a breach of their rights under Article 3 of the European Convention on Human Rights (ECHR) (prohibition of torture and ill-treatment), there may be little or indeed nothing that they can add to the expert reports, and it may be in such a case that no proof of evidence need be served. If, however, that person does have first-hand experience of prison conditions, or if they fall within a category of individual cited as being at risk in the reports (for example, because of illness or race), this is something that should be covered when taking instructions. In view of the most commonly raised bars, suggested areas to discuss with the requested person are covered below.

Rule against double jeopardy

9.16 Full instructions should be taken on the circumstances of the previous conviction/acquittal, together with any sentence imposed and the extent to which it has been served. It will also be important to obtain any documentary evidence from the court in the requesting state that dealt with the case: a local lawyer should be able to facilitate this. A signed letter of consent to enable the gathering of such information from third parties should be obtained.

Absence of prosecution decision

9.17 Where there is a lack of clarity on the face of the warrant as to whether a decision to charge or try has been taken, it will be for the requested person to satisfy the appropriate judge that there are reasonable grounds for believing that this decision has not been taken; in looking at this, the appropriate judge will be entitled to consider extraneous evidence. In appropriate circumstances, the requested person should therefore be asked whether or not they have any material which could support the contention that a decision to charge or try has not been made. In *Kandola*,[3] for example, in which a person's prosecution was

3 *Kandola and others v Generalstaatwaltschaft Frankfurt, Germany and others* [2015] EWHC 619 (Admin).

sought for offences of tax evasion, the requested person adduced letters from tax authorities seeking payment of the outstanding tax which post-dated the issue of the European Arrest Warrant (EAW). It should be noted that the Administrative Court discouraged elaborate expert evidence on this question.

9.18 If this first hurdle can be overcome, the court will then go on to consider EA 2003 s12A(1)(a)(ii) ie whether the sole reason for the decision to charge or try not having been made is the absence of the requested person. In considering this question, the court stated that 'it is likely that this could only be done by some sort of extraneous evidence from the requested person' but went on to say that, although the evidence need not be elaborate, mere assertion would be insufficient.[4]

Extraneous considerations

9.19 The requested person is likely to be able to provide useful scene setting information for extraneous considerations cases, and enough time should be provided to allow them to provide an account which can then be supplemented by research using objective material. Relying on either limb of this bar, the requested person should be asked about any past experience of prejudice or punishment experienced by them on account of race, religion, nationality, gender, sexual orientation or political opinion.

Passage of time

9.20 It will be essential to take detailed instructions on the reasons why the requested person left the jurisdiction in order to deal with any assertion that the requested person has deliberately fled the jurisdiction. The warrant may give an indication as to whether the requesting state will assert that the requested person is a fugitive. If the person faces an accusation warrant, it will be necessary to probe their knowledge (if any) of the offence and its aftermath. Lawyers will need to ask questions such as:

- whether they knew of the offence;
- whether they were arrested;
- what they had understood to have happened following arrest;
- whether any assertions were made by the authorities.

4 At para 33.

If, for example, the person was arrested and later released, why did they subsequently leave the jurisdiction? Were they under any obligation to return or abide by any bail conditions?

9.21 Similarly, for a conviction warrant the requested person should be asked:

- whether they were aware of the conviction;
- whether they were present when convicted;
- if so, why they then left the country;
- whether any assurance was given that led them to the belief that they were allowed to leave;
- if they were subject to a suspended sentence, whether they complied with any conditions imposed;
- what contact they had with the authorities.

Documentary evidence in support will lend weight to the requested person's case.

9.22 The second area that should be covered in detail is the person's current circumstances as this will go to the question of oppression. How has their life changed since the time of the alleged offence, in particular with regards to family, employment and health? Do they now have familial responsibilities such that extradition would cause particular hardship to a vulnerable person? An expert report from, for example, a social worker may be helpful in such a case.

9.23 In addition to this, requested persons should be asked whether they know of any reason why their extradition would be unjust, eg whether there are essential witnesses who are no longer available.

Forum

9.24 It will often be clear from the warrant or request when looking at 'the gateway' of the forum test (see para 5.61), whether a substantial measure of a person's relevant activity was performed in the UK. Instructions on this question should, however, be carefully sought from the requested person. In addition to this, the specified matters that the appropriate judge can look at when considering the interests of justice test include a number of matters which the requested person should be asked about, including under EA 2003 ss19B/83A(3)(f) the jurisdictions in which co-defendants and other suspects are located and, importantly, under EA 2003 ss19B/83A(3)(g), the person's connections with the UK.

Proportionality

9.25 In considering whether the extradition would be disproportionate under EA 2003 s21A, the appropriate judge is only permitted to take into account three specified matters, namely: the seriousness of the offence; the likely penalty; and the possibility of the foreign authorities taking less coercive measures.

9.26 In relation to the first of these, it will be noted that the Lord Chief Justice's (LCJ's) guidance[5] suggests that previous offending history will be relevant to the seriousness of the offence. Instructions on the circumstances of previous convictions should therefore be taken. In relation to the third specified matter, that is, whether less coercive measures are available, this should be explored with the requested person given that there is an evidential burden on the requested person to identify these.[6] At the same time, the requested person should also be asked about any knowledge they might have of their obligations to the requesting state's authorities: if they are in breach of these obligations, it will be unlikely that the appropriate judge will find less coercive measures appropriate.[7]

Human rights considerations

9.27 With regard to ECHR Articles 2 (right to life), 3 (prohibition of torture and ill-treatment), 5 (right to liberty and security) and 6 (right to a fair trial), there will often be limited instructions that can be taken from the requested person (see para 9.13 above) beyond their past experience of conditions in the requesting state. For Article 8 (right to respect for private and family life), however, detailed instructions should be taken on the requested person's personal and family circumstances, including children and any issues around being a sole carer, covering areas similar to those set out in para 9.13 above.

Conviction in absence

9.28 If the requested person was absent from their trial, instructions should be taken on their knowledge (or lack of knowledge) of the trial, covering the same areas as those set out in para 9.20 above. If

5 see Table 3.1
6 *Miraszewski and others v District Court in Torun, Poland and others* [2014] EWHC 4261 (Admin) at para 41.
7 *Miraszewski* at para 41.

instructions establish that the person was not deliberately absent and knew nothing of the criminal investigation, the requested person is unlikely to be able to provide any useful instructions on whether or not they will be entitled to a retrial: this will be a question for an expert to address. If the requested person was arrested or involved in the preliminary parts of the investigation, this should be covered.

Physical or mental health

9.29 While this is an area that will always require the commissioning of medical reports, it will often be the case (depending on the precise medical condition of the requested person) that useful instructions can be taken on the history of the requested person's medical complaints along with the effects that that condition has had on their life. In suicide risk cases, a full history of previous incidents of self-harm or attempts should be taken, in addition to information on psychiatric diagnoses. Again, a signed authority for the release of medical records should be obtained from the client along with details of the relevant GP, treating doctor and hospitals. As well as obtaining medical records from these sources, it may also be necessary to seek records of any medical treatment from the prison, if the requested person is in custody.

Statement of issues

9.30 A statement of issues will not be required in straightforward cases. Where a statement is required, the court will usually direct service. Its purpose is to notify the court and primarily the prosecution of the grounds on which extradition is contested. A statement of issues should set out the very basic facts about the arrest warrant (AW) or request, along with the challenges to be raised and an outline of the facts that support the grounds on which extradition is contested.

9.31 It is essential that it sets out any point on which the prosecution may wish to seek further information from the requesting state. If it does not, this may well lead to delay as the prosecution may seek time to obtain information to address issues that are raised late in proceedings. If it becomes apparent that an issue has arisen after the statement of issues has been served, it is good practice to notify the prosecution of this issue in writing at the first opportunity.

Drafting a proof of evidence

9.32 The proof of evidence is a crucial document in extradition proceedings. Particular time and care should be taken in its preparation. There are no rules or guidelines that dictate its form or content. While the court will direct that a 'proof of evidence' be served, this does not mean that a full statement setting out all of the client's instructions need necessarily be provided to the court. A proof of evidence in extradition cases is different from that which would be taken in usual criminal proceedings and that would be used by the defence team and not disclosed to the court or the other side. A proof of evidence for service in extradition proceedings will be more like a witness statement served in civil proceedings. In more complex cases, and where counsel is instructed, it may be useful to prepare the more typical 'proof of evidence' setting out the client's instructions in writing, and a shorter proof intended for service. In accusation cases in particular, care should be taken if anything is said about the offences in the requesting state, given that this could potentially prejudice a defence if extradited.

9.33 In terms of form, practice among solicitors varies: some favour serving the proof in the form of a section 9 statement;[8] others will serve it as a statement with numbered paragraphs signed and dated by the client. The authors prefer the latter approach. Given that there is no requirement to serve the statement in section 9 format,[9] there is no good reason for the requested person to provide a statement that carries a risk of prosecution for perjury if they do deviate from it under cross- examination.

9.34 The proof should be set out in chronological order, with subject headings at appropriate points. The content of the proof should set out relevant background information, along with current circumstances and the particular detail pertaining to the grounds upon which extradition is contested (as set out in paras 9.13–9.29). It is important that it is in the requested person's own words and that any comment that could be seen as legal argument is avoided.

9.35 There is no need to serve a full statement setting out detail that is irrelevant, and district judges dealing with cases that are frequently document-heavy are unlikely to welcome lengthy biographical histories.

8 Of the Criminal Justice Act (CJA) 1967.

9 EA 2003 s 205 states that CJA 1967 s9 (proof by witness statement) and s10 (proof by formal admission) apply to extradition proceedings as they do to proceedings for an offence.

Nevertheless, it is important that any fact that may be raised by the requested person in evidence is covered in the proof, and it may therefore be preferable to lean towards inclusion of detail if in doubt. Although no statutory inference will be drawn from failure to mention facts in a proof, requested persons should be aware that where facts not included are then elicited in live evidence, this may undermine their credibility. If there are parts of a client's case that are particularly problematic, it is tactically better to deal with this in the proof rather than to leave an obvious gap that will be exploited in cross-examination. Practitioners should be aware that some appropriate judges are reluctant to allow the defence advocate to ask questions that could have been covered in the proof of evidence. See *Germany v Parkes*[10] for a discussion of the status of the proof of evidence in extradition hearings.

Witness statements

9.36 Witnesses in extradition hearings range from friends and family of the requested person to professionals in the requesting state with, for example, knowledge of proceedings in that jurisdiction. Witness statements should be served in section 9 form,[11] given that there will always be a possibility that the witness will not attend the extradition hearing.

Obtaining expert evidence

9.37 While the courts have discouraged expert evidence in particular circumstances (see, for example, para 3.42 and para 5.91) evidence from an expert will be required in some cases. Use of an expert will usually be necessary in two areas. First, in support of arguments about the situation (legal, factual or political) in the requesting state, when challenging extradition on either extraneous considerations or human rights grounds. Second, experts are commonly relied upon to support cases where a requested person's personal circumstances are relevant to an issue in the case, for example doctors who can provide a report for the purposes of EA 2003 ss25/81 or psychologists who

10 [2021] EWHC 1655 (Admin).

11 EA 2003 s 205 states that CJA 1967 s9 (proof by witness statement) and s10 (proof by formal admission) apply to extradition proceedings as they do to proceedings for an offence.

can comment on the impact of a separation between parent and child for the purposes of an argument on ECHR Article 8.

9.38 As in other proceedings, an expert's duty is to the court, and they must be impartial and objective. Part 19 of the Criminal Procedure Rules (CrimPR) applies to expert witnesses in extradition cases and a copy of this should be provided to any expert along with the letter of instruction. Rule 19.4 sets out information that all expert reports should contain. Compliance with the rules should be verified upon receipt of the report. It is important that the statement includes enough detail for a court to be able to establish that the expert has complied with their duties.

9.39 An expert's opinion is 'admissible to furnish the court with ... information which is likely to be outside the experience of a judge and jury.'[12] An expert must have direct personal experience of, and proven expertise in, the issue upon which a report is sought.[13] Evidence tending simply to provide the expert's view of the credibility or reliability of a witness is generally inadmissible.[14]

9.40 Where a requested person is legally aided, an application for prior authority should be made to cover the expert's costs. Where counsel is instructed, an application for prior authority will often be supported by an advice from counsel. The hourly rates are set out in the Criminal Legal Aid (Remuneration) Regulations 2013 SI No 435 at Sch 5. If it is impossible to find an expert who can produce a report at the rates set out in the order, the LAA may increase the rates in exceptional circumstances. Exceptional circumstances are defined by the LAA as:

> ... where the expert's evidence is key to the client's case and either:
> a) the complexity of the material is such that an expert with a high level of seniority is required; or
> b) the material is of such a specialised and unusual nature that only very few experts are available to provide the necessary evidence.[15]

12 *R v Turner* (1975) QB 834.

13 *Brazuks and others v Prosecutor General's Office, Latvia* [2014] EWHC 1021 (Admin).

14 *Short v Falkland Islands* [2020] EWHC 438 (Admin) at para 40.

15 See LAA Guidance on Remuneration of Expert Witnesses, September 2020, para 2.2 (https://assets.publishing.service.gov.uk/government/uploads/system/uploads/attachment_data/file/925207/Guidance_on_the_Remuneration_of_Expert_Witnessesv6.pdf).

If prior authority is refused, legally aided clients can, in certain circumstances, pay for experts' reports.[16]

9.41 Letters of instruction should enclose the warrant or request along with any further information received from the prosecution, the proof of evidence and any pertinent witness statements. It may be useful in some cases for the expert to be provided with relevant case-law. The letter of instruction should set out a brief background before going through the questions to be addressed. These questions should be as specific as possible, and should direct the expert towards answering questions that are not addressed in the objective evidence. Funding matters and the timeframe should also be covered. It is advisable to require experts to submit reports at least a week prior to the deadline in order to allow sufficient time to address any issues. In drafting a letter of instruction, it is important to bear in mind that the letter and enclosures, as well as any correspondence between the solicitor and the expert, may be seen by the court and/or the prosecution, and careful thought should therefore be given as to both the content of the letter and any documents that are provided along with it.

9.42 Solicitors will be responsible for paying the costs of the commissioning of expert reports. Where a client is legally aided and the expert's attendance at court is required, this will be covered by the court. The rates for travel and attendance for expert witnesses are minimal,[17] and can only be claimed after attendance. It can take the court many months to process the expert's claim for payment. For this reason it is frequently impossible to secure the attendance of experts based in other jurisdictions and the use of video link evidence is becoming more frequent.

Receivable and admissible documents

9.43 An AW is a receivable document that is admissible in proceedings under the EA 2003.[18] But what about other documents adduced by the judicial authority/requesting state in the course of the proceed-

16 2017 Standard Criminal Contract Specification para 8.43.

17 See the Guide to Allowances under Part V of the Costs in Criminal Cases (General) Regulations 1986 SI No 1335, available at https://assets.publishing.service.gov.uk/government/uploads/system/uploads/attachment_data/file/592291/guide-allowances-under-part-v-costs-criminal-cases-general-september-2016.doc, for the applicable rates of payment.

18 EA 2003 s202(1).

ings? Section 202(2) and (3) state that any other document issued in a category 1 or 2 territory may be received in evidence if it has been 'duly authenticated.' Duly authenticated is defined in subsection 202(4):

> (4) A document issued in a category 1 or category 2 territory is duly authenticated if (and only if) one of these applies–
> (a) it purports to be signed by a judge, magistrate or officer of the territory;
> (b) it purports to be certified, whether by seal or otherwise, by the Ministry or Department of the territory responsible for justice or for foreign affairs;
> (c) it purports to be authenticated by the oath or affirmation of a witness.

A document that is not duly authenticated is not precluded from being admitted into evidence in extradition proceedings.[19] However, less weight may be afforded to it.

9.44 The hearsay provisions of the Criminal Justice Act 2003 do not apply to extradition proceedings as the route to a document being admitted into evidence is via EA 2003 s202.[20]

Evidence via video-link

9.45 It is possible to arrange with the court for evidence to be given remotely. This can be done in two ways:

- The first is by Cloud Video Platform (CVP), which is a secure video link. In order for evidence to be given via CVP, an application must be made to the court in accordance with CrimPR 18.24 and must be granted by an appropriate judge. Once granted, the proposed expert or witness will be sent a link which will enable them to connect their device to the CVP platform.
- The second way to facilitate video evidence is by using the Prison Video Link network. The majority of magistrates' and Crown courts in England and Wales are connected to this network and the expert/witness will need to attend their local court to access

19 In *Prendi (aka Aleks Kola) v Government of the Republic of Albania* [2015] EWHC 1809 (Admin), the court stated (at para 48) that the correct test to be applied as to the admissibility of an authenticated document is: 'is this document, which has not been authenticated in accordance with section 202(3), admissible as evidence of the facts stated in it, according to the English rules of criminal evidence?'

20 *Friesel v United States* [2009] EWHC 1659 (Admin).

the video-link network. The local court should therefore be contacted in advance to ensure that they have a booth available for the time that the evidence is to be given. This way of giving evidence is not available for witnesses based abroad.

9.46 An application for a live link should be made on the form set out in the Criminal Practice Direction.[21] Unless the court otherwise directs, the application should identify the place from which the witness will give evidence.[22] If the place is in the UK, the application must explain why it would be in the interests of the efficient and effective administration of justice for the witness to give evidence by live-link.[23] If the witness is to be accompanied by another person while giving evidence (such as an interpreter), then the application must name that other person[24] (if possible) and explain why it is appropriate for the witness to be accompanied.[25]

9.47 Once granted, the court will provide details to the representative of the relevant person to liaise with at the court to facilitate the link. In order to ensure that the CVP link works with the expert/witness, a test may be carried out five working days before the date of the hearing where the video evidence is to be given. Tests are carried out between 9 am and 4 pm, and can be arranged by contacting the IJO. A representative of the defence firm can attend on the test link. in case there are any difficulties arranged

Objective evidence

9.48 Reports from international organisations, if available, should be served as part of the hearing bundle in appropriate cases. If, for example, a requested person is arguing that their extradition will result in a breach of their human rights, reports from such organisations as Amnesty International, the US State Department or the European Committee for the Prevention of Torture will reinforce other evidence. Although criticism from independent international bodies may carry some weight, the court will also require expert evidence that is tailored to the specific facts of the case.

21 See: www.gov.uk/government/publications/application-for-a-witness-to-give-evidence-by-live-link.

22 CrimPR 18.24(a).

23 CrimPR 18.24(b).

24 CrimPR 18.24(c)(i).

25 CrimPR 18.24(c)(ii).

Further information from the issuing state

Overview

9.49 The court in this country cannot compel the requesting state to provide further information. It may, however, direct that further information, if it is to be provided, should be served by a particular date. While there is no obligation on the requesting state to serve further information, it is sometimes provided following service of defence documents where the requesting state 'wishes to resist the implications of evidence advanced and proffered by an appellant.'[26] Note, however, that a requesting state may rely on the presumption that it will comply with its ECHR obligations and serve no information in response.[27] Failure to provide a response could, in some circumstances lead to an inference being drawn.

9.50 When it is provided, further information is frequently served very late in the proceedings. Even if the Crown Prosecution Service (CPS) has acted diligently in communicating requests for information, the requesting state itself can be dilatory in responding. In some cases, there will be no comment that the requested person can usefully make on the further information, but they should nevertheless be provided with the opportunity to do so.

9.51 If it is a case in which expert reports have been commissioned, the expert's views on the further information should also be solicited; this may require a further application for prior authority if an addendum report is necessary.

Disclosure

9.52 The CPS does not have a general duty of disclosure as it does when conducting prosecutions in English criminal proceedings. However, the CPS owes the court a duty of candour and good faith.[28] It is accepted that, while it is for the requesting state to determine which evidence to put forward in support of its request for extradition, the CPS in accordance with its duty to the court must disclose evidence (but

26 *Baksys v Ministry of Justice of the Republic of Lithuania* [2007] EWHC 2838 (Admin) at para 11.

27 If the court has been satisfied that the 'presumption' has been rebutted in a case concerning a Council of Europe or EU state, an 'assurance' or 'guarantee' is a legitimate means by which such a state can 'dispel doubts' – *Ilia v Appeal Court in Athens, Greece* [2015] EWHC 547 (Admin) at para 38. See para 6.21.

28 *Knowles Jr v United States of America and another* [2006] UKPC 38 at para 35.

only if such material is brought to the attention of the CPS by the requesting state) which destroys, renders worthless or very severely undermines the evidence on which it relies.[29] In *R (Raissi) v Secretary of State for the Home Department*[30] the court said that the CPS's duty to the court includes a duty to ensure that the requesting state complies with its duty of disclosure.

9.53 The obligations of a requesting state were summarised by Mitting J in *Wellington v Governor of Belmarsh Prison*:[31]

1) It is for the requesting state alone to determine the evidence upon which it relies to seek a committal.
2) The requesting state is not under any general duty of disclosure similar to that imposed on the prosecution at any stage in domestic criminal proceedings.
3) The magistrates' court has the right to protect its process from abuse and the requesting state has a duty not to abuse that process. That is no different from saying that the requesting state must fulfil the duty which it has always had of candour in making applications for extradition.
4) In fulfilment of that duty, the requesting state must disclose any evidence which would render worthless the evidence on which it relies to seek committal.
5) It is for the person subject to the extradition process to establish that the requesting state is abusing the process of the court.
6) The requested state may be given power to request further evidence under the relevant Order in Council but, in the absence of evidence of abuse, the court is entitled to, and should generally, refuse to request the UK authorities to exercise that power or to adjourn to permit it to be exercised.

9.54 This approach was endorsed and re-stated by the Divisional Court in *R (Gambrah) v CPS*[32] as follows:

> The duties of the requesting state and of the CPS can, in my view, be summarised as follows: the duty of the requesting state includes, pursuant to its duty of candour and good faith, the obligation to disclose evidence which destroys or very seriously undermines the evidence on which it relies. The CPS has independently a similar duty. It also has a duty to ensure that the requesting state fulfills its duty. Finally, it has a duty to withdraw from the proceedings if it finds itself put in the position where its duty to the court conflicts with its

29 At para 35.
30 [2008] EWCA Civ 72.
31 [2014] EWHC 418 (Admin) at para 26.
32 [2013] EWHC 4126 (Admin) at para 8.

duties to the requesting state. That is, I believe, a full and accurate statement of the law as expounded in *Raissi*.

Closed material proceedings and secret evidence

9.55 A closed material proceeding can take place in certain types of immigration cases. It is a hearing in which the evidence is considered by the judge but not seen or disclosed to the other side. Closed material hearings are not permitted in extradition proceedings[33] and the judge at the extradition hearing has no power to limit disclosure to the requesting state of evidence relied upon by the requested person. All material relied upon must be served upon the CPS with the expectation that it will be disclosed to the requesting state. It is imperative that the requested person be made aware of this.

Drafting a skeleton argument

9.56 A skeleton argument is usually served well in advance of the extradition hearing. Those used to drafting skeleton arguments in usual criminal proceedings will recognise the format: in short, it should set out the facts, followed by the law, then the submissions. The headings below provide a suggested structure for a skeleton argument:

- Introduction and procedural chronology:
  - details of the AW (relevant dates, accusation/conviction, offence);
  - court proceedings since initial hearing.
- Issues for the court to determine: Set out the challenges to be raised.
- The law: Set out the statutory provisions and relevant case-law relied upon. It may be necessary to set out more of the case-law than in criminal proceedings.
- Submissions: Apply the law to the facts.
- Conclusion.

Preparation of the hearing bundle

9.57 A hearing bundle, preferably indexed with tabs and page numbering, should be served on the court prior to the extradition hearing. It

33 *VB and others v Westminster Magistrates' Court* [2014] UKSC 59.

should include all the documents set out in para 9.8, along with the documents relied upon by the prosecution (usually AW/extradition request, further information and skeleton argument) and the relevant statutory provisions and case-law. If a joint bundle is to be prepared, it should be properly paginated and indexed.

9.58 The general running order for such a joint bundle will be:

- opening note/skeleton argument of the judicial authority;
- AW/extradition request;
- witness statements from the judicial authority;
- expert reports;
- further information from judicial authority;
- statement of issues;
- defence skeleton argument;
- proof of requested person;
- witness statements;
- expert reports;
- authorities.

9.59 In cases that are complex and/or document heavy, it may be helpful for the hearing bundles to be separated into three volumes, comprising core documents, evidence and authorities.

9.60 Current practice at Westminster Magistrates' Court (WMC) is to assign a specific district judge to hear a case prior to the extradition hearing. When sending the hearing bundle to the court, it should be accompanied by a covering letter requesting that it be placed before the relevant district judge so that they have time to read it prior to the extradition hearing. The court and the CPS should be served with the hearing bundle electronically (as a PDF) where possible.

Timetable for hearing

9.61 In a case of any complexity, or with a number of witnesses, it may be helpful to agree a timetable with the prosecution in advance of the extradition hearing. This is particularly important where witnesses from different time zones will be giving evidence by video-link.

Certificate for counsel

9.62 Where a case is publicly funded, a certificate for counsel (including, in appropriate cases, Queen's Counsel) can be granted for extradition proceedings in the magistrates' court. The relevant legislation is the Criminal Legal Aid (Determinations by a Court and Choice of Representative) Regulations 2013 SI No 614. Regulation 16 reads:

> **16 Criminal proceedings before a magistrates' court**
> (1) Subject to paragraph (2), in relation to any criminal proceedings before a magistrates' court, the right of an individual conferred by section 27(4) of the Act does not include a right to select an advocate.
> (2) The relevant court may determine that the individual can select an advocate if–
> (a) the proceedings relate to an extradition hearing under the Extradition Act 2003 or an indictable offence; and
> (b) the relevant court determines that because there are circumstances which make the proceedings unusually grave or difficult, representation by an advocate would be desirable.

9.63 It is important to note that the Regulations use the word 'desirable' rather than, for example, 'necessary.' In order to apply for a certificate for counsel, a written application should be submitted to the IJO setting out the facts of the case and the reason that the proceedings are unusually grave or difficult. There is no prescribed form for an application, although they are frequently supplemented by a written advice from counsel. The application can be submitted to the LAA via its email address: extraditionapplica@legalaid.gsi.gov.uk. Once the application has been logged by the LAA, they will send the application to the IJO at WMC for it to be listed before an appropriate judge. An application that has been refused on the papers can be renewed at an oral hearing. If granted, the representation order will be amended accordingly from the date of grant.

CHAPTER 10

The contested extradition hearing

Introduction

10.1 The extradition hearing can vary in length depending on the complexity of the issues to be argued and the volume of evidence to be considered. Straightforward issues can be argued in as little as one hour of court time, whereas complex cases may require several days and occasionally weeks of the court's time.

Public hearing

10.2 The general rule is that the magistrates' court must hold hearings in public. However, the Criminal Procedure Rules (CrimPR) state that this is subject to the court's power to impose reporting restrictions, withhold information from the public or order a hearing in private.[1] Where such an application is to be made, it should ordinarily be done on notice, in advance of the hearing.

10.3 Closed material hearings are not permitted in extradition proceedings and the judge at the extradition hearing has no power to limit the disclosure of evidence relied upon by the requested person to the requesting state.[2] All material relied upon must be served upon the Crown Prosecution Service (CPS) with the expectation that it will be disclosed to the requesting state. The requested person must be made aware of this.

10.4 However, the court does have a discretion whether to admit anonymous evidence – but it must be 'an unusual exception to the general practice' and the judge must be satisfied that despite its admission the proceedings are 'nevertheless fair'.[3]

Proceeding in the absence of the requested person

10.5 Hearings should be held in the requested person's presence unless either (a) the case is being discharged or (b) the requested person is represented, and her presence is impracticable because of her ill health or disorderly conduct.[4]

1 CrimPR 50.3(1).
2 *VB and others v Westminster Magistrates' Court* [2014] UKSC 59.
3 *VB and others v Westminster Magistrates' Court* [2014] UKSC 59 at para 73.
4 CrimPR 50.3(2)(d).

10.6 Where the requested person is absent, the general rule is that the court must proceed as if the requested person were present and opposed extradition on any ground of which the court has been made aware.[5] Ordinarily, the court will not proceed and will instead issue a warrant of arrest for the requested person.

Burden and standard of proof

10.7 Unless any express provisions in the Extradition Act (EA) 2003 apply, the burden and standard of proof must be applied as if the person who is facing extradition is accused of an offence and the judicial authority/requesting state is the prosecution.[6] That is to say, it is for the requesting state to prove to the criminal standard.

Requests for further information

10.8 The CPS decides what will be disclosed in extradition proceedings. Domestic rules of disclosure do not apply to extradition proceedings,[7] although the CPS owes the court a duty of candour and good faith.

Applications to adjourn

10.9 The CrimPR set out a non-exhaustive list of the reasons for which an adjournment may be sought, as follows:[8]

- to allow there to be obtained information that the court requires;
- following a provisional arrest under Part 1 of the EA 2003, pending receipt of the warrant;
- following a provisional arrest under Part 2 of the Act, pending receipt of the extradition request;
- if the court is informed that the defendant has been charged with an offence in the United Kingdom;

5 CrimPR 50.3(3)(a)(i–ii)

6 EA 2003 s206.

7 *R (Raissi) v Secretary of State for the Home Department* [2008] EWCA Civ 72, [2008] QB 836.

8 CrimPR 50.3(4)(b)(i–viii).

- if the court is informed that the defendant is serving a custodial sentence in the UK;
- if it appears to the court that the defendant is not fit to be extradited, unless the court discharges the defendant for that reason;
- where a court dealing with a warrant to which Part 1 applies is informed that another such warrant has been received in the UK;
- where a court dealing with a warrant to which Part 1 applies is informed of a request for the temporary transfer of the requested person to the territory to which the defendant's extradition is sought, or for a request for the requested person to speak to the authorities of that territory; or
- during a hearing to which CrimPR 50.32 applies ('Application for consent to deal with another offence or for consent to further extradition').

10.10 Under CrimPR 50.3(6), the general rule is that, before exercising a power to adjourn, the court must give each party an opportunity to make representations, unless that party is deliberately absent.

10.11 Applications to adjourn should not be left until the day of the extradition hearing unless unavoidable. The court is unlikely to consider sympathetically an application to adjourn the extradition hearing if it is made on the day of the hearing. The court will be reluctant to lose court time, especially given the courts' listing difficulties. However, if an application to adjourn on the day of the extradition hearing is essential, it must be made on notice.

10.12 The CPS acting on behalf of the judicial authority/requesting state should be put on notice of an intention to seek an adjournment as soon as the need arises. The reasons that an adjournment is sought, and the proposed timetable for the case going forward should the court grant the application to adjourn, should be set out. If the CPS do not oppose the application or is 'neutral' to it, the application is more likely to be granted. In that case, the court will expect the parties to have agreed directions.

10.13 The court should be notified in writing of an application to adjourn the extradition hearing. This can be done by emailing the international office (Westminster.ij@justice.gov.uk) and should clearly outline the reason an adjournment is required and state why it is in the interests of justice for the case to be adjourned. The court will be referred to any previous applications to adjourn and will consider whether the parties have complied with directions set by the court. It is therefore important to apply to vary the directions where they cannot be complied with.

10.14 Where an application to adjourn is made on the day of the extradition hearing, advocates should be prepared for the application to be refused and for the hearing to proceed. Challenges to the refusal to grant adjournments are made by way of judicial review but the Administrative Court will be slow to interfere in a decision by the appropriate judge.

Housekeeping

10.15 Before the extradition hearing begins the advocate should ensure that both the court and the CPS have all the documents to which reference will be made. Ideally, these should all be in an indexed and paginated joint bundle (see chapter 9). If the judge has not had sight of the bundle or has not read it, the court should be invited to rise to allow the judge to read the key documents and skeleton arguments.

10.16 Any additional documents that were not included in the bundle should be handed up to the judge at the start of the hearing and the judge informed where in the bundle the documents should be inserted.

10.17 The order in which live witnesses are to be called should be outlined. If there is a witness who is to be called 'out of turn', the reason for this should be explained to the court.

10.18 Finally, if the time estimate does not appear sufficient, the court should be informed so that the judge can decide whether to begin to hear the case and adjourn the proceedings part-heard or to adjourn to a day when the hearing can be completed at one hearing.

Who goes first?

10.19 Those acting on behalf of the judicial authority/requesting state will open the hearing and take the court through the arrest warrant (AW)/extradition request. They will outline the issues that are raised by the requested person and invite the court to find matters not contested in their favour.

10.20 If the burden is on the judicial authority to prove the issue under EA 2003 (for example, the burden is on the judicial authority to prove to the criminal standard that the conduct contained in the AW/extradition request is an extradition offence) then they will go first in presenting their evidence (if any) and making submissions to the court.

10.21 In all other situations, it will be the requested person's case that is heard first, with their evidence called first, and the judicial authority/requesting state responding.

10.22 The structure of the EA 2003 envisages a 'step-by-step' approach by the judge to particular questions[9] and the answer to each particular question will determine the next question that has to be considered. Arguments should therefore be presented in sequence as a failure to do so could lead the court 'into error.'[10] The prescribed sequence is set out in CrimPR 50.6(2) for Part 1 cases, and CrimPR 50.13(2) for Part 2.

Calling your client – evidence in chief

10.23 The requested person is not obliged to give evidence, however where assertions are made by a requested person in a proof of evidence, but the requested person chooses not to give evidence in court, this may affect their credibility and in turn the weight to be attached to the poof of evidence.[11] Before the requested person gives evidence it is important to ensure that no other witness of fact is sitting in the courtroom. Any witness of fact should be asked to leave while the requested person is giving their testimony. This does not apply to expert witnesses who can sit in court throughout the proceedings while other evidence is being heard.

10.24 If the requested person is in custody, they will be brought to the witness box by the gaolers. If the requested person is on bail, they will be asked to make their way to the witness box by the court usher.

10.25 It is important that the requested person has with them the proof of evidence and any other documents to which reference will be made. If the court has a bundle of evidence for the hearing, the requested person should also be provided with one.

10.26 As with many types of proceeding, the requested person will be asked to affirm or to swear on oath before giving evidence. If the requested person is assisted by an interpreter, the interpreter will also be sworn in.

10.27 The advocate should ask the requested person to adopt their proof of evidence as part of their evidence-in-chief. In order for this to be

9 *Sonea v Mehedinti District Court* [2009] EWHC 89 (Admin).

10 *Bagri v Public Prosecutor Bordeaux Court of First Instance* [2014] EWHC 4066 (Admin).

11 See *Germany v Parkes* [2021] EWHC 1655 (Admin) for a discussion of the status of the proof of evidence in extradition hearings.

done, the requested person should be asked if the proof of evidence that is before the court is the person's statement and confirm that it is true to the best of their knowledge and belief. The requested person should be asked to confirm that it is, and that they have signed the statement.

10.28 Depending on the issues raised, there may be no supplementary questions for the requested person or they may be asked to address issues that have arisen subsequent to the proof of evidence being served. For example, the requested person may need to address further information served on behalf of the judicial authority. The court's preference is for this to be received in evidence by way of an addendum proof of evidence unless unpractical to do so, in which case any additional evidence should be addressed through examination in chief.

10.29 The advocate should be careful not to frustrate the court by asking questions where the answers are clearly contained in the proof of evidence: the judge should have read the papers ahead of the extradition hearing. If it is clear that the judge has not had an opportunity to read the papers in advance of the hearing, it may be necessary to summarise the main points covered in the proof of evidence with the requested person.

10.30 If there is a break in the proceedings and the requested person is in the middle of giving evidence, it is important to remember that the evidence cannot be discussed either with their legal representatives or with third parties.

10.31 Once the requested person has finished giving evidence in chief, they will likely be cross-examined and are also likely to be questioned by the judge. Re-examination follows, should there be a need for it. As in criminal proceedings, it is not an opportunity to address new topics, rather to address issues arising from cross-examination.

Expert evidence

10.32 If relying upon expert evidence, the report(s) of such experts should have been served ahead of the hearing to allow the judicial authority an opportunity to respond and adduce its own evidence in rebuttal. The requesting state may indicate that they do not require an expert to give oral evidence, although, as in other criminal proceedings, where a party wishes to challenge evidence given by a witness and contend that the evidence is either untruthful or inaccurate for reasons that would be within the knowledge of the witness, they are expected to put that case to the witness in cross-examination. If they do not do so, the inference may be drawn that the evidence is accepted as accurate.[12]

10.33 The reports of experts can be adopted into evidence – in the same manner as that presented by the requested person – and this can drastically reduce the time an expert spends in the witness box. The expert should have a copy of the report when giving evidence and any other documents that they will be asked to consider. If there is a bundle, this should be provided to the expert before giving evidence so that they can familiarise themselves with it.

10.34 With the permission of the court, the expert should be led through their qualifications and experience before addressing the main conclusion and findings. If the judicial authority/requesting state does not contest the expertise of an expert, there will be no need to establish their qualifications.

10.35 It is important that the expert addresses any points made by the judicial authority/requesting state in further information served in the proceedings if this has not been addressed in an addendum report. Once the expert has finished giving their evidence in chief, they may be subjected to questions from both the court and the judicial authority/requesting state.

10.36 If the judicial authority/requesting state call evidence, the defence expert should be invited to remain in court to address any issues arising.

Adducing other evidence

10.37 If other evidence is to be adduced, the time to do it is after the requested person and expert (if applicable) have given their evidence.

10.38 Other evidence could take the form of section 9 witness statements[13] to be read, or objective evidence. If the court admits written statements from a witness or expert as evidence, each relevant part of the statement must be read or summarised aloud[14] or the court must read the statement and its gist must be summarised aloud.[15]

12 *Eason v Government of the United States of America* [2020] EWHC 604 (Admin) at para 12.

13 Criminal Justice Act (CJA) 1967.

14 CrimPR 50.15(2)(a).

15 CrimPR 50.15(2)(b).

10.39 If lengthy objective evidence reports are being relied upon, relevant passages in the judge's bundle should be highlighted to ensure that they are easily found when reference is made to them.

Submissions

10.40 Once all the evidence has been called/adduced, the court will invite submissions from the parties. Some judges will invite the advocates to provide submissions in writing at the conclusion of the hearing. The skeleton argument that has already been served should address the submissions on behalf of the requested person. Closing submissions should expand upon the arguments presented and address the evidence that has been heard.

10.41 The court should be addressed on the relevant law. If the applicability of the law is agreed between the requested person and the judicial authority/requesting state, then the court can be informed of the agreed position.

10.42 Very often judges will be careful to avoid making decisions that will 'open the floodgates.' It is therefore important not to make general sweeping assertions (eg 'a fair trial is not possible in Malta') but rather to emphasise the points in the case being presented that are unique (eg 'a fair trial in Malta is not possible for this particular requested person because ...').

Authorities

10.43 The advocate should apply the facts of the case to the law. It may be necessary to distinguish the facts of the current case from reported case-law. When referring to reported cases the court should be taken to the relevant passages. Advocates should note that many of the core principles in extradition law are well known to the court. Highlighting key passages in the authorities bundle will bring them to the judge's attention in pre-hearing reading.

Judgment

10.44 After both the requested person and the judicial authority have made submissions, the judge may give their ruling in an 'ex tempore' judgment. The court may adopt this approach if the issue raised at the contested extradition hearing is straightforward.[16] As full a note as possible should be taken of an 'ex tempore' judgment. If the matter is to be appealed, a summary of the judgment should be agreed between the parties so that it can be provided to the Administrative Court Office with the application for permission to appeal (see chapter 11 on appeals).

10.45 If judgment is reserved to another date, the parties will have to return to court for a written ruling to be handed down. This is normally read out in full in open court. However, it is the practice of some judges to read the findings of fact and the conclusion rather than the whole judgment.

10.46 If there are any factual errors in the judgment, these should be noted and brought to the attention of the judge once it has been read out in full. The amendments (if any) can then be made by hand.

10.47 A copy of the written ruling in a reserved judgment will be provided to the parties and there is therefore no need to take a detailed note.

Information provided to the requested person after judgment

10.48 After reading out the judgment, the judge will then explain to the requested person the effect of their decision. If the result is to order the person's extradition (in an AW case) or to send the case to the Secretary of State for the Home Department (SSHD) (in a Part 2 case) the judge will explain the timeframe for appealing. The judge will then remand the person in custody or on bail.

10.49 If the decision of the judge is to order the person's discharge, and the CPS gives an indication to the judge of an intention to appeal the decision, then the judge must continue to remand the person in custody or on bail. If no such indication is given, and the requested person is in custody, the person will be released. If the requested person was subject to bail conditions then those conditions will cease to apply.

10.50 Whether the court's decision is to order extradition or to discharge, the CrimPR state that the court must also consider any ancillary application, such as those relating to reporting restrictions or costs.[17]

16 Practitioners should note that the Lord Chief Justice (LCJ) in *Polish Judicial Authorities v Celinski and others* [2015] EWHC 1274 (Admin) stated that the practice of giving oral judgments in Article 8 ECHR cases was 'unacceptable' as no official transcript of it would be available to the appellate court.

17 CrimPR 50.6(3) and (4).

Costs where extradition ordered

10.51 If the judge orders extradition, in the vast majority of cases where the requested person is on bail, the CPS will make an application for costs pursuant to EA 2003 s60. The costs sought by the CPS should be limited to the 'expenses reasonably incurred in conducting extradition proceedings' and can include:

- costs incurred through the preparation of the case by the CPS;
- counsel's fees and disbursements; and
- witness expenses.

10.52 However, the CPS memo on applying for costs states that 'it is impractical to maintain detailed time and costs records and in any event the requested person is generally only able to make a contribution to costs.' The contribution in 'standard cases' usually amounts to the following:

- £100 where extradition is ordered at the first hearing;
- £100 per interim and review hearing;
- £165 for a contested extradition hearing (each day).

10.53 The High Court has urged caution on the magistrates' court regarding the imposition of costs. Collins J in *Mencwel v Regional Court in Poznan, Poland,*[18] stated:

> The District Judge took a robust view of the circumstances put before him which were said to be a bar to extradition. He said it was a typical case of non-existent grounds and very flimsy arguments to resist it. He made a point that the court as from April this year will consider ordering costs against requested persons who pointlessly resist extradition in this way. I note that it is a jurisdiction which no doubt the court has but it is one which on the face of it should be exercised with the greatest possible care.

10.54 The appropriate route for challenging a costs order is by way of judicial review. In *Bizunowicz and others v Poland*[19] the Divisional Court concluded that the High Court had no jurisdiction to determine an appeal from a costs order where a person has challenged that order as part of an unsuccessful extradition appeal. However, the court does have jurisdiction to vary or quash a costs order where the appellant has successfully appealed the extradition order.

18 [2013] EWHC 1513 (Admin) at para 5.

19 *Bizunowicz and Florea v Koszalin District Court, Poland and Plzen Regional Court, Czech Republic* [2014] EWHC 3238 (Admin).

Costs in Part 2 cases

10.55 EA 2003 s133 allows the appropriate judge to award costs where extradition is ordered. In Part 2 cases, it is not the appropriate judge that orders extradition and therefore at the time the case is still with the appropriate judge they have no power to award costs.

Costs where discharge ordered

10.56 When discharge is ordered, the requested person is able to make an application for a costs order pursuant to EA 2003 ss61/134 for their out of pocket expenses (usually travel costs).

10.57 A requested person who has funded their case privately will be able to seek a costs order for recovery of costs from central funds subject to the rules of determination which state that the costs are capped at legal aid rates.

CHAPTER 11

Appeals

continued

continued

Introduction

11.1 Both the requested person whose extradition has been ordered and the requesting state can appeal against adverse decisions made at the extradition hearing, subject to being granted permission by the High Court.[1]

11.2 In Extradition Act (EA) 2003 Part 1 cases (known as 'arrest warrant (AW) cases') the appeal is against the decision of the appropriate judge who either ordered extradition or ordered the person's discharge.

11.3 In EA 2003 Part 2 cases, the appeal can be against the decision of the appropriate judge to send the case to the Secretary of State for the Home Department (SSHD) and/or the decision of the SSHD to order extradition or a decision by either to order the person's discharge from the extradition request.

11.4 The timeframe in which an application for permission to appeal must be lodged and served differs depending on the part of the Act under which proceedings are brought.

11.5 Appeals to the High Court under EA 2003 are also governed by rule 50 of the Criminal Procedure Rules 2020 (CrimPR) and Part 50 of the Criminal Practice Directions (CrimPD).[2]

Legal aid

11.6 There is no means testing in the High Court for extradition appeals. In order to apply for legal aid in extradition appeal proceedings before the High Court, a fully completed CRM14 form must be submitted to the Administrative Court Office (ACO).

11.7 CRM14s that were previously submitted to the magistrates' court will not be accepted.

11.8 A fresh CRM14 should be submitted at the same time that the appeal notice is lodged so that the issuing fee of £255 (at time of writing) can be recovered as a disbursement. The representation order only takes effect from the date on which the form, properly

1 This relates to a decision of the appropriate judge to a) order the requested person's extradition, b) send the requested person's case to the secretary of state and c) order the requested person's discharge. Any other decision must be challenged by way of judicial review.

2 The CrimPR and CrimPD are available here: www.gov.uk/guidance/rules-and-practice-directions-2020#rules-and-practice-directions-contents.

completed, is received.[3] The case lawyers at the ACO have delegated powers to grant a representation order. A copy of the representation order will usually be received by the legal representative two to three days after a CRM14 is submitted.

11.9 Although the CrimPD states that 'a Representation Order will cover junior advocate and solicitors for the preparation of the Notice of Appeal to determination of the appeal',[4] practitioners should be aware that it will only cover preparation of the notice of appeal after the grant of the representation order (for example, if the notice of appeal is perfected in the ten business days after service). Preparation of the notice of appeal prior to the grant of the High Court representation order will be covered by the magistrates' court representation order.

11.10 In order to obtain a representation order for leading counsel alone or for leading counsel and junior counsel, an application must be made to extend the representation order (see para 11.86 below).

11.11 The representation order can also be extended to cover disbursements such as experts' fees and translation fees (see paras 11.88 and 11.94 below).

Appeals under Part 1 (arrest warrant cases)

11.12 If a person's extradition is ordered, then that person has *seven days* in which to apply for permission[5] to appeal to the High Court. The seven days start with the day the extradition order is made. If, for example, the order is made on a Tuesday, the appeal must be filed and served by the following Monday. If the decision is made on a Monday, the deadline will be the following Monday as the seventh day falls on a Sunday when the ACO is closed. Similarly, if the seventh day falls on a bank holiday or a day when the ACO is shut, the deadline moves to the next working day.[6]

Preparing the permission to appeal application

11.13 The following documents should be put together in a bundle[7] to be lodged at the High Court:

3 There is no power to back-date legal representation orders.

4 CrimPD 50C.1.

5 The terms 'permission' and 'leave' to appeal are used interchangeably in the EA 2003 and Criminal Procedure Rules (CrimPR).

6 *Mucelli v Government of Albania* [2009] UKHL 2.

7 If lodging in person. Electronic applications can also be accepted.

- form EXN161 – appellant's notice – application for permission to appeal;
- grounds of appeal;
- the AW;
- judgment of the appropriate judge (or a detailed note if judgment issued 'ex tempore');
- any other documents relied upon[8] (eg witness statements, expert reports, further information[9]).

11.14 In total, four bundles should be prepared. The court will require three copies and one master copy should be retained by the defence so that copies can be made to be served upon the Crown Prosecution Service (CPS) and the National Crime Agency (NCA). If numerous 'other documents' are being relied on, then it may be appropriate to submit the bundles with dividers and an index. Electronic permission to appeal applications can be submitted (see guidance below).

Appellant's notice – application for permission to appeal – form EXN161

11.15 Guidance for the completion of the EXN161 is provided on the ACO website.[10]

11.16 Practitioners should note that it should be signed either by the appellant or a solicitor of the firm lodging the leave to appeal application.

11.17 Any documents not included at the time of lodging that should ordinarily be included (such as a copy of the AW or a copy of the judge's ruling) should be provided as soon as possible to the court and the respondents if they do not already have a copy.

Grounds of appeal

11.18 The grounds of appeal must be attached to the form EXN161 and contain the information provided for in the CrimPR 50.20. Form EXN161 states that the grounds of appeal must:

- specify the date of arrest;[11]

8 These documents can follow when serving the perfected grounds of appeal (see paras 11.33–11.34).

9 It is prudent to include all documents that the appropriate judge had before them at the extradition hearing.

10 https://assets.publishing.service.gov.uk/government/uploads/system/uploads/attachment_data/file/943393/exn161-notes-eng.pdf

11 CrimPR 50.20(3)(a)(i).

- specify the decision which the appellant wants to appeal and the date of the decision that is being appealed;[12]
- specify whether the appellant is in custody and if so where the appellant is detained, their prison number, date of birth and the date the appellant was remanded into custody;
- specify the issues raised in the court below;
- provide an explanation if the appellant is raising an issue not raised at the extradition hearing or seeking to adduce evidence which was not available at the extradition hearing;
- identify each ground of appeal on which the appellant relies, numbering them consecutively (if there is more than one) and concisely outlining each argument in support;[13]
- summarise the relevant facts;[14]
- identify any relevant authorities;
- identify any other document or information that the appellant thinks the court will need to decide the permission to appeal and the appeal, if the court grants permission;[15]
- include or attach a list of those on whom the appellant has served the notice of appeal and the date of service;[16]
- where an appellant is in custody, include an application for
  - bail pending appeal, or
  - a direction that an unrepresented appellant be produced for the hearing of the appeal.

11.19 Where the appeal is against the decision of the appropriate judge and the ground is that the judge ought to have decided a question of fact or law at the extradition hearing differently, the notice must:

- identify that question;[17]
- explain what decision the magistrates' court should have made, and why;[18] and
- explain why the magistrates' court would have been required not to make the order under appeal, if that question had been decided differently.[19]

12 CrimPR 50.20(3)(a)(ii).
13 CrimPR 50.20(3)(b).
14 CrimPR 50.20(3)(c).
15 CrimPR 50.20(3)(d).
16 CrimPR 50.20(3)(e).
17 CrimPR 50.20(6)(a)(i).
18 CrimPR 50.20(6)(a)(ii).
19 CrimPR 50.20(6)(a)(iii).

11.20 If the grounds of appeal are that there is an issue which was not raised at the extradition hearing or that there is evidence now available that was not before the appropriate judge at the extradition hearing, then the appeal notice must also:

- identify that issue or evidence;[20]
- explain why the issue was not raised or the evidence not available at the extradition hearing;[21]
- explain why that issue or evidence would have resulted in the magistrates' court deciding a question differently at the extradition hearing;[22] and
- explain why, if the court had decided that question differently, the court would have been required not to make the order it made.[23]

11.21 The EXN161 states that the grounds of appeal, if drafted by counsel, must be signed by counsel with the name of counsel printed underneath their signature. This does not appear to be a requirement of the CrimPR or CrimPD and it is also unclear if solicitors will have to comply with the same requirement if the grounds of appeal have been prepared by them.

Court fee

11.22 Court fees are payable in extradition appeals and a party lodging the application must pay that fee when lodging the application[24]. However, unless the court directs otherwise, failure to pay the relevant fee will not result in the High Court refusing to accept the application in respect of which the court fee is due or dismiss an application for permission to appeal. Instead, the High Court must serve a notice on the defaulting party requiring payment of the fee within a period specified in the notice.[25] A party must then comply with the notice by the expiry of the period specified in the notice or risk having the application dismissed.

11.23 The fee for lodging the application for permission to appeal is £255. If lodging the application in person, attendance at the fees

20 CrimPR 50.20(6)(b)(i).
21 CrimPR 50.20(6)(b)(ii).
22 CrimPR 50.20(6)(b)(iii).
23 CrimPR 50.20(6)(b)(iv).
24 CrimPR 50.31(2).
25 CrimPR 50.31(3)(a).

office counter is, at the time of writing, by appointment only.[26] If lodging the application electronically, the practitioner can pay by debit or credit card by contacting the Fees Office on 0203 936 8957 between the hours of 10 am and 4 pm, Monday to Friday (except bank holidays); or by emailing: RCJfeespayments@justice.gov.uk. Once the payment has been processed, a receipt will be received which should be submitted with the appellant's notice. Practitioners should always check the up-to-date guidance provided by the Fees Office, which can be found on the Judiciary website.[27]

Lodging and service of the permission to appeal application

11.24 The EXN161 and grounds of appeal must be served on the CPS (extradition.ijoc@cps. gov.uk) and the NCA (Manchester@nca.x.gsi. gov.uk) prior to being lodged with the ACO[28] and a declaration of service must be completed on the form.

11.25 There is no need to serve any other document on the CPS or NCA as the grounds of appeal will identify the documents which the appellant thinks the court will need to decide the permission to appeal stage.

11.26 On paying the fee, the EXN161 will be stamped to show the fee has been paid. A receipt will also be provided. The documents should then be taken to the ACO (if lodging in person). A directions map is available at the enquiries counter to help those unfamiliar with the court to navigate to the fees office and on to the ACO.[29]

11.27 The ACO will issue the appeal and 'seal' the EXN161 by stamping it with the court seal and retain three copies of the bundles. The ACO can become very busy at certain times, and in particular between 3 pm and 4 pm, especially on a Friday afternoon. It is therefore important to allow plenty of time to lodge the appeal.

11.28 If lodging the application electronically, the EXN161, grounds of appeal and receipt for the payment of the court fee should be sent to

26 To make an appointment to attend the counter contact the Fees Office, Monday to Friday 10.00 am to 4.00 pm (except Bank Holidays), by phone (0203 936 8957) or by email feesofficecounterbooking@justice.gov.uk.

27 See: www.gov.uk/court-fees-what-they-are.

28 CrimPR 50.20(3)(e).

29 As a result of the restrictions imposed during the Coronavirus pandemic, practitioners intending to lodge applications in person at the ACO should check that the ACO is open to the public.

crimex@administrativecourtoffice.justice.gov.uk where the EXN161 will be sealed and returned.

11.29 Once the EXN161 has been sealed, it (along with the grounds of appeal) should be served upon the CPS and the NCA within the same seven-day period.[30]

Service of appeal notice out of time

11.30 An out of time application for permission to appeal can be made. The EA 2003 states where a person gives notice of application for leave to appeal after the end of the permitted period, the High Court must not for that reason refuse to entertain the application if the person did everything reasonably possible to ensure that the notice was given as soon as it could be given.[31]

11.31 If an extension of time for service of the EXN161 is required, detailed reasons for the delay must be provided and attached to the grounds of appeal under a separate heading explaining what was done to ensure that the notice was served as soon as it could be; attaching such evidence as the defendant relies upon to support that explanation.

11.32 On receipt of the application, it will be sent to a single judge within 24 hours for a decision on whether the court has jurisdiction to hear the application. If the single judge refuses the application for an extension of time, there is no right to renew the application.[32]

Amendments to the leave to appeal notice

11.33 An application for leave to appeal can be amended by serving an amended application on the High Court and the respondents by no later than *ten business days* after the service of the original appeal notice.[33] If the ten-business-day period has expired, then the application for permission to appeal notice may not be amended without the permission of the court.[34]

30 Although there is no requirement for this, the authors believe it is best practice for this to be done, despite the unsealed EX161 and grounds of appeal having to be served prior to the appeal being issued by the ACO.

31 EA 2003 s26(5)

32 *Oleantu-Ursache v Judecatoris Bacau, Romania* [2021] EWHC 1437 (Admin).

33 CrimPR 50.20(5)(a) and (b) and CrimPD 50B.18.

34 CrimPD 50B.18(i).

If the application to amend is made prior to permission to appeal being determined, then the application will be determined without a hearing.[35]

11.34 Ordinarily, practitioners will lodge a 'bare bones' EXN161 and grounds of appeal and 'perfect' the grounds of appeal within the ten business days permitted. An extension of the ten business-day period for amending the grounds of appeal can be granted by the court on application.[36] The applicant must give reasons for the application for an extension of time when making the application.[37]

Electronic filing of permission to appeal bundles

11.35 After the period for lodging amended grounds of appeal has expired, the practitioner should lodge an electronic permission to appeal bundle with the ACO using the Document Upload Centre (DUC). Any request to upload documents must be made by email to: crimex@administrativecourtoffice.justice.gov.uk.

11.36 The ACO provides the following guidance[38] for filing applications electronically:

> In all cases where the application is filed by a legal representative the electronic bundle must be prepared as below and be suitable for use with all of Adobe Acrobat Reader and PDF Expert and PDF Xchange Editor. The document:
> (a) must be a single PDF;
> (b) must be paginated in ascending order from start to finish. The first page of the PDF will be numbered "1", and so on. (Any original page numbers of documents within the bundle are to be ignored.) Index pages must be numbered as part of the single PDF document, they are not to be skipped; they are part of the single PDF and must be numbered. If a hard copy of the bundle is produced, the pagination on the hard copy must correspond exactly to the pagination of the PDF.
> (c) Wherever possible pagination should be computer-generated; if this is not possible, pagination must be in typed form.
> (d) The index page must be hyperlinked to the pages or documents it refers to.

35 CrimPD 50B.18(ii).

36 CrimPR 50.20(5).

37 CrimPR 50.17(7).

38 'Administrative Court Office guidance – Information for Court Users', 31 May 2021. https://assets.publishing.service.gov.uk/government/uploads/system/uploads/attachment_data/file/1000961/RCJ_Administrative_Court_Information_for_Court_Users_6_July.pdf

(e) Each document within the bundle must be identified in the sidebar list of contents/bookmarks, by date and description (e.g., 'email 11.9.21 from [x] to [y]'). The sidebar list must also show the bundle page number of the document.
(f) All bundles must be text based, not a scan of a hard copy bundle. If documents within a bundle have been scanned, optical character recognition should be undertaken on the bundle before it is lodged. (This is the process which turns the document from a mere picture of a document to one in which the text can be read as text so that the document becomes word-searchable, and words can be highlighted in the process of marking them up.) The text within the bundle must therefore be selectable as text, to facilitate highlighting and copying.
(g) Any document in landscape format must be rotated so that it can be read from left to right.
(h) The default display view size of all pages must always be 100%.
(i) The resolution on the electronic bundle must be reduced to about 200 to 300 dpi to prevent delays whilst scrolling from one page to another.
(j) The index page must be hyperlinked to the pages or documents it refers to.
(k) If a bundle is to be added to after the document has been filed, it should not be assumed the judge will accept a new replacement bundle because he/she may already have started to mark up the original. Enquiries should be made of the judge as to what the judge would like to do about it. Absent a particular direction, any pages to be added to the bundle as originally filed should be provided separately, in a separate document, with pages appropriately sub-numbered.

11.37 If the papers in support of an extradition appeal exceed 20MB, the appellant should file:

a) a core bundle (no larger than 20MB) which includes:
   i) the appellant's notice;
   ii) grounds (or amended grounds of appeal);
   iii) the decision challenged (Ruling of the appropriate judge or decision by the secretary of state (Part 2 cases);
   iv) the arrest warrant (Part 1 cases) or the certification request by the secretary of state and arrest warrant (Part 2 cases);
   v) the respondent's notice;
   vi) the witness statement (or primary witness statement) relied on in support of the appeal; and
   vii) any other documents regarded as essential to the appeal.
b) a further bundle containing any remaining documents.

11.38 Any application filed that does not comply with the above rules on electronic bundles may not be considered by a judge. If the application is filed by a litigant in person the electronic bundle must if at all possible, comply with the above rules. If it is not possible for a litigant in person to comply with the rules on electronic bundles, the application must include a brief explanation of the reasons why.

The Document Upload Centre

11.39 The DUC allows users to upload bundles for use in court hearings where email restrictions do not allow for large attachments to be sent in a single email.

11.40 Guidance provided by HM Courts and Tribunals Service (HMCTS) on the use of the DUC can be found on the website.[39]

Applying for leave to appeal in Part 2 cases

11.41 Under EA 2003 Part 2, it is the appropriate judge that sends the case to the Secretary of State for the Home Department (SSHD), who then has a two-month period in which to make the extradition order, starting on the day on which the case is sent to the SSHD.[40] Once the extradition order has been signed by the SSHD, the requested person has *14 days* in which to lodge the application for permission to appeal starting from the date he is informed of the SSHD's decision.

11.42 An appeal can be against i) the decision of the appropriate judge and/or ii) the decision of the SSHD.

11.43 The following documents should be put together in a bundle to be lodged at the High Court either in person or electronically (see above):

- Form EXN161 – appellant's notice – application for permission to appeal;
- grounds of appeal;
- extradition request;
- judgment of the appropriate judge;
- decision of the SSHD (if the decision has been made);
- any other documents relied upon (witness statements, expert reports, further information).

39 https://assets.publishing.service.gov.uk/government/uploads/system/uploads/attachment_data/file/887109/Document_Upload_Centre_-_Professional_User.pdf

40 See *Zaporozhchenko and another v Westminster Magistrates' Court and others* [2011] EWHC 34 (Admin).

11.44 The EXN161 and grounds of appeal must be served on the CPS (extradition.ijoc@cps. gov.uk) and the SSHD[41] prior to being lodged with the ACO[42] and a declaration of service must be completed on the form.

11.45 The appellant's notice (EXN161) and grounds of appeal are to take the same form as that outlined at paras 11.15–11.21 above and the process for lodging the application for permission to appeal is the same as set out in paras 11.24–11.29. If the appeal is against the decision of the SSHD, the information set out in Crim PR 50.20(7) must also be provided in the appellant's notice and grounds of appeal.

11.46 The sealed appellant's notice and grounds of appeal should be served on the CPS and the SSHD regardless of whether there is an application to apply for permission to appeal the decision of the SSHD. An application for leave to appeal can be amended by serving an amended application on the High Court and the respondents by no later than ten business days after the service of the original appeal notice (see paras 11.33–11.34 above).

Service of appeal notice out of time

11.47 As with Part 1 appeals (see para 11.30), the High Court must not refuse to entertain the application where notice is given after the end of the permitted period if the person did everything reasonably possible to ensure that the notice was given as soon as it could be given.

11.48 The notes to CrimPR 50.19 go further and state that 'a defendant may apply out of time for permission to appeal to the High Court on human rights grounds against an order for extradition made by the Secretary of State'[43] but the notice must explain why:

- the appeal is necessary to avoid real injustice;[44] and
- the circumstances are exceptional and make it appropriate to consider the appeal.[45]

11.49 Application notices must be accompanied by a witness statement setting out the reasons for non- compliance with any previous order and the proposed timetable for compliance.[46]

41 Details of who to serve upon will be provided in the covering letter enclosing the Extradition Order.

42 CrimPR 50.20(3)(e).

43 CrimPR 50.20(4)(b).

44 CrimPR 50.20(4)(b)(i).

45 CrimPR 50.20(4)(b)(ii).

46 CrimPD 50D.1(iii).

11.50 If the single judge refuses the application for an extension of time, there is no right to renew the application.[47]

Respondent's notice – form EXN162

11.51 CrimPR 50.21(1) imposes an obligation upon a party to file a respondent's notice if they wish to make representations to the High Court or if the court so directs. The respondent's notice must be served on the High Court, the appellant and any other person on whom the appellant served the appeal notice and must be served no more than *ten business days* after:

- service on that party of an amended appeal notice under CrimPR 50.20(5), or
- the expiry of the time or service of any such amended appeal notice, whichever of those events happens first.

The High Court may extend or shorten the time limit for service of a respondent's notice under this rule.[48] Reasons must be given for the application to extend the time limit[49] and applications must be accompanied by a witness statement.

11.52 The respondent's notice should be completed using form EXN162. Guidance for the completion of form EXN162 can also be found on the ACO website.[50]

11.53 The respondent's notice must provide the information contained within CrimPR 50.21(4), namely:

(a) the date on which the respondent was served with, as appropriate:
  (i) the appeal notice;
  (ii) the appellant's notice renewing the application for permission to appeal;
  (iii) a direction to serve a respondent's notice;
(b) each ground of opposition on which the respondent relies, identifying the grounds of appeal to which each relates;
(c) summary of any relevant facts not already summarised in the appeal notice; and

47 *Oleantu-Ursache v Judecatoris Bacau, Romania* [2021] EWHC 1437 (Admin).

48 CrimPR 50.17(7).

49 CrimPR 50.17(7)(b).

50 See: www.justice.gov.uk/courts/procedure-rules/criminal/docs/october-2015/exn162-notes-eng.pdf.

(d) identification of any other document or material that the appellant thinks the court will need to decide the permission to appeal and the appeal, if the court grants permission.

11.54 Amendments to a respondent's notice cannot be made without permission of the court.[51]

11.55 Respondents' notices and bundles must be filed electronically with the ACO using the Document Upload Centre. Any request to upload documents must be made by the practitioner by email to crimex@administrativecourtoffice.justice.gov.uk (see para 11.39 above).

Consideration of the application for permission to appeal

11.56 An application for permission to appeal will usually be considered on the papers without a hearing[52] by a single judge of the High Court. There may be occasions where leave to appeal is determined at a hearing. The court has the power to refuse or grant permission to appeal, or to give permission, but not on every ground identified in the appeal notice.

11.57 The test applied to the permission stage is whether the ground(s) of appeal are 'reasonably arguable.'[53]

11.58 There does not appear to be any requirement on the High Court to give reasons for its decision, although in practice the single judge will give detailed reasons for their decision.

11.59 If permission is granted, then the court must give directions as are required for the preparation and hearing of the appeal.[54] In Part 2 cases, the court may direct that a case management hearing takes place (see para 11.74).

Renewing an application for permission to appeal (Parts 1 and 2 cases)

11.60 If the decision to refuse to give permission to appeal is made at an oral hearing, there is no right to renew that application.[55]

51 CrimPD 50B.19(i).
52 CrimPR 50.17(1)(b)(i).
53 CrimPR 50.17(4)(b).
54 CrimPR 50.17(4)(c).
55 CrimPR 50.22(2).

11.61 If the decision is made on the papers, then the appellant may renew the application to the High Court to be determined by a single judge of the High Court[56] (other than by the judge who determined permission) or a Divisional Court at an oral hearing.[57] No dates to avoid are taken into consideration when fixing the date for an oral hearing.

11.62 The renewal notice (form EXREN) must explain the grounds for renewal[58] and should comply with the guidance given in *Opalfvens v Public Prosecutor Antwerp, Belgium*[59] by addressing the decision of the single judge and submitting why it was wrong:

> It will be clear, once proper consideration is given to the rule, that renewal requires thought. The grounds for renewal must grapple with the reasons given by the single judge and set out, briefly and concisely, why it is said the judge's decision was wrong. If that is not done, the appellant may be held to have failed to lodge grounds for renewal, to have failed to have applied for renewal, and the matter may be dismissed without a renewal hearing.

11.63 No fee applies to the lodging of a renewed application for permission to appeal, although a fee is payable for an application to renew permission to appeal out of time.

11.64 If the court decides to give permission to appeal, but not on every ground identified in the appeal notice, then any application to renew must specify which ground or grounds are renewed and explain the grounds for renewal.

11.65 An application to renew is given by serving notice on the High Court, the respondent and the NCA in a Part 1 case; or the High Court, CPS and SSHD in a Part 2 case. This must be done no later than *five business days* after service of the court's decision on the appellant.[60] If the timeframe is not complied with, an application to renew out of time will need to be lodged. CrimPR 50.17 gives the High Court the power to extend or shorten the time limits specified for renewing an application for permission to appeal. A respondent's notice may be served not more than 5 business days after service of the appellant's notice renewing an application for permission to appeal (CrimPR 50.21(3)(b)(i)).

56 CrimPR 50.30(3)(a).
57 CrimPR 50.30(3)(b).
58 CrimPR 50.22(3).
59 [2015] EWHC 2808 (Admin) at para 14.
60 CrimPR 50.22(2).

Renewal application made out of time

11.66 If an application to renew is made out of time, and the judge who considers the papers refuses the application for an extension of time, there is no right to renew the application.[61]

There is no jurisdiction to entertain a renewed application for an extension of time for making a renewed application for permission to appeal against an extradition order.[62]

11.67 If an applicant does not seek to renew the refusal of permission to appeal on the original grounds, but seeks to renew so that they can raise a fresh ground of appeal, then (a) their grounds for renewal must make that position clear; and (b) the application for renewal must be accompanied by an application for an extension of time to apply for permission to amend the grounds of appeal, with full reasons provided. If this is not complied with, then the application is likely to be treated as inadequate and may be dismissed.

Permission granted – the appeal

11.68 Under EA 2003 s31, an appeal under Part 1 of the Act must begin to be heard within 40 days of the person's arrest.[63]

11.69 Appeals under Part 2 of the Act should begin within 76 days[64] after the later of:

- service of the appeal notice; or
- the day on which the SSHD informs the appellant of the SSHD's order, in a case in which:
  - the appeal is by the appellant against an order by the magistrate's court sending the case to the SSHD; and
  - the appeal notice is served before the SSHD decides whether the appellant should be extradited.

11.70 The above prescribed time limits for the hearing of appeals may be extended if the High Court believes it to be in the interests of justice to do so and the court may make such an order even if the time limit for the hearing of the appeal has expired.[65] The power to extend time

61 *Oleantu-Ursache v Judecatoris Bacau, Romania* [2021] EWHC 1437 (Admin).

62 *Oleantu-Ursache v Judecatoris Bacau, Romania* [2021] EWHC 1437 (Admin) at para 38.

63 CrimPR 50.23(1).

64 CrimPR 50.23(2).

65 CrimPD 50B.8.

may be exercised by a Lord Justice of Appeal, a single judge of the High Court, a Master of the Administrative Court or a nominated legal officer of the court.[66]

11.71 An appeal may be determined by a single judge of the High Court or a Divisional Court.[67]

Date for hearing

11.72 The Listing Office is responsible for the listing of appeal hearings under the guidance of the judge with overall responsibility for supervision of extradition appeal.[68] The Listing Office aims to fix a date for the substantive appeal within two weeks of receiving dates to avoid, and if a date has not been fixed within this timeframe then up-to-date dates to avoid will be requested.

11.73 If a party disagrees with a time estimate given by the court for a hearing, then they must, within 24 hours of the notification of the listing, inform the Listing Office and provide their time estimate.[69] Regard will not usually be given to counsel's existing commitments.[70]

Case management hearing

11.74 If the court so directs, a case management hearing will be listed after leave to appeal has been granted.

11.75 The case management hearing will be held before a Lord Justice of Appeal, a Single Judge of the High Court or a master or nominated legal officer of the Administrative Court.[71] The purpose of the case management hearing is to provide effective management of the appeal to ensure that the appeal takes place on the date fixed for hearing. Five days before the case management hearing, the parties will be expected to send to the court office a document providing the following information:

- a time estimate for the appeal hearing including delivery of the judgment;

66 CrimPD 50B.9.
67 CrimPR 50.30(4)(a) and (b).
68 Currently Lord Justice Holroyde.
69 CrimPD 50B.14.
70 CrimPD 50B.13.
71 CrimPD 50B.10.

- names of counsel and a list of dates to avoid for listing of the substantive appeal;
- a list of issues for the case management hearing (if any);
- a list of the legal points to be taken at the appeal (together with any relevant authorities, with page references to passages relied on);
- a chronology of events;
- a list of the essential documents for the advance reading of the court;
- the case for any further evidence to be adduced, having regard to the provisions set out in *The Szombathely City Court v Fenyvesi*;[72]
- a date for the exchange of evidence that the parties may be permitted to rely upon;
- a date for replies following exchange of evidence;
- a date for the parties to provide joint bundles;
- any further directions necessary for the appeal to proceed without delay that the master ought to consider.

11.76 The purpose of providing dates to avoid and a time estimate five days in advance of the case management hearing is to enable the list office to fix a date for the appeal so that all parties at the conference have an opportunity to consider whether it allows sufficient time for the preparation of the appeal. If insufficient time has been set aside for the appeal hearing, an application should be made at the case management conference for the date to be vacated and re-fixed. The reason that more time is required should be identified in the documents to be provided to the master ahead of the conference.

11.77 The court will expect the parties to the appeal to reach agreement (as far as is possible) as to the directions to be applied that are necessary to ensure that the appeal will be heard on the date fixed.

11.78 Case management hearings take place in open court and therefore only barristers or solicitors with higher rights of audience may appear.

Applications for bail

11.79 An application for bail is made by lodging an application notice (EX244) and paying a fee of £255. The application for bail will be treated as an interlocutory application within the appeal and will therefore attract the same court reference number as the existing appeal.

72 [2009] EWHC 231 (Admin).

Compliance with directions made by the High Court

11.80 It is important to comply with all directions made by the High Court (as with any court). Where a direction cannot be complied with, the court should be notified of the reasons why and an extension sought in a formal application by lodging form EX244 application notice, together with the relevant fee.

11.81 Any application to vary directions should be made promptly before the deadline for compliance has passed in order to seek further directions. An application to vary directions attracts a fee and the application must:

- provide full and proper explanations as to why the current directions have not been complied with;
- set out the views of the other parties to the appeal; and
- include a draft order with the timetable for directions going forward.[73]

11.82 A failure to seek a variation in directions before the expiry of the deadline will generally result in the refusal of the application unless good reasons are shown.[74] It is therefore important to provide a detailed application setting out the reasons why the directions could not be complied with and saying why no application to vary was made prior to the expiry of the deadline. Practitioners' attention is specifically drawn to CrimPD 50F.2 and 50F.3 which state:

> 50F.2 Judges dealing with extradition appeals will seek full and proper explanations for any breaches of the rules and the provisions of this Practice Direction.
>
> 50F.3 If no good explanation can be given immediately by counsel or solicitors, the senior partner of the departmental head responsible is likely to be called to court to explain any failure to comply with a court order. Where counsel or solicitors fail to obey orders of the court and are unable to provide proper and sufficient reasons for their disobedience they may anticipate the matter being formally referred to the President of the Queen's Bench Division with a recommendation that the counsel or solicitors involved be reported to their professional bodies.

11.83 Whenever corresponding with the ACO, it is important to ensure that the case reference number is included so that court staff can

73 CrimPD 50D.7.

74 CrimPD 50D.8.

identify the case more easily. Misspelt names can cause delays and result in misfiling. If documents are to be sent to the judge's clerk, these should be copied to the extradition team by email: crimex@administrativecourtoffice.justice.gov.uk.

Applying to extend the representation order

11.84 The representation order covers the work of a solicitor and junior counsel. Applications to extend the representation order for a Queen's Counsel (QC) and junior, QC alone, translation of documents or the cost of an expert, must be made in writing to the ACO. Applications to extend representation orders are not subject to any court fee[75] and can be sent via email to: crimex@administrativecourtoffice.justice.gov.uk.

11.85 The applications will be considered by a Lord Justice of Appeal, a single judge of the High Court, a master of the Administrative Court or a nominated Court Officer on the papers although they may order that the matter be dealt with at a case management hearing.

Application to instruct a QC

11.86 An application can be made to extend the representation order to cover a QC and junior counsel or a QC alone. The application must include the following information:[76]

- the substantial novel or complex issues of law or fact in the case;
- why these may only be adequately presented by a QC;
- whether a QC has been instructed on behalf of the respondent;
- an explanation for any delay in making the request.

11.87 The application must be supported by an advice from junior or leading counsel.

Expert evidence

11.88 An application to extend the representation order to include the cost of obtaining expert evidence must include[77] (where applicable):

75 CrimPD 50B.27.

76 CrimPD 50C.3.

77 In accordance with CrimPD 50C.4.

- confirmation that the evidence sought has not been considered in any previous appeals determined by the appellate courts;
- an explanation of why the new evidence was not called at the extradition hearing at WMC and what evidence can be produced to support that;
- an explanation of why the new evidence would have resulted in the district judge deciding a question at the extradition hearing differently and whether, if so, the district judge would have been required to make a different order as to discharge of the requested person;
- an explanation of why the evidence was not raised when the case was being considered by the SSHD or information was available that was not available at the time;
- an explanation of why the new evidence would have resulted in the SSHD deciding a question differently, and why, had the question been decided differently, the SSHD would not have ordered the person's extradition;
- an indication of when the need for the new evidence first became known;
- an explanation of any delay in making the request;
- an explanation of what relevant factual (as opposed to expert) evidence is being given, and by whom, to create the factual basis for the expert's opinion;
- an explanation of why this particular area of expertise is relevant: for example, why a child psychologist should be appointed as opposed to an independent social worker;
- an indication of whether the requested person has capacity;
- in legal aid cases, a full breakdown of all costs involved including any VAT or other tax payable, including alternative quotes or explaining why none are available;
- a list of all previous extensions of the representation order and the approval of expenditure to date;
- a timetable for the production of the evidence and its anticipated effect on the time estimate and hearing date;
- an indication of the level of compliance to date with any directions order.

Expert status

11.89 Only experts that have direct personal experience of and proven expertise in the issue upon which a report is sought will be considered for expert status[78]. In *Brazuks and Others v Prosecutor General's Office, Latvia*[79] Collins J provided guidance for expert reports and experts. He stated, at para 42:

> I should say a word about the experts' reports which have been put forward. No doubt it is helpful to identify the material available in reports on prison conditions in any requesting state. That material can then be produced to the court and any relevant matters referred to in support of any submissions. The views of an expert are not relevant and probably not admissible since it is for the judge to decide on the evidence produced whether there is a real risk of any material ill-treatment. Approval should not be given to pay such experts who have no direct personal experience of the conditions in a particular country. If they do have such experience and it is relevant, they can of course give evidence of what they have observed. They may also have knowledge of the economic situation or of any views expressed by government officials which may mean that any shortcomings will not be likely to be dealt with. Thus their knowledge of the existing situation and their added knowledge of the prospects of improvements may entitle them to put forward expert opinions. But if they do not have any such expertise, they will be doing no more than giving factual evidence.

11.90 The fact that the court has extended a representation order to include the costs of an expert does not necessarily mean the expert report will be admitted into evidence. The normal rules of having new evidence admitted on appeal apply[80] (see para 11.101).

Other disbursements

11.91 Other reasons for applying to extend the representation order could be to cover the cost of disbursements such as the translation of long documents. Such an application to the court will act as 'prior authority' but will not enable the solicitors to obtain an interim payment.

11.92 The application must:[81]

- explain the importance of the document for which a translation is being sought and the justification for obtaining it;
- explain the contents of the document and the issues those contents will address to assist the court in hearing the appeal;

78 CrimPD 50C.5.
79 [2014] EWHC 1021 (Admin).
80 CrimPD 50C.8.
81 CrimPD 50C.7.

- confirm that the evidence sought has not been considered in any previous appeals determined by the appellate courts;
- confirm that the evidence sought was not called at the extradition hearing;
- explain why the evidence sought would have resulted in the district judge deciding a question at the extradition hearing differently and, if this were the case, whether the district judge would have been required to make a different order as to discharge the requested person;
- confirm that the new evidence was not raised when the case was being considered by the SSHD (Part 2 cases only);
- explain why the new evidence would have resulted in the SSHD deciding a question differently, and if the question had been decided differently, that the SSHD would not have ordered the person's extradition (Part 2 cases only);
- confirm when the need for the new evidence first became known;
- explain any delay in making the request;
- explain fully the evidential basis for incurring the expenditure;
- explain why the appellant cannot produce the evidence himself or herself in the form of a statement of truth;
- in legal aid cases, set out a full breakdown of all costs involved including any VAT or other tax payable, including alternative quotes or explaining why none are available;
- provide a list of all previous extensions of the representation order and the approval of expenditure to date.

11.93 The party seeking to rely on the new evidence, notwithstanding the extension of a representation order, must still persuade the court that the new evidence should be admitted.[82]

Applications to adjourn

11.94 Once a date has been fixed, it can only be vacated on written application to the court. Any application to adjourn should be made on form EX244 and be accompanied by a signed witness statement. If the issue is relatively straightforward, the witness statement can be contained within the EX244. The application must comply with CrimPD 50D.4 and must therefore:

82 CrimPD 50C.8.

i) explain the reasons why the application to vacate the hearing is being made;
ii) detail the views of the other parties to the appeal; and
iii) include a draft order, attached to the application notice setting out the orders sought.

Exceptional circumstances must be shown if a date for the hearing has been fixed or the adjournment (if granted) will result in material delay to the determination of the appeal.[83]

11.95 A fee is applicable if the application to adjourn is made within 14 days of the hearing date.[84]

11.96 The EX244 should be lodged with the ACO and served upon the CPS and NCA in Part 1 matters; or the CPS and SSHD for Part 2 matters.

11.97 An application to adjourn will normally be dealt with on the papers by a nominated court officer unless the papers are already with the single judge or Divisional Court, in which case the decision will be made by the single judge or the presiding judge of the Divisional Court. If the parties to an appeal both seek an adjournment the application must be submitted for consideration by a Lord Justice of Appeal, a Single Judge of the High Court or a Master of the Administrative Court.[85]

Applications to amend the appeal notice or grounds of appeal

11.98 An application to amend the appeal notice or grounds of appeal after permission has been granted will normally be dealt with at the hearing unless there is any risk that the proposed amendment may lead to the hearing being adjourned.[86] If the application to amend is likely to lead to the other party having to seek time to answer the proposed amendment, then the application to amend must be made as soon as practicable and in any event, well in advance of the appeal hearing. A failure to make the application as soon as possible may lead to a refusal to amend.

11.99 Practitioners must inform the court at the time the application to amend is made if the time estimate is likely to be affected by the

83 CrimPD 50D.5.
84 CrimPD 50D.4.
85 CrimPD 50D.5.
86 CrimPD 50B.18(iii).

proposed amendment[87] and must attempt to agree a revised time estimate with the other party no later than five business days after service of the application.[88]

11.100 Applications to amend the appeal notice and/or the grounds of appeal must be made using form EX244 and be accompanied by the relevant fee.

Introduction of new evidence

11.101 Strict rules apply to the introduction of new evidence being adduced on appeal. The introduction of fresh evidence was considered in *The Szombathely City Court v Fenyvesi*.[89]

11.102 The Divisional Court considered the provisions in EA 2003 s29(4), in particular where evidence was available on appeal that was not available at the extradition hearing. The court held that 'not available at the extradition hearing' was to be interpreted as evidence which either did not exist at the time of the extradition hearing, or was not at the disposal of the party wishing to adduce it and that they could not with reasonable diligence have produced.

11.103 Following the case of *Fenyvesi*, a party wishing to adduce fresh evidence must submit a witness statement explaining why the evidence was not available at the extradition hearing.

11.104 When considering whether to admit fresh evidence, the court must consider it to be decisive – in other words, the court must be satisfied that the evidence would have resulted in the appropriate judge deciding the relevant question differently.

11.105 Appellants should not 'keep their powder dry' and adduce fresh evidence on appeal or raise new issues that could have been presented before the appropriate judge at first instance. However, there is a material difference between seeking to adduce fresh evidence on appeal that could have been available before the appropriate judge and raising a new issue that was not argued at first instance. In *Hoholm v Government of Norway*[90] Stanley Burnton LJ held:

> ... it seems to me to be significant that section 104 distinguishes between a new issue and new evidence. I would therefore hold that where an issue was available to be raised by an appellant on the

87 CrimPD 50B.18(iv)(a).
88 CrimPD 50B.18(iv)(b).
89 [2009] EWHC 231 (Admin).
90 [2009] EWHC 1513 (Admin) at para 19.

evidence adduced at the extradition hearing, she is in general, if not always, entitled to raise that issue on appeal to this Court, even though the issue was not raised at that hearing. In any event, I see no good reason why the Appellant should not be permitted to argue the issue before this Court. Extradition is an infringement of liberty, and while the Court is concerned to ensure that those who are the subject of conforming requests for extradition are lawfully extradited, the legal requirements for extradition are safeguards that must be observed.

11.106 It is therefore possible to raise an issue on appeal (such as dual criminality, validity of the warrant) that was not raised at the extradition hearing, provided no new evidence is to be adduced. However, practitioners should be aware of the opposing views proffered in *Khan v Government of the United States of America*[91] and *Koziel v Poland*[92] and take note of the ruling of Bean, J in *R (Soltysiak) v Judicial Authority of Poland*[93] in which he said:[94]

> I am also in no doubt that until or unless this issue is resolved authoritatively, possibly by a three judge Divisional Court or perhaps by a still higher court, it is the duty of advocates to ensure that this court, when it is sought to raise a point of law not taken below, is made aware of both Hoholm and Khan.

11.107 If new evidence is to be adduced, then the criteria in *Fenyvesi* must be satisfied.

11.108 If a new issue and/or fresh evidence are to be raised on appeal that was not raised at the extradition hearing by previous legal representatives, and if specific criticism of the previous legal representatives is being levelled, then the guidance set out in *Sondy v Crown Prosecution Service*[95] should be followed. Openshaw J stated:

> In my judgment, the practice commonly followed in the Court of Appeal Criminal Division should have been followed here; the appellant should have been formally invited to waive his privilege and, whether he did so or not, the lawyers should have been asked by the court to deal with the points made against them, having regard to whether privilege has been waived or not. If the appellant did not waive privilege, then of course an adverse inference could in any event be drawn against him.

91 [2010] EWHC 1127 (Admin).
92 [2011] EWHC 3781 (Admin).
93 [2011] EWHC 1338 (Admin).
94 At para 18.
95 [2010] EWHC 108 (Admin) at para 6.

Withdrawing the appeal

11.109 If the appellant wishes to withdraw an appeal, the solicitor must notify the High Court, other parties to the appeal and any other person on whom the appeal notice was served.[96]

11.110 When serving notice of withdrawal of the appeal on form EX244, a joint notice consenting to the dismissal of the appeal must be included that sets out an agreement between the parties about costs. The wording of the consent order will differ depending on the stage when proceedings are withdrawn. A fee is applicable for the application.

Applying to come off the record

11.111 It may sometimes be necessary for the solicitors instructed to withdraw from the case for professional reasons, for example if the client wishes to pursue an appeal against the advice of the solicitor.

11.112 Any application made to come off the record must be made at least seven business days before the hearing of the appeal.[97]

11.113 An application to come off the record must be accompanied by a statement of truth and contain:

- proper and sufficient reasons why the solicitor wishes to come off record (without breaching client confidentiality);
- confirmation that the solicitor has complied with orders made by the High Court before the application to come off the record was made or an explanation as to why there has been non-compliance;
- confirmation that where the appellant is on bail, they have been advised of the time and date of the appeal hearing and the need to attend in person;
- identifying, where the appellant is in custody, the prison in which they are held, their prison number and date of birth.

11.114 Once submitted with the relevant fee, the application will be determined by a Lord Justice of Appeal, a single judge of the High Court, a master of the Administrative Court or a nominated legal officer of the court.

96 CrimPR 50.24(2).
97 CrimPD 50D.2.

Preparing the appeal

Skeleton arguments

11.115 Skeleton arguments will normally be drafted by instructed counsel but should be considered (and amended where necessary, by agreement with counsel) by the solicitor before it is submitted. Skeleton arguments can be submitted electronically to: crimex@administrativecourtoffice.justice.gov.uk.

11.116 CrimPD 50E.2 sets out guidance as to the format of the skeleton argument. A skeleton argument must:

- not normally exceed 25 pages (excluding front sheets and back sheets) and be concise;
- be printed on A4 paper in not less than 12 point font and 1.5 line spacing;
- define the issues in the appeal;
- be set out in numbered paragraphs;
- be cross-referenced to any relevant document in the bundle;
- be self-contained and not incorporate by reference material from previous skeleton arguments;
- not include extensive quotations from documents or authorities.

11.117 Where skeleton arguments refer to an authority, they must also:[98]

- state the proposition of law the authority demonstrates; and
- identify but not quote the parts of the authority that support the proposition.

11.118 If more than one authority is cited in support of a given proposition, the skeleton argument must state why.[99]

11.119 A chronology of relevant events will be necessary in most appeals and should be incorporated into the skeleton argument.[100]

11.120 If a skeleton argument has been submitted in support of the application for leave to appeal then it may be relied upon in the appeal upon notice being given to the court. Alternatively, a replacement skeleton argument may be lodged not less than *ten business days* before the hearing of the appeal.[101]

98 CrimPD 50E.3.
99 CrimPD 50E.4.
100 CrimPD 50E.5.
101 CrimPD 50E.6.

11.121 Practitioners should take note that the court may refuse to hear submissions on a point if it is not included in the skeleton argument served within the prescribed time.[102]

Bundles for the appeal hearing

11.122 Practitioners should check with the ACO whether the judge(s) hearing the appeal would like hard copy bundles, electronic bundles, or both. If the court requests electronic bundles (in addition to or in lieu of hard copy bundles) they should be submitted via the Document Upload Centre (see para 11.39).

11.123 A joint bundle should be provided to the court that has been agreed between the parties. If the appeal is to be heard by a single judge, two bundles should be provided to the court. If the case has been allocated to a Divisional Court, three bundles will be required.

11.124 The bundle should be paginated and indexed[103] and should include the following documents:[104]

- a copy of the appellant's notice;
- a copy of any respondent's notice;
- a copy of any appellant's or respondent's skeleton argument;
- a copy of the order under appeal;
- a copy of any order made by the court in the exercise of its case management powers;
- any judgment of the court made in a previous appeal involving the party or parties which is relevant to the present proceedings.

11.125 Where the bundle of papers in the joint bundle exceeds 200 pages, the parties must agree a core appeal[105] bundle that must include the documents set out above.

11.126 Authorities relied upon should also be included in the bundle. If there is a law report of the authority, that should be provided to the court.

Role of the appellate court and test to be applied

11.127 In determining the statutory provisions relating to an appeal (see below), the single question for the appellate court to answer is

102 CrimPD 50E.7.
103 CrimPD 50E.9.
104 CrimPD 50E.10.
105 CrimPD 50E.10(vii).

whether or not the appropriate judge made the wrong decision. Lord Neuberger in *Re B (a child) (FC)*[106] set out at paras 93–94 the ways in which an appellate court might consider a trial judge's conclusions:

> 93. There is a danger in over-analysis, but I would add this. An appellate judge may conclude that the trial judge's conclusion on proportionality was (i) the only possible view, (ii) a view which she considers was right, (iii) a view on which she has doubts, but on balance considers was right, (iv) a view which she cannot say was right or wrong, (v) a view on which she has doubts, but on balance considers was wrong, (vi) a view which she considers was wrong, or (vii) a view which is unsupportable. The appeal must be dismissed if the appellate judge's view is in category (i) to (iv) and allowed if it is in category (vi) or (vii).
> 94. As to category (iv), there will be a number of cases where an appellate court may think that there is no right answer, in the sense that reasonable judges could differ in their conclusions. As with many evaluative assessments, cases raising an issue on proportionality will include those where the answer is in a grey area, as well as those where the answer is in a black or a white area. An appellate court is much less likely to conclude that category (iv) applies in cases where the trial judge's decision was not based on his assessment of the witnesses' reliability or likely future conduct. So far as category (v) is concerned, the appellate judge should think very carefully about the benefit the trial judge had in seeing the witnesses and hearing the evidence, which are factors whose significance depends on the particular case. However, if, after such anxious consideration, an appellate judge adheres to her view that the trial judge's decision was wrong, then I think that she should allow the appeal.

11.128 This approach was endorsed in an extradition context by the Lord Chief Justice in *Polish Judicial Authorities v Celinski and others*:[107]

> It is only if the court concludes that the decision was wrong, applying what Lord Neuberger said [in *Re B (a child)*], that the appeal can be allowed. Findings of fact, especially if evidence has been heard, must ordinarily be respected. In answering the question whether the district judge, in the light of those findings of fact, was wrong to decide that extradition was or was not proportionate, the focus must be on the outcome, that is on the decision itself. Although the district judge's reasons for the proportionality decision must be considered with care, errors and omissions do not of themselves necessarily show that the decision on proportionality itself was wrong.

106 [2013] UKSC 33.
107 [2015] EWHC 1274 (Admin) at para 24.

11.129 The LCJ reiterated that findings of fact, especially if live evidence has been heard and evaluated by the appropriate judge, should ordinarily be respected.

11.130 The rationale for this was expressed by Knowles J in the case of *Kotsev v Bulgaria*:[108]

> ... an appellate court which does not hear evidence is often at a disadvantage in relation to the court which did hear the evidence and so had an opportunity to assess the witnesses' demeanour etc, as part of its fact-finding function ...

11.131 The summary of the test to apply on appeal was set out in the decision in *India v Chawla*:[109]

> It is established that when considering what approach to take to a challenge to a District Judge's findings about real risks of infringement of human rights the Court must have 'a very high respect for the findings of fact', 'we must also have respect for the DJ's evaluation of the expert evidence', and 'the decision of the DJ can only be successfully challenged if it is demonstrated that it is "wrong"', see *United States of America v Giese* at paragraph 15 and *Dzgoev v Russian Federation* [2017] EWHC 735 (Admin) at paragraphs 23 and 24.

11.132 In *Mallya v Government of India*[110] the court observed:

> [T]he applicant faces the potential difficulty that it is, of course, not the function of an appellate court in an extradition case, any more than in any other type of case, to repeat the fact-finding exercise undertaken by the lower court. In order to persuade an appellate court to interfere with findings of fact made by a lower court after hearing and receiving evidence, particularly in a case such as this involving a very substantial volume of evidence, it is necessary to identify a material error of law or other demonstrable error in the lower court's process of reasoning, or to persuade the appellate court that the lower court has made findings for which there was no reasonable evidential basis or otherwise reached a conclusion which no reasonable judge could have reached.

11.133 An appellate court will only interfere with the judge's decision if it concludes that the statutory question 'ought to have been decided differently because the overall evaluation was wrong: crucial factors should have been weighed so significantly differently as to make the decision wrong, such that the appeal in consequence should be allowed.'[111]

108 [2018] EWHC 3087 (Admin) at para 26.
109 [2018] EWHC 1050 (Admin) at para 35.
110 [2020] EWHC 924 (Admin) at para 21.
111 *Love v Government of the United States of America* [2018] EWHC 172 (Admin) at para 26.

11.134 If fresh evidence is admitted into evidence on appeal, then the appellate court may have to conduct the balancing exercise itself so as to determine whether it would have altered the appropriate judge's decision. Note, however, the comments of the Divisional Court in *Belbin*[112] in which the court refused to admit fresh evidence as it would not have resulted in the appropriate judge deciding the question differently.[113] Any fresh evidence submitted must therefore be decisive (see para 11.104).

11.135 It is clear from the above that the threshold for overturning a decision made by an appropriate judge is a high one, not easily surmounted.

Court's powers on appeal in Part 1 cases

11.136 On appeal under section 26 the High Court may either allow or dismiss the appeal. The court can only allow the appeal if the conditions in EA 2003 s27(3) or (4) are satisfied.

11.137 The conditions in section 27(3) are that:

(a) the appropriate judge ought to have decided a question before him at the extradition hearing differently;
(b) if he had decided the question in the way he ought to have done, he would have been required to order the person's discharge.

11.138 The conditions in section 27(4) are that:

(a) an issue is raised that was not raised at the extradition hearing or evidence is available that was not available at the extradition hearing;
(b) the issue or evidence would have resulted in the appropriate judge deciding a question before him at the extradition hearing differently;
(c) if he had decided the question in that way, he would have been required to order the person's discharge.

11.139 On allowing the appeal, the court must order the person's discharge and quash the order for their extradition.[114]

Appeal against discharge at extradition hearing

11.140 If the judicial authority has appealed the decision of the appropriate judge to discharge the requested person, then the appeal is brought

112 [2015] EWHC 149 (Admin).
113 At para 70.
114 EA 2003 s27(5).

under EA 2003 s28.[115] On appeal under section 28, the High Court may either allow the appeal or dismiss it. Section 29(3) and (4) set out the powers of the court on appeal.

11.141 If the appeal is allowed, the court must quash the order discharging the requested person and remit the case back to the judge, directing the judge to proceed as they would have been required to had they decided the relevant question differently at the extradition hearing.[116]

Court's powers on appeal in Part 2 cases

11.142 On appeal under EA 2003 s103 (appeal against the decision of the appropriate judge to send the case to the SSHD) the court may:

- allow the appeal;
- direct the judge to decide again a question (or questions) which they decided at the extradition hearing; or
- dismiss the appeal.[117]

11.143 The court may only allow the appeal if the conditions in section 104(3) or subsection (4) are satisfied. The conditions in subsection (3) are:

- the judge ought to have decided a question before them at the extradition hearing differently;
- if the judge had decided the question in the way they ought to have done, they would have been required to order the person's discharge.

11.144 The conditions in subsection (4) are:

- an issue is raised that was not raised at the extradition hearing or evidence is available that was not available at the extradition hearing;
- the issue or evidence would have resulted in the judge deciding a question before them at the extradition hearing differently;
- if the judge had decided the question in that way, they would have been required to order the person's discharge.

11.145 If the court allows the appeal, then it must make an order for the person's discharge and quash the order for their extradition.[118]

115 There is no ability for the judicial authority to apply for permission of appeal out of time.

116 EA 2003 s29(5)(a)–(c).

117 EA 2003 s104(1)(a)–(c).

118 EA 2003 s104(5).

11.146 If the court directs the judge to decide again a question (or questions) which they decided at the extradition hearing, then the case will be remitted back to the appropriate judge to consider the case again on the point remitted (and only that point).[119] If the judge comes to a different decision on any question that is the subject of a direction under EA 2003 s104(1)(b), the judge must order the person's discharge.[120] If the judge comes to the same decision as they did at the extradition hearing on the question that is (or all the questions that are), the subject of a direction under EA 2003 s104(1)(b) the appeal must be taken to have been dismissed by a decision of the High Court.[121]

Appeal against decision of the secretary of state to order extradition

11.147 Under EA 2003 s109(1) the High Court may either allow the requested person's appeal or dismiss the appeal.

11.148 The court may allow the appeal only if the conditions in section 109(3) or the conditions in subsection (4) are satisfied.

11.149 The conditions in subsection (3) are that:

- the SSHD ought to have decided a question before them differently;
- if the SSHD had decided the question in the way they ought to have done, they would not have ordered the person's extradition.

11.150 The conditions in subsection (4) are that:

- an issue is raised that was not raised when the case was being considered by the SSHD or information is available that was not available at that time;
- the issue or information would have resulted in the SSHD deciding a question before them differently;
- had the SSHD decided the question in that way, they would not have ordered the person's extradition.

11.151 If the court allows the appeal, it must order the person's discharge and quash the order for extradition.[122]

119 *Dempsey v Government of the United States of America* [2020] EWHC 603 (Admin).

120 EA 2003 s104(6).

121 EA 2003 s104(7).

122 EA 2003 s109(5).

11.152 The same conditions apply to an appeal against the decision of the SSHD under section 110 to order the person's discharge. If the appeal is allowed against the decision to discharge the person, the court must quash the order discharging the person and order the person's extradition.[123]

Appeal against discharge at extradition hearing

11.153 On appeal under EA 2003 s105, the High Court may allow the appeal, direct the judge to decide the relevant question again or dismiss the appeal.[124] The court may allow the appeal only if the conditions in subsection (4) or the conditions in subsection (5) are satisfied. There is no provision which allows an application for permission to appeal to be lodged out of time.

11.154 If the appeal is allowed, the court must quash the order discharging the person; remit the case to the judge; and direct the judge to proceed as they would have been required to do if they had decided the relevant question differently at the extradition hearing.[125]

11.155 If the court makes a direction that the judge is to decide the relevant question again and the judge subsequently decides the relevant question differently, they must proceed as they would have been required to do had they decided that question differently at the extradition hearing. If the court makes a direction that the judge is to decide the relevant question again and the judge does not subsequently decide the relevant question differently, the appeal must be taken to have been dismissed by a decision of the High Court.

Reserved judgments

11.156 In many cases, the court will make its decision 'ex tempore' at the conclusion of the hearing. In other cases, judgment will be reserved and handed down at a later date that will be notified to the parties. The parties to the appeal will receive a draft copy of the judgment about a week before it is due to be handed down. The parties must provide any amendments to the judgment by a specified date and nil returns[126]

123 EA 2003 s111(5).
124 EA 2003 s106(1)(a)–(c).
125 EA 2003 s106(6)(a)–(c)
126 A reply of zero to a request for a quantified reply.

will be required. It is important to note that draft copies of the judgment will be embargoed and disclosure of its content could constitute a contempt of court.[127] This means that the client cannot be informed of the decision unless express agreement is given by the court.

11.157 Attendance is not usually required at the handing down of judgment by the client or their representatives.

11.158 Once the court has adjourned for judgment, no further submissions or evidence should be submitted without the consent of the court. In *Ilia v Appeal Court in Athens, Greece*,[128] Aikens LJ held at para 15:

> We appreciate that the circumstances of this case are unusual, but we strongly deprecate the practice adopted by the appellant and her advisors in this case ... of serving further evidence and submissions after the hearing has been completed, without asking the court whether it wished or permitted such further materials to be adduced. When a hearing has been concluded, unless there is a particular matter that has been left outstanding, that must be the end of submitting further materials or observations to the court, unless the court specifically asks for, or agrees to accept, further observations.

11.159 Practitioners should therefore enquire with the court whether it wishes to receive further submissions and/or evidence should the need to serve arise and should not just serve the additional submissions and/or evidence without the court's agreement. If the court invites further submissions, they should be sent to the judge via the ACO using the crimex@administrativecourtoffice.justice.gov.uk email address or via the judge's clerk.

Appeals to the Supreme Court[129]

11.160 In order to appeal to the Supreme Court, the High Court must have certified that there is a point of law of general public importance involved in the decision and it must appear to the court granting leave that the point is one that ought to be considered by the Supreme Court.[130]

11.161 An application to certify a point of law must be made within *14 days* starting with the day on which the High Court makes its decision on

127 See *Attorney General v Crosland* [2021] UKSC 15.

128 [2015] EWHC 547 (Admin).

129 If permission to appeal is refused following an oral renewal hearing, that is the end of the appeal process and there is no possibility of applying to the court to certify a point of law of general public importance.

130 EA 2003 s114(4).

the appeal.[131] Such an application can be made orally after judgment has been handed down,[132] but where an application is made orally, there has to be an application in writing filed with the court. The usual course is for an application to certify to be made in writing[133] within the permitted period and then dealt with on the papers. Only in exceptional circumstances would the court agree to an oral hearing to determine certification. However, the decision will always be pronounced in open court (no attendance required) so there is no confusion as to when time runs from for removal/appeal to the Supreme Court.

11.162 A refusal to certify a point of law of general public importance does not make the High Court's decision final or abridge the 14-day period.[134] Theoretically, it would therefore be possible to submit additional points of law for certification, provided that such application was made within the permitted period.

11.163 If the High Court certifies that there is a point of law of general public importance, it can then also grant or refuse leave to appeal. If the High Court refuses leave to appeal then an application for leave can be made to the Supreme Court within 14 days starting with the day on which the High Court refuses to grant leave.[135] It is rare for the High Court to grant leave to appeal to the Supreme Court.

11.164 The Supreme Court has no power to grant a representation order. If a point of law of general public importance is certified, an application for a representation order to be extended to cover an application to the Supreme Court for leave to appeal should be made at the time of certification.

Making the application to certify a point of law

11.165 A formal application must be submitted (form EX244) with the fee of £255. It is usual for counsel to draft the application to certify and for it to be attached to the application notice.

11.166 Although the application must be lodged and served within *14 days*, there is no time limit within which the application must be determined by the High Court.

11.167 The application to certify a point of law must:

131 EA 2003 s114(5).

132 CrimPR 50.25(2)(a).

133 CrimPR 50.25(2)(b).

134 *Ownes v City of Westminster Magistrates' Court and others* [2009] EWHC 1343 (Admin) at paras 31 and 32.

135 EA 2003 s114(6).

- identify the point of law of general public importance;[136]
- serve on the High Court officer a statement of that point of law,[137] and give reasons why:
  - the point of law ought to be considered by the Supreme Court;[138] and
  - the High Court ought to give permission to appeal.[139]

11.168 Any response to the application to certify a point of law of general public importance must be made within *ten business days.*[140]

11.169 Notification of the decision on the application to certify a point of law of general public importance and permission to appeal to the Supreme Court will be notified to the legal representatives ahead of the proposed pronouncement, but legal representatives are prohibited form notifying the requested person until one hour before pronouncement is made in open court[141].

11.170 If leave is granted by the High Court, then the appeal must be lodged with the Supreme Court within *28 days* of the date on which the High Court granted leave.[142]

11.171 If leave to appeal is granted by the Supreme Court, the appeal must also be lodged with them within *28 days* of leave being granted.

11.172 The Supreme Court has strict rules[143] and practice directions[144] relating to appeals brought before it and the practitioner is referred to the Supreme Court website for further information.[145]

11.173 The Supreme Court has the power to allow an appeal, dismiss an appeal or remit[146] the matter back to the appropriate judge.[147]

136 CrimPR 50.25(3)(a).
137 CrimPR 50.25(3)(b)
138 CrimPR 50.25(3)(c)(i).
139 CrimPR 50.25(3)(c)(ii).
140 CrimPD 50D.10.
141 CrimPD 50D.13.
142 EA 2003 s114(7).
143 See: www.supremecourt.uk/procedures/rules-of-the-court.html.
144 See: www.supremecourt.uk/procedures/practice-directions.html.
145 See: www.supremecourt.uk/index.html
146 In *Norris v Government of the United States of America* [2008] UKHL 16, their Lordships stated at para 110: 'we have no doubt that the House has an inherent power to remit determination of an issue to an inferior tribunal where the interests of justice so require, and that is a power which nothing in the 2003 Act purports to abrogate.'
147 EA 2003 s115(7).

Re-opening the appeal

11.174 An application to re-open an appeal must be referred to the court that determined the appeal unless circumstances require it to be considered by a different judge or judges.[148] Applications are made on form EX244 in accordance with CrimPR 50.27, and attracts a fee. A party wishing to apply for permission to re-open an appeal must do so in writing, as soon as practicable after becoming aware of the grounds for doing so.[149] The application must specify the decision which the party wishes to re-open and give reasons[150] why:

- it is necessary for the court to reopen that decision in order to avoid real injustice;
- the circumstances are exceptional and make it appropriate to reopen the decision; and
- there is no alternative effective remedy.

The requirements in CrimPR 50.27(3)(b) are cumulative.[151]

11.175 Each party must have an opportunity to make representations before the court determines permission to re-open an appeal.[152]

Judge informed after extradition hearing or order that the person is charged with offence in UK

11.176 The Anti-social Behaviour, Crime and Policing Act 2014 inserted section 36A in Part 1 of the EA 2003 and section 118A in Part 2.

11.177 If the requested person is charged with an offence in the UK after an order for extradition has been made, but before removal is effected, then on application the appropriate judge *must* order the extradition not to be carried out until:

- the charge is disposed of;
- the charge is withdrawn;
- proceedings in respect of the charge are discontinued; or
- an order is made for the charge to lie on the file.

148 CrimPD 50D.15.
149 CrimPR 50.27(2)(a).
150 CrimPR 50.27(3)(b).
151 *Dempsey v Government of the United States of America* [2020] EWHC 603 (Admin).
152 CrimPR 50.27(4).

11.178 If the requested person has appealed the decision of the appropriate judge to order extradition, then the application is made to the High Court.[153] If a requested person has been charged with an offence in the UK after the High Court's decision to dismiss the application for permission/appeal has become final, but before removal takes place, then the application is made to the appropriate judge.

Judge informed after extradition hearing or order that person is serving a sentence in the UK

11.179 EA 2003 s36B and s118B were inserted by the Anti-social Behaviour, Crime and Policing Act 2014 to deal with cases where a person has been sentenced to a term of imprisonment after an extradition order has been made but who has yet to be removed.

11.180 On being informed of such, the appropriate judge (or High Court if the matter is on appeal) *may* order that the extradition is not carried out until the person is released from detention (on licence or otherwise).

Extradition (or not) following appeal

11.181 Practitioners should familiarise themselves with the provisions in the EA2003 that deal with extradition following appeal. It is not unusual for the authorities to fail to remove the requested person within the statutory timeframe, and in such situations a judge must discharge the requested person unless reasonable cause can be shown for the delay. Practitioners should therefore diarise the date by which their client should be removed and if the deadline is missed (and no application has been made to extend the time for removal), then an application for discharge should be made without delay.

11.182 EA 2003 s36 (s118 for Part 2 cases) provides the basis for such an application to be made and also allows the judicial authority an opportunity to agree a later starting date for removal than that set out in the legislation.

11.183 Applications for discharge must be made in accordance with the CrimPR that state that the application must be in writing[154] and

153 EA 2003 s36A(4) (Part 1); s118A(4) (Part 2).
154 CrimPR 50.16(2)(a).

served upon the court officer[155] and the prosecutor.[156] The application must explain the grounds on which it is made.[157] The hearing of the application should be listed as soon as practicable, and in any event no later than the second business day after the application has been served.[158]

11.184 Section 36(3) sets out the 'required period' within which a requested person is to be extradited:

(a) 10 days starting with the day on which the decision of the relevant court on the appeal becomes final or proceedings on the appeal are discontinued, or
(b) if the relevant court and the authority which issued the Part 1 warrant agree a later date, 10 days starting with the later date.

The required period in Part 2 cases within which a requested person is to be extradited is 28 days starting with the day on which the decision of the relevant court becomes final, or the day on which proceedings on the appeal are discontinued

11.185 Where section 36(2) (or section 118(2)) is not complied with, section 36(8) (or section 118(7)) provides a mechanism for the requested person's discharge:

> If subsection (2) is not complied with and the person applies to the appropriate judge to be discharged the judge must order his discharge, unless reasonable cause is shown for the delay.

11.186 The reference in section 36(8) and section 118(7) to 'appropriate judge' means a judge sitting at Westminster Magistrates' Court (WMC). Therefore, despite the High Court having been seized of the appeal, the section 36(8) or 118(7) application for discharge is dealt with at the magistrates' court.

11.187 Applications for the required period to be extended are made ex parte by the NCA (in Part 1 cases) to the Administrative Court (if there have been appeal proceedings) or to WMC where there has been no appeal. The applicant (in part 1 cases the NCA and the SSHD in Part 2 cases) will make the application through the CPS. The EA 2003 does not contain any requirement that the requested person be notified of an extension request, nor confer any right to the requested person to participate in the process.[159] An application to extend the required period within which to extradite a requested

155 CrimPR 50.16(2)(a)(i).
156 CrimPR 50.16(2)(a)(iii).
157 CrimPR 50.16(2)(b).
158 CrimPR 50.16(2)(c).
159 *Cosar v Governor of Wandsworth Prison* [2020] EWHC 1142 (Admin).

person must be accompanied by a witness statement explaining why it has not been possible to remove the requested person within the required period and setting out the proposed timetable for removal.[160] The application must also be accompanied by a draft order.[161]

11.188 An application to extend the required period for removal can be made before or after the expiry of the required period for extradition to take place, however the court will scrutinise with particular care any application made after its expiry.[162] Indeed, the granting of an extension does not affect the task of the court to consider the discharge application.[163]

11.189 If the application is granted, the ten-day period (in AW cases) then starts on a date nominated by the applicant and agreed by the court. The defence do not have any part to play in this application process unless the expiry for the period of removal has expired and the requested person has made an application to be discharged. Multiple extension periods can be granted.[164]

Reasonable cause for delay?

11.190 If an application under EA 2003 s36(8) or s118(7) is made, the appropriate judge must discharge[165] unless 'reasonable cause' is shown for

160 CrimPD 50D.16(i).

161 CrimPD 50D.16(ii).

162 CrimPD 50D.17.

163 *Jane v Westminster Magistrates' Court* [2019] EWHC 394 (Admin).

164 *Cosar v Governor of Wandsworth Prison* [2020] EWHC 1142 (Admin).

165 Despite the CJEU in the case of *Criminal Proceedings against Vilkas* (C-640/15) stating that 'the mere expiry of the time limits prescribed in Article 23 of the Framework Decision cannot relieve the executing Member State of its obligation to carry on with the procedure for executing a European arrest warrant and to surrender the requested person, and the authorities concerned must agree, for that purpose, on a new surrender date' (para 72): the Divisional Court in *Jane v Westminster Magistrates' Court* concluded that the EA 2003 Act had been interpreted in several decisions in the UK and there was nothing in EU law which required a different interpretation. Discharge from the extradition request therefore continues to be the remedy where a time limit for removal has not been complied with and there is no reasonable cause for the delay. Practitioners should note however that, as stated in chapter 5, the duty of conforming interpretation no longer applies, further strengthening the reasoning in *Jane*. However, interpretative questions will arise from European Union (Future Relationship) Act 2020 s29 which states that existing domestic law has effect with such modifications as are required for the purposes of implementing the 2021 Trade and Cooperation Agreement, so far as the agreement concerned is not otherwise so implemented.

the delay. The 'reasonable cause' provision has been given a broad construction.[166] An administrative error[167] can amount to a reasonable cause, as can negligence,[168] but not in all cases. Each case will turn on its own facts. The seriousness of the offence is not a factor the appropriate judge is entitled to take into account when determining whether reasonable cause has been shown. The onus is on those representing the requesting state to explain and justify the delay. The appropriate judge, when considering an application to discharge, must give a rigorous approach to the reasons put forward for any delay.[169]

11.191 A challenge to a decision of the appropriate judge not to discharge should be made by way of judicial review, rather than issuing a writ for habeas corpus[170] even if the requested person is in custody.

Application to the European Court of Human Rights for rule 39 interim measures

11.192 On exhaustion of all domestic avenues of appeal, an appellant can apply to the European Court of Human Rights (ECtHR) under rule 39 of the Rules of Court for interim measures to be applied. The ECtHR will only grant rule 39 relief in exceptional circumstances. In the period 2018–2020, 226 applications for rule 39 relief were made from the UK, and only three of these applications were granted, two preventing removal to the US.[171] If an application is granted, the ECtHR will issue interim measures to the UK against the removal of the person until the ECtHR directs otherwise.

166 Practitioners should consider the impact of the CJEU case of *Criminal Proceedings against Vilkas* (C-640/15) (as discussed in *Jane v Westminster Magistrates' Court*) as to whether a more stringent test is to be applied as to what constitutes 'reasonable cause' for a delay in removal.

167 *Owens* [2009] EWHC 1343 (Admin) at para 50.

168 In *Desai* [2014] EWHC 4631 (Admin), Laws, LJ stated that: 'Administrative error may be covered and in my judgment may, I emphasize the word may, encompass cases where there has been negligence: not, of course, any negligence.'

169 *R (Mechlinski) v Westminster Magistrates' Court* [2015] EWHC 2043 (Admin).

170 *Jane v Westminster Magistrates' Court* [2019] EWHC 394 (Admin) at paras 45–67; *Verde v Governor of HMP Wandsworth* [2020] EWHC 1219 (Admin) at para 39; and *Cosar v Governor of Wandsworth Prison* [2020] EWHC 1142 (Admin).

171 Figures provided by the ECtHR: www.echr.coe.int/Documents/Stats_art_39_01_ENG.pdf.

11.193 The ECtHR will only impose interim measures where, having reviewed all the relevant information, it considers that the applicant faces a real risk of serious, irreversible harm if the measure is not applied. Typically such cases are ones in which there are fears of a) a threat to life (situation falling under Article 2 (right to life) of the European Convention on Human Rights (ECHR)) or b) ill-treatment prohibited by ECHR Article 3 (prohibition of torture and inhuman or degrading treatment). In highly exceptional cases they can also be applied in respect of certain requests relating to the right to respect for private and family life (ECHR Article 8).

11.194 Any application for a rule 39 interim measure must state reasons and, in particular, must specify in detail the grounds on which the applicant's particular fears are based, the nature of the alleged risks and the ECHR provisions that are alleged to have been violated or will be violated if the measures are not imposed.

11.195 The application must be accompanied by the final decision of the domestic court (if available).

11.196 The expected date and time of removal must be provided in the application together with the applicant's place of detention, if in custody. If the final decision of the court is imminent and there is a risk of immediate removal, an application for rule 39 interim measures can be made without the need to await the final decision of the domestic court, but the application must indicate that the request is subject to an adverse decision of the domestic court.

11.197 Requests for interim measures must be submitted to the court with the applicant's consent and should preferably be accompanied by a properly completed application form. If the request is made by a representative, an authority form must be completed and sent immediately or within the next few days.

11.198 Practitioners should consider carefully the practice directions on requests for interim measures.[172]

11.199 The ECtHR recommends that an application for rule 39 interim measures should be sent by fax and all requests should be marked in bold on the face of the request:

Rule 39 – Urgent
Person to contact (name and contact details)
Date and time of removal and destination

172 See: www.echr.coe.int/Documents/PD_interim_measures_ENG.pdf.

11.200 The ECtHR has a dedicated fax number for sending requests for rule 39 interim measures: +33 (0)3 90 21 43 50 or + 33 (0)3 88 41 39 00.[173]

11.201 Applications are only received Monday to Friday from 8 am to 4.30 pm.[174] Requests sent after 4.30 pm will normally be dealt with the next working day.

11.202 It is recommended that any faxes exceeding ten pages (which most are) should be sent in several parts so that they can be received in the best possible condition.

11.203 The result of the application will be communicated to the parties relatively quickly (by fax and post) and, if such application is refused, there are no further steps that can be taken to prevent removal unless a supervening event occurs.

173 Correct as of time of writing. Those wishing to apply for rule 39 interim measures from the ECtHR should check the court website for up-to-date contact information: www.echr.coe.int/ECHR.

174 The times given are local time (GMT+1).

CHAPTER 12

Ancillary matters

Introduction

12.1 This chapter seeks to deal with matters that are generally outside the scope of the Extradition Act (EA) 2003, but nonetheless are matters that practitioners need to be aware of when conducting (and concluding) extradition proceedings: compromising the extradition request; temporary transfer; 'iron letters'; INTERPOL Red Notices; transfer of prisoners; and funding and billing.

Compromising the extradition request

12.2 As the preceding pages show, resisting extradition is difficult. Very often a requested person will be more likely to avoid extradition by attempting to persuade the requesting state to withdraw the request for extradition. In order to do this, it will be necessary to secure the assistance of a lawyer in the requesting state. This lawyer can then apply to the court in the requesting state for the case to be dealt with without the requested person having to return. For example, on an 'accusation warrant' it may be possible for the requested person to plead guilty and be sentenced to a non-custodial sentence in their absence. In a conviction case, it may be possible for a lawyer in the requesting state to apply to the court to suspend or defer a sentence of imprisonment.

12.3 A lawyer in the requesting state will not be funded by the representation order: it is very often the requested person or their family who fund this. Very occasionally, lawyers may agree to carry out the work on a pro bono basis, particularly where the requested person is a former client.

12.4 Practitioners may sometimes be asked to assist in finding a lawyer in the requesting state. Given the likelihood of language difficulties, it is unlikely that a lawyer in this country will be able to offer any real help unless they have had previous dealings with a lawyer in the issuing state. It is therefore worth retaining details of those lawyers who have been effective in securing the withdrawal of a warrant for future use.

12.5 The court is often reluctant to adjourn extradition proceedings while attempts are being made to compromise a warrant. In order to persuade the court to adjourn, the defence will have to demonstrate that the attempt to compromise is at an advanced stage and stands a chance of success. Evidence from the lawyer instructed in the requesting state will assist such an application.

Temporary transfer

12.6 EA 2003 s21B was inserted by Anti-social Behaviour, Crime and Policing Act 2014 s159 and provides a mechanism, at the request of the judicial authority[1] or requested person,[2] for either temporary transfer to the requesting territory or arrangements to be made for discussions with investigators/prosecutors from the requesting territory. It was anticipated that the effect of this provision section would. in some cases, be likely to lead to withdrawal of the arrest warrant (AW), or to the requested person spending less time in pre-trial detention.[3] It applies only to EA 2003 Part 1 cases and those who are accused within the meaning of section 2(3).

12.7 EA 2003 s21B can be invoked at any time before or in the extradition hearing.[4] It does not apply at the appeal stage of extradition proceedings.[5] A request is made to the appropriate judge by either the judicial authority or the requested person and should be clearly expressed and particularised.[6]

12.8 If such a request is made, then the appropriate judge must order the extradition proceedings to be adjourned if they think it necessary to do so to enable the judicial authority or requested person to consider whether to consent to the request.[7] The discretion to adjourn must be exercised judicially and there is a duty on the judge to give reasons explaining why the discretion has been exercised in a particular way.[8] The timing and appropriateness of the request will have a bearing on whether the judge considers it necessary to grant the adjournment.[9] However, an adjournment must not be for more than seven days.

12.9 Once consent is given, the appropriate judge must make whatever orders and directions are appropriate to give effect to the request.[10]

1 EA 2003 s21B(2).
2 EA 2003 s21B(3).
3 See explanatory notes to Anti-social Behaviour, Crime and Policing Act 2014 s159.
4 EA 2003 s21B(1)(b).
5 *Lidak v Poland* [2020] EWHC 1321 (Admin) at paras 2–3.
6 *Duncan v Presiding Magistrate, Malaga, Spain* [2015] EWHC 3466 (Admin) at para 27.
7 EA 2003 s21B(4).
8 *Duncan v Presiding Magistrate, Malaga, Spain* [2015] EWHC 3466 (Admin) at para 26.
9 At para 28.
10 EA 2003 s21B(5)(a).

The judge must also adjourn the extradition proceedings for however long seems necessary to enable the orders and directions to be carried out.[11]

12.10 If a request is made before the extradition hearing has been fixed then the proceedings will be adjourned and when they resume, the permitted period for fixing the date of the hearing is extended by the same number of days for which the extradition proceedings have been adjourned.[12]

12.11 A requested person cannot make a further request if the request is withdrawn or the judicial authority does not consent.[13] Furthermore, a requested person cannot make a request if the judicial authority has made a counter-request that has been dealt with.[14]

'Iron letters'

12.12 Some jurisdictions will withdraw an extradition request on an application by the requested person to a court upon payment of a security to guarantee the requested person's return. This is known as an 'iron letter.' Although it can result in the withdrawal of the extradition request, it requires the requested person to appear voluntarily at the court in the requesting state when summoned to appear (unlike the scenarios at para 12.2).

12.13 Arranging for an iron letter to be issued will require close liaison with a lawyer in the requesting state; it will only be issued after a bail security has been deposited in the requesting state. After this has been paid in, the extradition request will be withdrawn resulting in the discharge of the requested person in the UK.

INTERPOL Red Notices

12.14 An INTERPOL (International Criminal Police Organization) Red Notice may be issued at the request of a member country. It is a request to locate and provisionally arrest a person pending extradition or surrender. In many extradition cases, a person will be facing an INTERPOL Red Notice alongside an extradition request. Save in

11 EA 2003 s21B(5)(b).
12 EA 2003 s21B(9).
13 EA 2003 s21B(8).
14 EA 2003 s21B(7).

the case of requests from those countries mentioned in para 8.13, it does not amount to a warrant of arrest in the UK, although it will do so in many other jurisdictions. A Red Notice could have a significant impact, not only on a person's ability to travel, but also on other aspects of their life (for example, reputation and banking), particularly if a Red Notice is published online.

12.15 An application may be made to the Commission for the Control of INTERPOL's files (CCF) for removal of a Red Notice, if it fails to comply with INTERPOL's constitution or technical requirements.[15] The process is a lengthy one, and strategic consideration must be given as to the timing of an application for removal, and any interplay with extradition and/or asylum proceedings.

Transfer of prisoners

12.16 It is, in some cases, possible for a sentence to be transferred across jurisdictions. Where a person is serving a sentence of imprisonment in another state, the Repatriation of Prisoners Act (RPA) 1984 will in some cases allow that person to be repatriated to complete that sentence in the UK. The person must be a British citizen, or in some circumstances, the relevant provisions of the RPA 1984 will apply where the person has close ties to the UK.[16] Using these provisions, it is possible to seek to transfer a sentence of a requested person prior to their extradition, thus obviating the need for return.

12.17 Currently there are significant practical difficulties involved in negotiating such a transfer of a sentence.

12.18 RPA 1984 s1(1) sets out the circumstances in which a transfer can take place as follows:

(a) the United Kingdom is a party to international arrangements providing for the transfer between the United Kingdom and a country or territory outside the British Islands of persons ..., and
(b) the relevant Minister and the appropriate authority of that country or territory have each agreed to the transfer under those arrangements of a particular person (in this Act referred to as 'the prisoner'), and

15 See:www.interpol.int/en/Who-we-are/Commission-for-the-Control-of-INTERPOL-s-Files-CCF/How-to-submit-a-request. See also the very useful website of the organisation Fair Trials: www.fairtrials.org/campaign/interpol#frequently-asked-questions.

16 See RPA 1984 s1(3), which also provides for the temporary return of a prisoner to the UK.

(c) in a case in which the terms of those arrangements provide for the prisoner to be transferred only with his consent, the prisoner's consent has been given.

12.19 The international arrangements referred to under RPA 1984 s1(1)(a) are as follows:

- Council of Europe Convention on the Transfer of Sentenced Persons and the Additional Protocol;[17]
- Commonwealth Scheme for the Transfer of Convicted Offenders;
- bilateral agreements.[18]

12.20 Transfers of sentence are dealt with by the Interventions and Operational Services department of Her Majesty's Prison and Probation Service, who can be contacted at crossbordertransfers@justice.gov.uk.

Funding and billing

12.21 Where a case is privately funded, it will be possible to obtain an order for costs from central funds if the requested person is discharged; but costs will be capped at legal aid rates.[19]

12.22 All extradition cases conducted in the magistrates' court that are the subject of public funding are to be submitted for taxation to the Legal Aid Agency (LAA) within three months of conclusion. A CRM7 must be completed for all cases and lodged with the file of papers. If a certificate for counsel has been granted in the proceedings then counsel's claim for costs must be completed on a CRM8 and submitted at the same time as the CRM7.

12.23 Given that the claim will be for a non-standard fee, it is possible to apply for an uplift in costs.[20] An enhancement to the hourly rate will be allowed if:

- the work was done with exceptional competence, skill or expertise; or

17 ETS 112.

18 See prison service instruction (PSI) 52/2011 'Immigration, repatriation and removal services' at Annex S for a list of countries with which the UK has a repatriation agreement (www.gov.uk/government/publications/repatriation-and-removal-of-foreign-nationals-psi-522011).

19 Legal Aid, Sentencing and Punishment of Offenders Act (LASPO) 2012 Sch 7.

20 2017 Standard Crime Contract para 10.99 (www.gov.uk/government/publications/standard-crime-contract-2017).

- the work was done with exceptional dispatch; or
- the case involved exceptional circumstances or complexity.

12.24 In deciding whether to grant an enhancement in fees, and in determining the appropriate percentage enhancement, the LAA will have regard to:

- the degree of responsibility;
- the care, speed and economy with which the case was prepared;
- the novelty, weight and complexity of the case.[21]

The percentage enhancement is capped at 100 per cent.

12.25 If applying for an enhancement, a covering letter stating why the case meets the above criteria should be sent to the LAA when the claim is submitted.

12.26 Cases that have concluded before the Administrative Court must be submitted for taxation to the Senior Courts Cost Office (SCCO) at the Royal Courts of Justice (DX 44454 Strand). It is usual for a bill of costs to be drafted by an experienced costs draftsman. The bill of costs, representation order and disbursement invoices are the only documents that need to be sent to the SCCO.

12.27 Again, an uplift can be applied to the solicitor's costs. Counsel instructed in these cases are able to submit their bills directly to the SCCO and need not submit them at the same time as the solicitor submits his or her bill.

12.28 Publicly funded judicial review proceedings will be funded under a civil legal aid certificate. Firms without a civil legal aid contract but holding a 2017 Standard Crime Contract are entitled to apply for community legal services certificates for this work: judicial review and habeas corpus are classified as 'associated Civil Work carried out under the provisions governing civil Legal Aid in Part 1 of[LASPO].'[22]

12.29 Practitioners must ensure that they adhere to the Funding Code criteria as set out on the LAA website. Applications should be made using forms CIV APP1 and the relevant means form (usually CIV MEANS 1 or 2) and sent to the regional LAA office. An advice from counsel setting out the merits of the case will usually be required. It can take many weeks for such applications to be processed. If the application is urgent, the form CIV APP6 should be made to the Special Cases Unit of the LAA.

21 2017 Standard Crime Contract para 10.101.

22 See 2017 Standard Crime Contract – Specification para 1.3.

12.30 The more detailed CIV APP1 must be submitted to the regional office within five working days of the grant of a certificate. A certificate will then be issued that permits work to a given stage of the case and with a limitation on costs. If the work is to proceed beyond that permitted in the funding certificate, a further application should be made to the LAA using form CIV APP8. This form should also be used to apply to extend funding to cover the cost of experts or leading counsel.

APPENDICES

APPENDIX A

Extradition Act 2003 ss1–25, 64, 65, 70–75, 137–138[1]

PART 1: EXTRADITION TO CATEGORY 1 TERRITORIES

Introduction

Extradition to category 1 territories

1 (1) This Part deals with extradition from the United Kingdom to the territories designated for the purposes of this Part by order made by the Secretary of State.

(2) In this Act references to category 1 territories are to the territories designated for the purposes of this Part.

(3) A territory may not be designated for the purposes of this Part if a person found guilty in the territory of a criminal offence may be sentenced to death for the offence under the general criminal law of the territory.

Part 1 warrant and certificate

2 (1) This section applies if the designated authority receives a Part 1 warrant in respect of a person.

(2) A Part 1 warrant is an arrest warrant which is issued by a judicial authority of a category 1 territory and which contains–

(a) the statement referred to in subsection (3) and the information referred to in subsection (4), or

(b) the statement referred to in subsection (5) and the information referred to in subsection (6).

(3) The statement is one that–

(a) the person in respect of whom the Part 1 warrant is issued is accused in the category 1 territory of the commission of an offence specified in the warrant, and

(b) the Part 1 warrant is issued with a view to his arrest and extradition to the category 1 territory for the purpose of being prosecuted for the offence.

(4) The information is–

(a) particulars of the person's identity;

(b) particulars of any other warrant issued in the category 1 territory for the person's arrest in respect of the offence;

(c) particulars of the circumstances in which the person is alleged to have committed the offence, including the conduct alleged to constitute the offence, the time and place at which he is alleged to have committed the offence and any provision of the law of the category 1 territory under which the conduct is alleged to constitute an offence;

(d) particulars of the sentence which may be imposed under the law of the category 1 territory in respect of the offence if the person is convicted of it.

(5) The statement is one that–

(a) the person in respect of whom the Part 1 warrant is issued has been convicted of an offence specified in the warrant by a court in the category 1 territory, and

(b) the Part 1 warrant is issued with a view to his arrest and extradition to the category 1 territory for the purpose of being sentenced for the offence or of serving a sentence of imprisonment or another form of detention imposed in respect of the offence.

(6) The information is–

(a) particulars of the person's identity;

(b) particulars of the conviction;

(c) particulars of any other warrant issued in the category 1 territory for the person's arrest in respect of the offence;

(d) particulars of the sentence which may be imposed under the law of the category 1 territory in respect of the offence, if the person has not been sentenced for the offence;

(e) particulars of the sentence which has been imposed under the law of the category 1 territory in respect of the offence, if the person has been sentenced for the offence.

(7) The designated authority may issue a certificate under this section if it believes that the authority which issued the Part 1 warrant has the function of issuing arrest warrants in the category 1 territory.

(7A) But in the case of a Part 1 warrant containing the statement referred to in subsection (3), the designated authority must not issue a certificate under this section if it is clear to the designated authority that a judge proceeding under section 21A would be required to order the person's discharge on the basis that extradition would be disproportionate.

In deciding that question, the designated authority must apply any general guidance issued for the purposes of this subsection.

(7B) Any guidance under subsection (7A) may be revised, withdrawn or replaced.

(7C) The function of issuing guidance under subsection (7A), or of revising, withdrawing or replacing any such guidance, is exercisable by the Lord Chief Justice of England and Wales with the concurrence of–

(a) the Lord Justice General of Scotland, and

(b) the Lord Chief Justice of Northern Ireland.

(8) A certificate under this section must certify that the authority which issued the Part 1 warrant has the function of issuing arrest warrants in the category 1 territory.

(9) The designated authority is the authority designated for the purposes of this Part by order made by the Secretary of State.

(10) An order made under subsection (9) may–

(a) designate more than one authority;

(b) designate different authorities for different parts of the United Kingdom.

Arrest

Arrest under certified Part 1 warrant

3 (1) This section applies if a certificate is issued under section 2 in respect of a Part 1 warrant issued in respect of a person.

(2) The warrant may be executed by a constable or a customs officer in any part of the United Kingdom.

(3) The warrant may be executed by a service policeman anywhere, but only if the person is subject to service law or is a civilian subject to service discipline.

(5) The warrant may be executed even if neither the warrant nor a copy of it is in the possession of the person executing it at the time of the arrest.

Person arrested under Part 1 warrant

4 (1) This section applies if a person is arrested under a Part 1 warrant.

(2) A copy of the warrant must be given to the person as soon as practicable after his arrest.

(3) The person must be brought as soon as practicable before the appropriate judge.

(4) If subsection (2) is not complied with and the person applies to the judge to be discharged, the judge may order his discharge.

(5) If subsection (3) is not complied with and the person applies to the judge to be discharged, the judge must order his discharge.

(6) A person arrested under the warrant must be treated as continuing in legal custody until he is brought before the appropriate judge under subsection (3) or he is discharged under subsection (4) or (5).

Provisional arrest

5 (1) A constable, a customs officer or a service policeman may arrest a person without a warrant if he has reasonable grounds for believing–

(a) that a Part 1 warrant has been or will be issued in respect of the person by an authority of a category 1 territory, and

(b) that the authority has the function of issuing arrest warrants in the category 1 territory.

(2) A constable or a customs officer may arrest a person under subsection (1) in any part of the United Kingdom.

(3) A service policeman may arrest a person under subsection (1) only if the person is subject to service law or is a civilian subject to service discipline.

(4) If a service policeman has power to arrest a person under subsection (1) he may exercise the power anywhere.

Person arrested under section 5

6 (1) This section applies if a person is arrested under section 5.

(2) The person must be brought before the appropriate judge within 48 hours starting with the time when the person is arrested.

(2A) The documents specified in subsection (4) must be produced to the judge within 48 hours starting with the time when the person is arrested but this is subject to any extension under subsection (3B).

(2B) Subsection (3) applies if–

(a) the person has been brought before the judge in compliance with subsection (2); but

(b) documents have not been produced to the judge in compliance with subsection (2A).

(3) The person must be brought before the judge when the documents are produced to the judge.

(3A) While the person is before the judge in pursuance of subsection (2), the authority of the category 1 territory may apply to the judge for an extension of the 48 hour period mentioned in subsection (2A) by a further 48 hours.

(3B) The judge may grant an extension if the judge decides that subsection (2A) could not reasonably be complied with within the initial 48 hour period.

(3C) The judge must decide whether that subsection could reasonably be so complied with on a balance of probabilities.

(3D) Notice of an application under subsection (3A) must be given in accordance with rules of court.

(4) The documents are–

(a) a Part 1 warrant in respect of the person;

(b) a certificate under section 2 in respect of the warrant.

(5) A copy of the warrant must be given to the person as soon as practicable after his arrest.

(5A) Subsection (5B) applies if–

(a) the person is before the judge in pursuance of subsection (2); and

(b) the documents specified in subsection (4) have not been produced to the judge.

(5B) The judge must remand the person in custody or on bail (subject to subsection (6)).

(6) If subsection (2), (2A) or (3) is not complied with and the person applies to the judge to be discharged, the judge must order his discharge.

(7) If subsection (5) is not complied with and the person applies to the judge to be discharged, the judge may order his discharge.

(8) The person must be treated as continuing in legal custody until he is brought before the appropriate judge under subsection (2) or he is discharged under subsection (6) or (7).

(8A) In calculating a period of 48 hours for the purposes of this section no account is to be taken of–

(a) any Saturday or Sunday;

(b) Christmas Day;

(c) Good Friday; or

(d) any day falling within subsection (8B).

(8B) The following days fall within this subsection–

(a) in Scotland, any day prescribed under section 8(2) of the Criminal Procedure (Scotland) Act 1995 as a court holiday in the court of the appropriate judge;

(b) in any part of the United Kingdom, any day that is a bank holiday under the Banking and Financial Dealings Act 1971 in that part of the United Kingdom.

(9) Subsection (10) applies if–

(a) a person is arrested under section 5 on the basis of a belief that a Part 1 warrant has been or will be issued in respect of him;

(b) the person is discharged under subsection (6) or (7).

(10) The person must not be arrested again under section 5 on the basis of a belief relating to the same Part 1 warrant.

The initial hearing

Identity of person arrested

7 (1) This section applies if–

(a) a person arrested under a Part 1 warrant is brought before the appropriate judge under section 4(3), or

(b) a person arrested under section 5 is brought before the appropriate judge under section 6 and section 6(2A) is complied with in relation to him.

(2) The judge must decide whether the person brought before him is the person in respect of whom–

(a) the warrant referred to in subsection (1)(a) was issued, or

(b) the warrant referred to in section 6(4) was issued.

(3) The judge must decide the question in subsection (2) on a balance of probabilities.

(4) If the judge decides the question in subsection (2) in the negative he must order the person's discharge.

(5) If the judge decides that question in the affirmative he must proceed under section 8.

(6) In England and Wales, the judge has the same powers (as nearly as may be) as a magistrates' court would have if the proceedings were the summary trial of an information against the person.

(7) In Scotland–

(a) the judge has the same powers (as nearly as may be) as if the proceedings were summary proceedings in respect of an offence alleged to have been committed by the person; but

(b) in his making any decision under subsection (2) evidence from a single source shall be sufficient.

(8) In Northern Ireland, the judge has the same powers (as nearly as may be) as a magistrates' court would have if the proceedings were the hearing and determination of a complaint against the person.

(9) If the judge exercises his power to adjourn the proceedings he must remand the person in custody or on bail.

(10) If the person is remanded in custody, the appropriate judge may later grant bail.

Remand etc

8 (1) If the judge is required to proceed under this section he must–

(a) fix a date on which the extradition hearing is to begin;

(b) inform the person of the contents of the Part 1 warrant;

(c) give the person the required information about consent;

(d) remand the person in custody or on bail.

(2) If the person is remanded in custody, the appropriate judge may later grant bail.

(3) The required information about consent is–

(a) that the person may consent to his extradition to the category 1 territory in which the Part 1 warrant was issued;

(b) an explanation of the effect of consent and the procedure that will apply if he gives consent;
(c) that consent must be given before the judge and is irrevocable.

(4) The date fixed under subsection (1) must not be later than the end of the permitted period, which is 21 days starting with the date of the arrest referred to in section 7(1)(a) or (b).

(4A) But if proceedings in respect of the extradition are adjourned under section 8A or 8B, the permitted period is extended by the number of days for which the proceedings are so adjourned.

(5) If before the date fixed under subsection (1) (or this subsection) a party to the proceedings applies to the judge for a later date to be fixed and the judge believes it to be in the interests of justice to do so, he may fix a later date; and this subsection may apply more than once.

(6) Subsections (7) and (8) apply if the extradition hearing does not begin on or before the date fixed under this section.

(7) If the person applies to the judge to be discharged the judge must order his discharge, unless reasonable cause is shown for the delay.

(8) If no application is made under subsection (7) the judge must order the person's discharge on the first occasion after the date fixed under this section when the person appears or is brought before the judge, unless reasonable cause is shown for the delay.

Person charged with offence in United Kingdom before extradition hearing

8A(1) This section applies if–
(a) a person has been brought before the appropriate judge under section 4(3) or 6(2) but the extradition hearing has not begun; and
(b) the judge is informed that the person is charged with an offence in the United Kingdom.

(2) The judge must order further proceedings in respect of the extradition to be adjourned until one of these occurs–
(a) the charge is disposed of;
(b) the charge is withdrawn;
(c) proceedings in respect of the charge are discontinued;
(d) an order is made for the charge to lie on the file, or in relation to Scotland, the diet is deserted ***pro loco et tempore***.

(3) If a sentence of imprisonment or another form of detention is imposed in respect of the offence charged, the judge may order further proceedings in respect of the extradition to be adjourned until the person is released from detention pursuant to the sentence (whether on licence or otherwise).

Person serving sentence in United Kingdom before extradition hearing

8B(1) This section applies if–
(a) a person has been brought before the appropriate judge under section 4(3) or 6(2) but the extradition hearing has not begun; and
(b) the judge is informed that the person is in custody serving a sentence of imprisonment or another form of detention in the United Kingdom.

(2) The judge may order further proceedings in respect of the extradition to be

adjourned until the person is released from detention pursuant to the sentence (whether on licence or otherwise).

(3) In a case where further proceedings in respect of the extradition are adjourned under subsection (2)–
  (a) section 131 of the Magistrates' Courts Act 1980 (remand of accused already in custody) has effect as if a reference to 28 clear days in subsection (1) or (2) of that section were a reference to six months;
  (b) Article 47(2) of the Magistrates' Courts (Northern Ireland) Order 1981 (period of remand in custody) has effect as if a reference to 28 days in–
    (i) sub-paragraph (a)(iii), or
    (ii) the words after sub-paragraph (b),
  were a reference to six months.

The extradition hearing

Judge's powers at extradition hearing

9 (1) In England and Wales, at the extradition hearing the appropriate judge has the same powers (as nearly as may be) as a magistrates' court would have if the proceedings were the summary trial of an information against the person in respect of whom the Part 1 warrant was issued.
(2) In Scotland, at the extradition hearing the appropriate judge has the same powers (as nearly as may be) as if the proceedings were summary proceedings in respect of an offence alleged to have been committed by the person in respect of whom the Part 1 warrant was issued.
(3) In Northern Ireland, at the extradition hearing the appropriate judge has the same powers (as nearly as may be) as a magistrates' court would have if the proceedings were the hearing and determination of a complaint against the person in respect of whom the Part 1 warrant was issued.
(4) If the judge adjourns the extradition hearing he must remand the person in custody or on bail.
(5) If the person is remanded in custody, the appropriate judge may later grant bail.

Initial stage of extradition hearing

10 (1) This section applies if a person in respect of whom a Part 1 warrant is issued appears or is brought before the appropriate judge for the extradition hearing.
(2) The judge must decide whether the offence specified in the Part 1 warrant is an extradition offence.
(3) If the judge decides the question in subsection (2) in the negative he must order the person's discharge.
(4) If the judge decides that question in the affirmative he must proceed under section 11.

Bars to extradition

11 (1) If the judge is required to proceed under this section he must decide whether the person's extradition to the category 1 territory is barred by reason of–
  (a) the rule against double jeopardy;
  (aa) absence of prosecution decision;
  (b) extraneous considerations;
  (c) the passage of time;
  (d) the person's age;

(e) [***Repealed***]
(f) speciality;
(g) the person's earlier extradition to the United Kingdom from another category 1 territory;
(h) the person's earlier extradition to the United Kingdom from a non-category 1 territory;
(i) the person's earlier transfer to the United Kingdom by the International Criminal Court;
(j) forum.

(1A) But the judge is to decide whether the person's extradition is barred by reason of–
(a) absence of prosecution decision, or
(b) forum,
only in a case where the Part 1 warrant contains the statement referred to in section 2(3) (warrant issued for purposes of prosecution for offence in category 1 territory).

(2) Sections 12 to 19F apply for the interpretation of subsection (1).

(3) If the judge decides any of the questions in subsection (1) in the affirmative he must order the person's discharge.

(4) If the judge decides those questions in the negative and the person is alleged to be unlawfully at large after conviction of the extradition offence, the judge must proceed under section 20.

(5) If the judge decides those questions in the negative and the person is accused of the commission of the extradition offence but is not alleged to be unlawfully at large after conviction of it, the judge must proceed under section 21A.

Rule against double jeopardy

12 A person's extradition to a category 1 territory is barred by reason of the rule against double jeopardy if (and only if) it appears that he would be entitled to be discharged under any rule of law relating to previous acquittal or conviction on the assumption–
(a) that the conduct constituting the extradition offence constituted an offence in the part of the United Kingdom where the judge exercises jurisdiction;
(b) that the person were charged with the extradition offence in that part of the United Kingdom.

Absence of prosecution decision

12A(1) A person's extradition to a category 1 territory is barred by reason of absence of prosecution decision if (and only if)–
(a) it appears to the appropriate judge that there are reasonable grounds for believing that–
(i) the competent authorities in the category 1 territory have not made a decision to charge or have not made a decision to try (or have made neither of those decisions), and
(ii) the person's absence from the category 1 territory is not the sole reason for that failure,
and
(b) those representing the category 1 territory do not prove that–

(i) the competent authorities in the category 1 territory have made a decision to charge and a decision to try, or

(ii) in a case where one of those decisions has not been made (or neither of them has been made), the person's absence from the category 1 territory is the sole reason for that failure.

(2) In this section 'to charge' and 'to try', in relation to a person and an extradition offence, mean–

(a) to charge the person with the offence in the category 1 territory, and

(b) to try the person for the offence in the category 1 territory.

Extraneous considerations

13 A person's extradition to a category 1 territory is barred by reason of extraneous considerations if (and only if) it appears that–

(a) the Part 1 warrant issued in respect of him (though purporting to be issued on account of the extradition offence) is in fact issued for the purpose of prosecuting or punishing him on account of his race, religion, nationality, gender, sexual orientation or political opinions, or

(b) if extradited he might be prejudiced at his trial or punished, detained or restricted in his personal liberty by reason of his race, religion, nationality, gender, sexual orientation or political opinions.

Passage of time

14 A person's extradition to a category 1 territory is barred by reason of the passage of time if (and only if) it appears that it would be unjust or oppressive to extradite him by reason of the passage of time since he is alleged to have–

(a) committed the extradition offence (where he is accused of its commission), or

(b) become unlawfully at large (where he is alleged to have been convicted of it).

Age

15 A person's extradition to a category 1 territory is barred by reason of his age if (and only if) it would be conclusively presumed because of his age that he could not be guilty of the extradition offence on the assumption–

(a) that the conduct constituting the extradition offence constituted an offence in the part of the United Kingdom where the judge exercises jurisdiction;

(b) that the person carried out the conduct when the extradition offence was committed (or alleged to be committed);

(c) that the person carried out the conduct in the part of the United Kingdom where the judge exercises jurisdiction.

16 [*repealed*]

Speciality

17 (1) A person's extradition to a category 1 territory is barred by reason of speciality if (and only if) there are no speciality arrangements with the category 1 territory.

(2) There are speciality arrangements with a category 1 territory if, under the law of that territory or arrangements made between it and the United Kingdom, a person who is extradited to the territory from the United Kingdom may be

dealt with in the territory for an offence committed before his extradition only if–

(a) the offence is one falling within subsection (3), or
(b) the condition in subsection (4) is satisfied.

(3) The offences are–

(a) the offence in respect of which the person is extradited;
(b) an extradition offence disclosed by the same facts as that offence;
(c) an extradition offence in respect of which the appropriate judge gives his consent under section 55 to the person being dealt with;
(d) an offence which is not punishable with imprisonment or another form of detention;
(e) an offence in respect of which the person will not be detained in connection with his trial, sentence or appeal;
(f) an offence in respect of which the person waives the right that he would have (but for this paragraph) not to be dealt with for the offence.

(4) The condition is that the person is given an opportunity to leave the category 1 territory and–

(a) he does not do so before the end of the permitted period, or
(b) if he does so before the end of the permitted period, he returns there.

(5) The permitted period is 45 days starting with the day on which the person arrives in the category 1 territory.

(6) Arrangements made with a category 1 territory which is a Commonwealth country or a British overseas territory may be made for a particular case or more generally.

(7) A certificate issued by or under the authority of the Secretary of State confirming the existence of arrangements with a category 1 territory which is a Commonwealth country or a British overseas territory and stating the terms of the arrangements is conclusive evidence of those matters.

Earlier extradition to United Kingdom from category 1 territory

18 A person's extradition to a category 1 territory is barred by reason of his earlier extradition to the United Kingdom from another category 1 territory if (and only if)–

(a) the person was extradited to the United Kingdom from another category 1 territory (the extraditing territory);
(b) under arrangements between the United Kingdom and the extraditing territory, that territory's consent is required to the person's extradition from the United Kingdom to the category 1 territory in respect of the extradition offence under consideration;
(c) that consent has not been given on behalf of the extraditing territory.

Earlier extradition to United Kingdom from non-category 1 territory

19 A person's extradition to a category 1 territory is barred by reason of his earlier extradition to the United Kingdom from a non-category 1 territory if (and only if)–

(a) the person was extradited to the United Kingdom from a territory that is not a category 1 territory (the extraditing territory);
(b) under arrangements between the United Kingdom and the extraditing territory, that territory's consent is required to the person's being dealt

with in the United Kingdom in respect of the extradition offence under consideration;

(c) consent has not been given on behalf of the extraditing territory to the person's extradition from the United Kingdom to the category 1 territory in respect of the extradition offence under consideration.

Earlier transfer to United Kingdom by International Criminal Court

19A(1) A person's extradition to a category 1 territory is barred by reason of his earlier transfer by the International Criminal Court if (and only if)–

(a) the person was transferred to the United Kingdom to serve a sentence imposed by the Court;

(b) under arrangements between the United Kingdom and the Court, the consent of the Presidency of the Court is required to the person's extradition from the United Kingdom to the category 1 territory in respect of the extradition offence under consideration;

(c) that consent has not been given.

(2) Subsection (1) does not apply if the person has served the sentence imposed by the Court and has subsequently–

(a) remained voluntarily in the United Kingdom for more than 30 days, or

(b) left the United Kingdom and returned to it.

Forum

19B(1) The extradition of a person ('D') to a category 1 territory is barred by reason of forum if the extradition would not be in the interests of justice.

(2) For the purposes of this section, the extradition would not be in the interests of justice if the judge–

(a) decides that a substantial measure of D's relevant activity was performed in the United Kingdom; and

(b) decides, having regard to the specified matters relating to the interests of justice (and only those matters), that the extradition should not take place.

(3) These are the specified matters relating to the interests of justice–

(a) the place where most of the loss or harm resulting from the extradition offence occurred or was intended to occur;

(b) the interests of any victims of the extradition offence;

(c) any belief of a prosecutor that the United Kingdom, or a particular part of the United Kingdom, is not the most appropriate jurisdiction in which to prosecute D in respect of the conduct constituting the extradition offence;

(d) were D to be prosecuted in a part of the United Kingdom for an offence that corresponds to the extradition offence, whether evidence necessary to prove the offence is or could be made available in the United Kingdom;

(e) any delay that might result from proceeding in one jurisdiction rather than another;

(f) the desirability and practicability of all prosecutions relating to the extradition offence taking place in one jurisdiction, having regard (in particular) to–

(i) the jurisdictions in which witnesses, co-defendants and other suspects are located, and

(ii) the practicability of the evidence of such persons being given in the United Kingdom or in jurisdictions outside the United Kingdom;

(g) D's connections with the United Kingdom.

(4) In deciding whether the extradition would not be in the interests of justice, the judge must have regard to the desirability of not requiring the disclosure of material which is subject to restrictions on disclosure in the category 1 territory concerned.

(5) If, on an application by a prosecutor, it appears to the judge that the prosecutor has considered the offences for which D could be prosecuted in the United Kingdom, or a part of the United Kingdom, in respect of the conduct constituting the extradition offence, the judge must make that prosecutor a party to the proceedings on the question of whether D's extradition is barred by reason of forum.

(6) In this section 'D's relevant activity' means activity which is material to the commission of the extradition offence and which is alleged to have been performed by D.

Effect of prosecutor's certificates on forum proceedings

19C(1) The judge hearing proceedings under section 19B (the 'forum proceedings') must decide that the extradition is not barred by reason of forum if (at a time when the judge has not yet decided the proceedings) the judge receives a prosecutor's certificate relating to the extradition.

(2) That duty to decide the forum proceedings in that way is subject to the determination of any question relating to the prosecutor's certificate raised in accordance with section 19E.

(3) A designated prosecutor may apply for the forum proceedings to be adjourned for the purpose of assisting that or any other designated prosecutor–

(a) in considering whether to give a prosecutor's certificate relating to the extradition,

(b) in giving such a certificate, or

(c) in sending such a certificate to the judge.

(4) If such an application is made, the judge must–

(a) adjourn the forum proceedings until the application is decided; and

(b) continue the adjournment, for such period as appears to the judge to be reasonable, if the application is granted.

(5) But the judge must end the adjournment if the application is not granted.

Prosecutor's certificates

19D(1) A 'prosecutor's certificate' is a certificate given by a designated prosecutor which–

(a) certifies both matter A and matter B, and

(b) certifies either matter C or matter D.

(2) Matter A is that a responsible prosecutor has considered the offences for which D could be prosecuted in the United Kingdom, or a part of the United Kingdom, in respect of the conduct constituting the extradition offence.

(3) Matter B is that the responsible prosecutor has decided that there are one or more such offences that correspond to the extradition offence (the 'corresponding offences').

(4) Matter C is that–

(a) the responsible prosecutor has made a formal decision as to the prosecution of D for the corresponding offences,

(b) that decision is that D should not be prosecuted for the corresponding offences, and

(c) the reason for that decision is a belief that–
  (i) there would be insufficient admissible evidence for the prosecution; or
  (ii) the prosecution would not be in the public interest.

(5) Matter D is that the responsible prosecutor believes that D should not be prosecuted for the corresponding offences because there are concerns about the disclosure of sensitive material in–
(a) the prosecution of D for the corresponding offences, or
(b) any other proceedings.

(6) In relation to the extradition of any person to a category 1 territory, neither this section nor any other rule of law (whether or not contained in an enactment) may require a designated prosecutor–
(a) to consider any matter relevant to giving a prosecutor's certificate; or
(b) to consider whether to give a prosecutor's certificate.

(7) In this section 'sensitive material' means material which appears to the responsible prosecutor to be sensitive, including material appearing to be sensitive on grounds relating to–
(a) national security,
(b) international relations, or
(c) the prevention or detection of crime (including grounds relating to the identification or activities of witnesses, informants or any other persons supplying information to the police or any other law enforcement agency who may be in danger if their identities are revealed).

Questioning of prosecutor's certificate

19E(1) No decision of a designated prosecutor relating to a prosecutor's certificate in respect of D's extradition (a 'relevant certification decision') may be questioned except on an appeal under section 26 against an order for that extradition.

(2) In England and Wales, and Northern Ireland, for the purpose of–
(a) determining whether to give permission for a relevant certification decision to be questioned, and
(b) determining any such question (if that permission is given),
the High Court must apply the procedures and principles which would be applied by it on an application for judicial review.

(3) In Scotland, for the purpose of determining any questioning of a relevant certification decision, the High Court must apply the procedures and principles that would be applied by it on an application for judicial review.

(4) In a case where the High Court quashes a prosecutor's certificate, the High Court is to decide the question of whether or not the extradition is barred by reason of forum.

(5) Where the High Court is required to decide that question by virtue of subsection (4)–
(a) sections 19B to 19D and this section apply in relation to that decision (with the appropriate modifications) as they apply to a decision by a judge; and
(b) in particular–
  (i) a reference in this section to an appeal under section 26 has effect as a reference to an appeal under section 32 to the Supreme Court;

(ii) a reference in this section to the High Court has effect as a reference to the Supreme Court.

Interpretation of sections 19B to 19E

19F (1) This section applies for the purposes of sections 19B to 19E (and this section).

(2) These expressions have the meanings given–

'D' has the meaning given in section 19B(1);

'designated prosecutor' means–

(a) a member of the Crown Prosecution Service, or

(b) any other person who–

(i) is a prosecutor designated for the purposes of this section by order made by the Secretary of State, or

(ii) is within a description of prosecutors so designated;

'extradition offence' means the offence specified in the Part 1 warrant (including the conduct that constitutes the extradition offence);

'forum proceedings' has the meaning given in section 19C(1);

'part of the United Kingdom' means–

(a) England and Wales;

(b) Scotland;

(c) Northern Ireland;

'prosecutor' means a person who has responsibility for prosecuting offences in any part of the United Kingdom (whether or not the person also has other responsibilities);

'prosecutor's certificate' has the meaning given in section 19D(1);

'responsible prosecutor', in relation to a prosecutor's certificate, means–

(a) the designated prosecutor giving the certificate, or

(b) another designated prosecutor.

(3) In determining for any purpose whether an offence corresponds to the extradition offence, regard must be had, in particular, to the nature and seriousness of the two offences.

(4) A reference to a formal decision as to the prosecution of D for an offence is a reference to a decision (made after complying with, in particular, any applicable requirement concerning a code of practice) that D should, or should not, be prosecuted for the offence.

Case where person has been convicted

20 (1) If the judge is required to proceed under this section (by virtue of section 11) he must decide whether the person was convicted in his presence.

(2) If the judge decides the question in subsection (1) in the affirmative he must proceed under section 21.

(3) If the judge decides that question in the negative he must decide whether the person deliberately absented himself from his trial.

(4) If the judge decides the question in subsection (3) in the affirmative he must proceed under section 21.

(5) If the judge decides that question in the negative he must decide whether the person would be entitled to a retrial or (on appeal) to a review amounting to a retrial.

(6) If the judge decides the question in subsection (5) in the affirmative he must proceed under section 21.

(7) If the judge decides that question in the negative he must order the person's discharge.

(8) The judge must not decide the question in subsection (5) in the affirmative unless, in any proceedings that it is alleged would constitute a retrial or a review amounting to a retrial, the person would have these rights–

(a) the right to defend himself in person or through legal assistance of his own choosing or, if he had not sufficient means to pay for legal assistance, to be given it free when the interests of justice so required;

(b) the right to examine or have examined witnesses against him and to obtain the attendance and examination of witnesses on his behalf under the same conditions as witnesses against him.

Person unlawfully at large: human rights

21 (1) If the judge is required to proceed under this section (by virtue of section 20) he must decide whether the person's extradition would be compatible with the Convention rights within the meaning of the Human Rights Act 1998.

(2) If the judge decides the question in subsection (1) in the negative he must order the person's discharge.

(3) If the judge decides that question in the affirmative he must order the person to be extradited to the category 1 territory in which the warrant was issued.

(4) If the judge makes an order under subsection (3) he must remand the person in custody or on bail to wait for his extradition to the category 1 territory.

(5) If the person is remanded in custody, the appropriate judge may later grant bail.

Person not convicted: human rights and proportionality

21A(1) If the judge is required to proceed under this section (by virtue of section 11), the judge must decide both of the following questions in respect of the extradition of the person ('D')–

(a) whether the extradition would be compatible with the Convention rights within the meaning of the Human Rights Act 1998;

(b) whether the extradition would be disproportionate.

(2) In deciding whether the extradition would be disproportionate, the judge must take into account the specified matters relating to proportionality (so far as the judge thinks it appropriate to do so); but the judge must not take any other matters into account.

(3) These are the specified matters relating to proportionality–

(a) the seriousness of the conduct alleged to constitute the extradition offence;

(b) the likely penalty that would be imposed if D was found guilty of the extradition offence;

(c) the possibility of the relevant foreign authorities taking measures that would be less coercive than the extradition of D.

(4) The judge must order D's discharge if the judge makes one or both of these decisions–

(a) that the extradition would not be compatible with the Convention rights;

(b) that the extradition would be disproportionate.

(5) The judge must order D to be extradited to the category 1 territory in which the warrant was issued if the judge makes both of these decisions–

(a) that the extradition would be compatible with the Convention rights;

(b) that the extradition would not be disproportionate.

(6) If the judge makes an order under subsection (5) he must remand the person in custody or on bail to wait for extradition to the category 1 territory.
(7) If the person is remanded in custody, the appropriate judge may later grant bail.
(8) In this section 'relevant foreign authorities' means the authorities in the territory to which D would be extradited if the extradition went ahead.

Matters arising before end of extradition hearing

Request for temporary transfer etc

21B(1) This section applies if–
(a) a Part 1 warrant is issued which contains the statement referred to in section 2(3) (warrant issued for purposes of prosecution for offence in category 1 territory), and
(b) at any time before or in the extradition hearing, the appropriate judge is informed that a request under subsection (2) or (3) has been made.
(2) A request under this subsection is a request by a judicial authority of the category 1 territory in which the warrant is issued ('the requesting territory')–
(a) that the person in respect of whom the warrant is issued be temporarily transferred to the requesting territory, or
(b) that arrangements be made to enable the person to speak with representatives of an authority in the requesting territory responsible for investigating, prosecuting or trying the offence specified in the warrant.
(3) A request under this subsection is a request by the person in respect of whom the warrant is issued–
(a) to be temporarily transferred to the requesting territory, or
(b) that arrangements be made to enable the person to speak with representatives of an authority in the requesting territory responsible for investigating, prosecuting or trying the offence specified in the warrant.
(4) The judge must order further proceedings in respect of the extradition to be adjourned if the judge thinks it necessary to do so to enable the person (in the case of a request under subsection (2)) or the authority by which the warrant is issued (in the case of a request under subsection (3)) to consider whether to consent to the request.
An adjournment under this subsection must not be for more than 7 days.
(5) If the person or authority consents to the request, the judge must–
(a) make whatever orders and directions seem appropriate for giving effect to the request;
(b) order further proceedings in respect of the extradition to be adjourned for however long seems necessary to enable the orders and directions to be carried out.
(6) If the request, or consent to the request, is withdrawn before effect (or full effect) has been given to it–
(a) no steps (or further steps) may be taken to give effect to the request;
(b) the judge may make whatever further orders and directions seem appropriate (including an order superseding one made under subsection (5)(b)).
(7) A person may not make a request under paragraph (a) or (b) of subsection (3) in respect of a warrant if the person has already given consent to a request

under the corresponding paragraph of subsection (2) in respect of that warrant (even if that consent has been withdrawn).

(8) A person may not make a further request under paragraph (a) or (b) of subsection (3) in respect of a warrant if the person has already made a request under that paragraph in respect of that warrant (even if that request has been withdrawn).

(9) If–

(a) a request under subsection (2) or (3) is made before a date has been fixed on which the extradition hearing is to begin, and

(b) the proceedings are adjourned under this section,

the permitted period for the purposes of fixing that date (see section 8(4)) is extended by the number of days for which the proceedings are so adjourned.

Person charged with offence in United Kingdom

22 (1) This section applies if at any time in the extradition hearing the judge is informed that the person in respect of whom the Part 1 warrant is issued is charged with an offence in the United Kingdom.

(2) The judge must adjourn the extradition hearing until one of these occurs–

(a) the charge is disposed of;

(b) the charge is withdrawn;

(c) proceedings in respect of the charge are discontinued;

(d) an order is made for the charge to lie on the file, or in relation to Scotland, the diet is deserted ***pro loco et tempore***.

(3) If a sentence of imprisonment or another form of detention is imposed in respect of the offence charged, the judge may adjourn the extradition hearing until the person is released from detention pursuant to the sentence (whether on licence or otherwise).

(4) If before he adjourns the extradition hearing under subsection (2) the judge has decided under section 11 whether the person's extradition is barred by reason of the rule against double jeopardy, the judge must decide that question again after the resumption of the hearing.

Person serving sentence in United Kingdom

23 (1) This section applies if at any time in the extradition hearing the judge is informed that the person in respect of whom the Part 1 warrant is issued is in custody serving a sentence of imprisonment or another form of detention in the United Kingdom.

(2) The judge may adjourn the extradition hearing until the person is released from detention pursuant to the sentence (whether on licence or otherwise).

(3) In a case where an extradition hearing is adjourned under subsection (2)–

(a) section 131 of the Magistrates' Courts Act 1980 (remand of accused already in custody) has effect as if a reference to 28 clear days in subsection (1) or (2) of that section were a reference to six months;

(b) Article 47(2) of the Magistrates' Courts (Northern Ireland) Order 1981 (SI No 1675 (NI 26)) (period of remand in custody) has effect as if a reference to 28 days in–

(i) paragraph (a)(iii), or

(ii) the words after paragraph (b),

were a reference to six months.

Extradition request

24 (1) This section applies if at any time in the extradition hearing the judge is informed that–

(a) a certificate has been issued under section 70 in respect of a request for the person's extradition;

(b) the request has not been disposed of;

(c) an order has been made under section 179(2) for further proceedings on the warrant to be deferred until the request has been disposed of.

(2) The judge must remand the person in custody or on bail.

(3) If the person is remanded in custody, the appropriate judge may later grant bail.

Physical or mental condition

25 (1) This section applies if at any time in the extradition hearing it appears to the judge that the condition in subsection (2) is satisfied.

(2) The condition is that the physical or mental condition of the person in respect of whom the Part 1 warrant is issued is such that it would be unjust or oppressive to extradite him.

(3) The judge must–

(a) order the person's discharge, or

(b) adjourn the extradition hearing until it appears to him that the condition in subsection (2) is no longer satisfied.

. . .

Interpretation

Extradition offences: person not sentenced for offence

64 (1) This section sets out whether a person's conduct constitutes an 'extradition offence' for the purposes of this Part in a case where the person–

(a) is accused in a category 1 territory of an offence constituted by the conduct, or

(b) has been convicted in that territory of an offence constituted by the conduct but not sentenced for it.

(2) The conduct constitutes an extradition offence in relation to the category 1 territory if the conditions in subsection (3) or (4) are satisfied.

(3) The conditions in this subsection are that–

(a) the conduct occurs in the category 1 territory;

(b) the conduct would constitute an offence under the law of the relevant part of the United Kingdom if it occurred in that part of the United Kingdom;

(c) the conduct is punishable under the law of the category 1 territory with imprisonment or another form of detention for a term of 12 months or a greater punishment.

(4) The conditions in this subsection are that–

(a) the conduct occurs outside the category 1 territory;

(b) in corresponding circumstances equivalent conduct would constitute an extra-territorial offence under the law of the relevant part of the United Kingdom;

(c) the conduct is punishable under the law of the category 1 territory with imprisonment or another form of detention for a term of 12 months or a greater punishment.

(5) [Repealed.]
(6) For the purposes of subsections (3)(b) and (4)(b)–
(a) if the conduct relates to a tax or duty, it does not matter whether the law of the relevant part of the United Kingdom imposes the same kind of tax or duty or contains rules of the same kind as those of the law of the category 1 territory;
(b) if the conduct relates to customs or exchange, it does not matter whether the law of the relevant part of the United Kingdom contains rules of the same kind as those of the law of the category 1 territory.

Extradition offences: person sentenced for offence

65 (1) This section sets out whether a person's conduct constitutes an 'extradition offence' for the purposes of this Part in a case where the person–
(a) has been convicted in a category 1 territory of an offence constituted by the conduct, and
(b) has been sentenced for the offence.
(2) The conduct constitutes an extradition offence in relation to the category 1 territory if the conditions in subsection (3) or (4) are satisfied.
(3) The conditions in this subsection are that–
(a) the conduct occurs in the category 1 territory;
(b) the conduct would constitute an offence under the law of the relevant part of the United Kingdom if it occurred in that part of the United Kingdom;
(c) a sentence of imprisonment or another form of detention for a term of 4 months or a greater punishment has been imposed in the category 1 territory in respect of the conduct.
(4) The conditions in this subsection are that–
(a) the conduct occurs outside the category 1 territory;
(b) in corresponding circumstances equivalent conduct would constitute an extra-territorial offence under the law of the relevant part of the United Kingdom;
(c) a sentence of imprisonment or another form of detention for a term of 4 months or a greater punishment has been imposed in the category 1 territory in respect of the conduct.
(5) [Repealed.]
(6) For the purposes of subsections (3)(b) and (4)(b)–
(a) if the conduct relates to a tax or duty, it does not matter whether the law of the relevant part of the United Kingdom imposes the same kind of tax or duty or contains rules of the same kind as those of the law of the category 1 territory;
(b) if the conduct relates to customs or exchange, it does not matter whether the law of the relevant part of the United Kingdom contains rules of the same kind as those of the law of the category 1 territory.

. . .

PART 2: EXTRADITION TO CATEGORY 2 TERRITORIES

Extradition request and certificate

70 (1) The Secretary of State must (subject to subsection (2)) issue a certificate under this section if he receives a valid request for the extradition of a person to a category 2 territory.

(2) The Secretary of State may refuse to issue a certificate under this section if–
  (a) he has power under section 126 to order that proceedings on the request be deferred,
  (b) the person whose extradition is requested has been recorded by the Secretary of State as a refugee within the meaning of the Refugee Convention, or
  (c) the person whose extradition is requested has been granted leave to enter or remain in the United Kingdom on the ground that it would be a breach of Article 2 or 3 of the Human Rights Convention to remove him to the territory to which extradition is requested.

(3) A request for a person's extradition is valid if–
  (a) it contains the statement referred to in subsection (4) or the statement referred to in subsection (4A), and
  (b) it is made in the approved way.

(4) The statement is one that–
  (a) the person is accused in the category 2 territory of the commission of an offence specified in the request, and
  (b) the request is made with a view to his arrest and extradition to the category 2 territory for the purpose of being prosecuted for the offence.

(4A) The statement is one that–
  (a) the person has been convicted of an offence specified in the request by a court in the category 2 territory, and
  (b) the request is made with a view to his arrest and extradition to the category 2 territory for the purpose of being sentenced for the offence or of serving a sentence of imprisonment or another form of detention imposed in respect of the offence.

(5) A request for extradition to a category 2 territory which is a British overseas territory is made in the approved way if it is made by or on behalf of the person administering the territory.

(6) A request for extradition to a category 2 territory which is the Hong Kong Special Administrative Region of the People's Republic of China is made in the approved way if it is made by or on behalf of the government of the Region.

(7) A request for extradition to any other category 2 territory is made in the approved way if it is made–
  (a) by an authority of the territory which the Secretary of State believes has the function of making requests for extradition in that territory, or
  (b) by a person recognised by the Secretary of State as a diplomatic or consular representative of the territory.

(8) A certificate under this section must–
  (a) certify that the request is made in the approved way, and
  (b) identify the order by which the territory in question is designated as a category 2 territory.

(9) If a certificate is issued under this section the Secretary of State must send the request and the certificate to the appropriate judge.

(10) Subsection (11) applies at all times after the Secretary of State issues a certificate under this section.

(11) The Secretary of State is not to consider whether the extradition would be compatible with the Convention rights within the meaning of the Human Rights Act 1998.

Arrest

Arrest warrant following extradition request

71 (1) This section applies if the Secretary of State sends documents to the appropriate judge under section 70.

(2) The judge may issue a warrant for the arrest of the person whose extradition is requested if the judge has reasonable grounds for believing that–

(a) the offence in respect of which extradition is requested is an extradition offence, and

(b) there is evidence falling within subsection (3).

(3) The evidence is–

(a) evidence that would justify the issue of a warrant for the arrest of a person accused of the offence within the judge's jurisdiction, if the person whose extradition is requested is accused of the commission of the offence;

(b) evidence that would justify the issue of a warrant for the arrest of a person unlawfully at large after conviction of the offence within the judge's jurisdiction, if the person whose extradition is requested is alleged to be unlawfully at large after conviction of the offence.

(4) But if the category 2 territory to which extradition is requested is designated for the purposes of this section by order made by the Secretary of State, subsections (2) and (3) have effect as if 'evidence' read 'information'.

(5) A warrant issued under this section may–

(a) be executed by any person to whom it is directed or by any constable or customs officer;

(b) be executed even if neither the warrant nor a copy of it is in the possession of the person executing it at the time of the arrest.

(6) If a warrant issued under this section–

(a) is directed to a service policeman, and

(b) is in respect of a person subject to service law or a civilian subject to service discipline,

it may be executed anywhere.

(7) In any other case, a warrant issued under this section may be executed in any part of the United Kingdom.

Person arrested under section 71

72 (1) This section applies if a person is arrested under a warrant issued under section 71.

(2) A copy of the warrant must be given to the person as soon as practicable after his arrest.

(3) The person must be brought as soon as practicable before the appropriate judge.

(4) But subsection (3) does not apply if–

(a) the person is granted bail by a constable following his arrest, or

(b) the Secretary of State decides under section 126 that the request for the person's extradition is not to be proceeded with.

(5) If subsection (2) is not complied with and the person applies to the judge to be discharged, the judge may order his discharge.

(6) If subsection (3) is not complied with and the person applies to the judge to be discharged, the judge must order his discharge.

(7) When the person first appears or is brought before the appropriate judge, the judge must–
(a) inform him of the contents of the request for his extradition;
(b) give him the required information about consent;
(c) remand him in custody or on bail.

(8) The required information about consent is–
(a) that the person may consent to his extradition to the category 2 territory to which his extradition is requested;
(b) an explanation of the effect of consent and the procedure that will apply if he gives consent;
(c) that consent must be given in writing and is irrevocable.

(9) If the person is remanded in custody, the appropriate judge may later grant bail.

(10) Subsection (4)(a) applies to Scotland with the omission of the words 'by a constable'.

Provisional warrant

73 (1) This section applies if a justice of the peace is satisfied on information in writing and on oath that a person within subsection (2)–
(a) is or is believed to be in the United Kingdom, or
(b) is or is believed to be on his way to the United Kingdom.

(2) A person is within this subsection if–
(a) he is accused in a category 2 territory of the commission of an offence, or
(b) he is alleged to be unlawfully at large after conviction of an offence by a court in a category 2 territory.

(3) The justice may issue a warrant for the arrest of the person (a provisional warrant) if he has reasonable grounds for believing that–
(a) the offence of which the person is accused or has been convicted is an extradition offence, and
(b) there is written evidence falling within subsection (4).

(4) The evidence is–
(a) evidence that would justify the issue of a warrant for the arrest of a person accused of the offence within the justice's jurisdiction, if the person in respect of whom the warrant is sought is accused of the commission of the offence;
(b) evidence that would justify the issue of a warrant for the arrest of a person unlawfully at large after conviction of the offence within the justice's jurisdiction, if the person in respect of whom the warrant is sought is alleged to be unlawfully at large after conviction of the offence.

(5) But if the category 2 territory is designated for the purposes of this section by order made by the Secretary of State, subsections (3) and (4) have effect as if 'evidence' read 'information'.

(6) A provisional warrant may–
(a) be executed by any person to whom it is directed or by any constable or customs officer;
(b) be executed even if neither the warrant nor a copy of it is in the possession of the person executing it at the time of the arrest.

(7) If a warrant issued under this section–
  (a) is directed to a service policeman, and
  (b) is in respect of a person subject to service law or a civilian subject to service discipline,

it may be executed anywhere.

(8) In any other case, a warrant issued under this section may be executed in any part of the United Kingdom.

(9) . . .

(10) The preceding provisions of this section apply to Scotland with these modifications–
  (a) in subsection (1) for 'justice of the peace is satisfied on information in writing and on oath' substitute 'sheriff is satisfied, on an application by a procurator fiscal,';
  (b) in subsection (3) for 'justice' substitute 'sheriff';
  (c) in subsection (4) for 'justice's', in paragraphs (a) and (b), substitute 'sheriff's'.

(11) Subsection (1) applies to Northern Ireland with the substitution of 'a complaint' for 'information'.

Person arrested under provisional warrant

74 (1) This section applies if a person is arrested under a provisional warrant.

(2) A copy of the warrant must be given to the person as soon as practicable after his arrest.

(3) The person must be brought as soon as practicable before the appropriate judge.

(4) But subsection (3) does not apply if–
  (a) the person is granted bail by a constable following his arrest, or
  (b) in a case where the Secretary of State has received a valid request for the person's extradition, the Secretary of State decides under section 126 that the request is not to be proceeded with.

(5) If subsection (2) is not complied with and the person applies to the judge to be discharged, the judge may order his discharge.

(6) If subsection (3) is not complied with and the person applies to the judge to be discharged, the judge must order his discharge.

(7) When the person first appears or is brought before the appropriate judge, the judge must–
  (a) inform him that he is accused of the commission of an offence in a category 2 territory or that he is alleged to be unlawfully at large after conviction of an offence by a court in a category 2 territory;
  (b) give him the required information about consent;
  (c) remand him in custody or on bail.

(8) The required information about consent is–
  (a) that the person may consent to his extradition to the category 2 territory in which he is accused of the commission of an offence or is alleged to have been convicted of an offence;
  (b) an explanation of the effect of consent and the procedure that will apply if he gives consent;
  (c) that consent must be given in writing and is irrevocable.

(9) If the person is remanded in custody, the appropriate judge may later grant bail.

(10) The judge must order the person's discharge if the documents referred to in section 70(9) are not received by the judge within the required period.
(11) The required period is–
(a) 45 days starting with the day on which the person was arrested, or
(b) if the category 2 territory is designated by order made by the Secretary of State for the purposes of this section, any longer period permitted by the order.
(12) Subsection (4)(a) applies to Scotland with the omission of the words 'by a constable'.

Provisional arrest without warrant

74A Provisional arrest where certificate issued under section 74B

(1) A constable, a customs officer or a service policeman may arrest a person without a warrant if a certificate has been issued under section 74B in respect of the person.
(2) A copy of the certificate must be given to the person as soon as practicable after the arrest.
(3) The person must be brought as soon as practicable before the appropriate judge (see further, section 74D).
(4) A constable or a customs officer may arrest a person under subsection (1) in any part of the United Kingdom.
(5) A service policeman may arrest a person under subsection (1) only if the person is subject to service law or is a civilian subject to service discipline.
(6) A service policeman who has power to arrest a person under subsection (1) may exercise the power anywhere.
(7) A person arrested under subsection (1) may not be arrested again in reliance on the same certificate.

74B Certificates enabling provisional arrest under section 74A

(1) The designated authority may issue a certificate under this section in respect of a person if–
(a) it receives a valid request, made by an authority of a specified category 2 territory, for the person's arrest (for more about requests, see section 74C),
(b) it is satisfied that the request is made under arrangements which allow such a request to be made only if–
(i) a warrant for the person's arrest has been issued in the category 2 territory in respect of an offence, or
(ii) the person is alleged to be unlawfully at large after conviction of an offence by a court in the category 2 territory,
(c) it has reasonable grounds for believing that the offence specified in the request is a serious extradition offence, and
(d) it is satisfied that the seriousness of the conduct constituting the offence makes it appropriate to issue the certificate.
(2) A certificate issued by the designated authority under this section must–
(a) state the category 2 territory in respect of which the request is made, the form of the request and the date on which the request was made,

(b) certify that the category 2 territory is a specified category 2 territory,
(c) certify that the request is a valid request,
(d) certify the matters in subsection (1)(c) and (d), and
(e) set out the statement and information mentioned in section 74C(1)(a) or (b) (as the case may be).

(3) A certificate (or purported certificate) may be withdrawn and a new one issued on the basis of the same request at any time before the person has been arrested in reliance on it.

(4) The "designated authority" is the National Crime Agency.

(5) The Secretary of State may by regulations amend this section so as to change the meaning of "designated authority".

(6) Regulations made under subsection (5) may–
(a) designate more than one authority;
(b) designate different authorities for different parts of the United Kingdom.

(7) A "specified category 2 territory" is a category 2 territory that is specified in Schedule A1.

(8) The Secretary of State may by regulations–
(a) amend Schedule A1 so as to add, vary or remove a reference to a territory, and
(b) in consequence, amend section 74C so as to change what it means to make a request in the approved way for the purposes of that section.

(9) The reference in subsection (1)(b) to a warrant for a person's arrest includes a reference to a judicial document authorising the person's arrest.

(10) For the purposes of determining whether an offence is a "serious extradition offence", sections 137 and 138 apply as if–
(a) a reference to an "extradition offence" were to a "serious extradition offence",
(b) a reference to the relevant part of the United Kingdom were to any part of the United Kingdom (and, accordingly, each of sections 137 and 138 have effect as if subsection (8) were omitted),
(c) a reference to the request for the person's extradition were a reference to the request for the person's arrest,
(d) the references in sections 137(3)(b) and (4)(b) and 138(3)(b) to "12 months" were to "3 years", and
(e) the references in section 137(3)(c) and (4)(c) to conduct that is "so punishable" were to conduct that is punishable with imprisonment or another form of detention for a term of 12 months or a greater punishment.

74C Section 74B supplementary: valid requests for arrest

(1) For the purposes of section 74B a request for a person's arrest is valid if it is made in the approved way and it contains–
(a) the statement referred to in subsection (2) and the information referred to in subsection (3), or
(b) the statement referred to in subsection (4) and the information referred to in subsection (5).

(2) The statement is one that–
(a) the person is accused in the category 2 territory of the commission of an offence specified in the request, and

(b) the request is made with a view to the arrest and extradition of the person to the category 2 territory for the purpose of being prosecuted for the offence.

(3) The information is–

(a) particulars of the person's identity;

(b) particulars of the circumstances in which the person is alleged to have committed the offence, including the conduct alleged to constitute the offence, the time and place at which the person is alleged to have committed the offence and any provision of the law of the category 2 territory under which the conduct is alleged to constitute an offence;

(c) particulars of the sentence which may be imposed under the law of the category 2 territory in respect of the offence if the person is convicted of it.

(4) The statement is one that–

(a) the person has been convicted of an offence specified in the request by a court in the category 2 territory, and

(b) the request is made with a view to the arrest and extradition of the person to the category 2 territory for the purpose of being sentenced for the offence or of serving a sentence of imprisonment or another form of detention imposed in respect of the offence.

(5) The information is–

(a) particulars of the person's identity;

(b) particulars of the conviction;

(c) particulars of the sentence which may be imposed under the law of the category 2 territory in respect of the offence, if the person has not been sentenced for the offence;

(d) particulars of the sentence which has been imposed under the law of the category 2 territory in respect of the offence, if the person has been sentenced for the offence.

(6) A request is made in the approved way for the purposes of this section if it is made by an authority of the category 2 territory which the designated authority believes has the function of making such requests in that territory.

74D Person provisionally arrested under section 74A

(1) The judge before whom a person is brought following arrest under section 74A must decide, on the basis of any evidence or information produced to the judge, whether a warrant would be issued under section 73 if the person were not already under arrest.

(2) If the judge decides the question in subsection (1) in the negative, the judge must order the person's discharge.

(3) If the judge decides that question in the affirmative, the judge must proceed under section 74E.

(4) The judge may adjourn the proceedings to allow more evidence or information to be produced if–

(a) an application for the adjournment is made in accordance with rules of court, and

(b) the judge is satisfied, on the balance of probabilities, that evidence or information could not reasonably have been produced in time to avoid the need for the adjournment.

(5) If the judge grants an adjournment under subsection (4), the judge must remand the person in custody or on bail.

(6) If the person is remanded in custody, the judge may later grant bail.

(7) More than one adjournment may be granted under subsection (4) but the total period of any adjournments must not exceed 72 hours.

(8) In calculating that 72-hour period, no account is to be taken of any day falling within section 6(8A)(a) to (d) (weekends, bank holidays etc).

(9) If the judge has granted an adjournment or further adjournment, the question in subsection (1) must be decided by the appropriate judge on the next occasion when the person is brought or appears before the appropriate judge (unless a further adjournment is granted on that occasion).

(10) If the person applies to the judge to be discharged–

(a) the judge may order the person's discharge if–

(i) section 74A(2) (copy of certificate to be given to arrested person) was not complied with, or

(ii) the certificate did not comply with section 74B(2);

(b) the judge must order the person's discharge if–

(i) the judge is satisfied that there were no reasonable grounds on which the designated authority could have issued the certificate under section 74B(1), or

(ii) section 74A(3) (person to be brought before judge as soon as practicable after arrest) was not complied with.

74E Person provisionally arrested under section 74A: next steps

(1) If the appropriate judge is required by section 74D(3) to proceed under this section, the judge must–

(a) inform the person that they are accused of the commission of an offence in a category 2 territory or are alleged to be unlawfully at large after conviction of an offence by a court in a category 2 territory,

(b) give the person the required information about consent, and

(c) remand the person in custody or on bail.

(2) The required information about consent is–

(a) that the person may consent to extradition to the category 2 territory in which the person is accused of the commission of an offence or is alleged to have been convicted of an offence;

(b) an explanation of the effect of consent and the procedure that will apply if the person gives consent;

(c) that consent must be given in writing and is irrevocable.

(3) If the person is remanded in custody, the appropriate judge may later grant bail.

(4) The judge must order the person's discharge if the documents referred to in section 70(9) are not received by the judge within the required period as defined by section 74(11).

The extradition hearing

Date of extradition hearing: arrest under section 71

75 (1) When a person arrested under a warrant issued under section 71 first appears or is brought before the appropriate judge, the judge must fix a date on which the extradition hearing is to begin.

(2) The date fixed under subsection (1) must not be later than the end of the permitted period, which is 2 months starting with the date on which the person first appears or is brought before the judge.

(3) If before the date fixed under subsection (1) (or this subsection) a party to the proceedings applies to the judge for a later date to be fixed and the judge believes it to be in the interests of justice to do so, he may fix a later date; and this subsection may apply more than once.

(4) If the extradition hearing does not begin on or before the date fixed under this section and the person applies to the judge to be discharged, the judge must order his discharge.

. . .

Interpretation

Extradition offences: person not sentenced for offence

137 (1) This section sets out whether a person's conduct constitutes an 'extradition offence' for the purposes of this Part in a case where the person–

(a) is accused in a category 2 territory of an offence constituted by the conduct, or

(b) has been convicted in that territory of an offence constituted by the conduct but not sentenced for it.

(2) The conduct constitutes an extradition offence in relation to the category 2 territory if the conditions in subsection (3), (4) or (5) are satisfied.

(3) The conditions in this subsection are that–

(a) the conduct occurs in the category 2 territory;

(b) the conduct would constitute an offence under the law of the relevant part of the United Kingdom punishable with imprisonment or another form of detention for a term of 12 months or a greater punishment if it occurred in that part of the United Kingdom;

(c) the conduct is so punishable under the law of the category 2 territory.

(4) The conditions in this subsection are that–

(a) the conduct occurs outside the category 2 territory;

(b) in corresponding circumstances equivalent conduct would constitute an extra-territorial offence under the law of the relevant part of the United Kingdom punishable with imprisonment or another form of detention for a term of 12 months or a greater punishment;

(c) the conduct is so punishable under the law of the category 2 territory.

(5) The conditions in this subsection are that–

(a) the conduct occurs outside the category 2 territory;

(b) no part of the conduct occurs in the United Kingdom;

(c) the conduct constitutes, or if committed in the United Kingdom would constitute, an offence mentioned in subsection (6);

(d) the conduct is punishable under the law of the category 2 territory with imprisonment or another form of detention for a term of 12 months or a greater punishment.

(6) The offences are–

(a) an offence under section 51 or 58 of the International Criminal Court Act 2001 (genocide, crimes against humanity and war crimes);

(b) an offence under section 52 or 59 of that Act (conduct ancillary to genocide etc committed outside the jurisdiction);

(c) an ancillary offence, as defined in section 55 or 62 of that Act, in relation to an offence falling within paragraph (a) or (b);

(d) an offence under section 1 of the International Criminal Court (Scotland) Act 2001 (asp 13) (genocide, crimes against humanity and war crimes);

(e) an offence under section 2 of that Act (conduct ancillary to genocide etc committed outside the jurisdiction);

(f) an ancillary offence, as defined in section 7 of that Act, in relation to an offence falling within paragraph (d) or (e).

(7) If the conduct constitutes an offence under the military law of the category 2 territory but does not constitute an offence under the general criminal law of the relevant part of the United Kingdom it does not constitute an extradition offence; and subsections (1) to (6) have effect subject to this.

(7A) References in this section to 'conduct'(except in the expression 'equivalent conduct') are to the conduct specified in the request for the person's extradition.

(8) The relevant part of the United Kingdom is the part of the United Kingdom in which–

(a) the extradition hearing took place, if the question of whether conduct constitutes an extradition offence is to be decided by the Secretary of State;

(b) proceedings in which it is necessary to decide that question are taking place, in any other case.

Extradition offences: person sentenced for offence

138 (1) This section applies in relation to conduct of a person if–

(a) he is alleged to be unlawfully at large after conviction by a court in a category 2 territory of an offence constituted by the conduct, and

(b) he has been sentenced for the offence.

(2) The conduct constitutes an extradition offence in relation to the category 2 territory if these conditions are satisfied–

(a) the conduct occurs in the category 2 territory;

(b) the conduct would constitute an offence under the law of the relevant part of the United Kingdom punishable with imprisonment or another form of detention for a term of 12 months or a greater punishment if it occurred in that part of the United Kingdom;

(c) a sentence of imprisonment or another form of detention for a term of 4 months or a greater punishment has been imposed in the category 2 territory in respect of the conduct.

(3) The conduct also constitutes an extradition offence in relation to the category 2 territory if these conditions are satisfied–
  (a) the conduct occurs outside the category 2 territory;
  (b) a sentence of imprisonment or another form of detention for a term of 4 months or a greater punishment has been imposed in the category 2 territory in respect of the conduct;
  (c) in corresponding circumstances equivalent conduct would constitute an extra-territorial offence under the law of the relevant part of the United Kingdom punishable with imprisonment or another form of detention for a term of 12 months or a greater punishment.

(4) The conduct also constitutes an extradition offence in relation to the category 2 territory if these conditions are satisfied–
  (a) the conduct occurs outside the category 2 territory and no part of it occurs in the United Kingdom;
  (b) the conduct would constitute an offence under the law of the relevant part of the United Kingdom punishable with imprisonment or another form of detention for a term of 12 months or a greater punishment if it occurred in that part of the United Kingdom;
  (c) a sentence of imprisonment or another form of detention for a term of 4 months or a greater punishment has been imposed in the category 2 territory in respect of the conduct.

(5) The conduct also constitutes an extradition offence in relation to the category 2 territory if these conditions are satisfied–
  (a) the conduct occurs outside the category 2 territory and no part of it occurs in the United Kingdom;
  (b) a sentence of imprisonment or another form of detention for a term of 4 months or a greater punishment has been imposed in the category 2 territory in respect of the conduct;
  (c) the conduct constitutes or if committed in the United Kingdom would constitute an offence mentioned in subsection (6).

(6) The offences are–
  (a) an offence under section 51 or 58 of the International Criminal Court Act 2001 (genocide, crimes against humanity and war crimes);
  (b) an offence under section 52 or 59 of that Act (conduct ancillary to genocide etc committed outside the jurisdiction);
  (c) an ancillary offence, as defined in section 55 or 62 of that Act, in relation to an offence falling within paragraph (a) or (b);
  (d) an offence under section 1 of the International Criminal Court (Scotland) Act 2001 (genocide, crimes against humanity and war crimes);
  (e) an offence under section 2 of that Act (conduct ancillary to genocide etc committed outside the jurisdiction);
  (f) an ancillary offence, as defined in section 7 of that Act, in relation to an offence falling within paragraph (d) or (e).

(7) If the conduct constitutes an offence under the military law of the category 2 territory but does not constitute an offence under the general criminal law of the relevant part of the United Kingdom it does not constitute an extradition offence; and subsections (1) to (6) have effect subject to this.

(7A) References in this section to “conduct” (except in the expression ‘equivalent conduct’) are to the conduct specified in the request for the person’s extradition.

(8) The relevant part of the United Kingdom is the part of the United Kingdom in which–

(a) the extradition hearing took place, if the question of whether conduct constitutes an extradition offence is to be decided by the Secretary of State;

(b) proceedings in which it is necessary to decide that question are taking place, in any other case.

APPENDIX B

Surrender provisions of the Trade and Cooperation Agreement 2021

Part III, Title VII: Surrender provisions of the Trade and Cooperation Agreement between the European Union and the European Atomic Energy Community, of the one part, and the United Kingdom of Great Britain and Northern Ireland, of the other Part [2021] OJ L 149/10 [the TCA]

TITLE VII
SURRENDER

Article 596
Objective

The objective of this Title is to ensure that the extradition system between the Member States, on the one side, and the United Kingdom, on the other side, is based on a mechanism of surrender pursuant to an arrest warrant in accordance with the terms of this Title.

Article 597
Principle of proportionality

Cooperation through the arrest warrant shall be necessary and proportionate, taking into account the rights of the requested person and the interests of the victims, and having regard to the seriousness of the act, the likely penalty that would be imposed and the possibility of a State taking measures less coercive than the surrender of the requested person particularly with a view to avoiding unnecessarily long periods of pre-trial detention.

Article 598
Definitions

For the purposes of this Title, the following definitions apply:

(a) 'arrest warrant' means a judicial decision issued by a State with a view to the arrest and surrender by another State of a requested person, for the purposes of conducting a criminal prosecution or executing a custodial sentence or detention order;

(b) 'judicial authority' means an authority that is, under domestic law, a judge, a court or a public prosecutor. A public prosecutor is considered a judicial authority only to the extent that domestic law so provides;

(c) 'executing judicial authority' means the judicial authority of the executing State which is competent to execute the arrest warrant by virtue of the domestic law of that State;

(d) 'issuing judicial authority' means the judicial authority of the issuing State which is competent to issue an arrest warrant by virtue of the domestic law of that State.

Article 599
Scope

1. An arrest warrant may be issued for acts punishable by the law of the issuing State by a custodial sentence or a detention order for a maximum period of at least 12 months or, where a sentence has been passed or a detention order has been made, for sentences or detention orders of at least four months.
2. Without prejudice to paragraphs 3 and 4, surrender is subject to the condition that the acts for which the arrest warrant has been issued constitute an offence under the law of the executing State, whatever the constituent elements or however it is described.
3. Subject to Article 600, points (b) to (h) of Article 601(1), and Articles 602, 603 and 604, a State shall not refuse to execute an arrest warrant issued in relation to the following behaviour where such behaviour is punishable by deprivation of liberty or a detention order of a maximum period of at least 12 months:
   (a) the behaviour of any person who contributes to the commission by a group of persons acting with a common purpose of one or more offences in the field of terrorism referred to in Articles 1 and 2 of the European Convention on the Suppression of Terrorism, done at Strasbourg on 27 January 1977, or in relation to illicit trafficking in narcotic drugs and psychotropic substances, or murder, grievous bodily injury, kidnapping, illegal restraint, hostage-taking or rape, even where that person does not take part in the actual execution of the offence or offences concerned; such contribution must be intentional and made with the knowledge that the participation will contribute to the achievement of the group's criminal activities; or
   (b) terrorism as defined in Annex 45.
4. The United Kingdom and the Union, acting on behalf of any of its Member States, may each notify the Specialised Committee on Law Enforcement and Judicial Cooperation that, on the basis of reciprocity, the condition of double criminality referred to in paragraph 2 will not be applied, provided that the offence on which the warrant is based is:
   (a) one of the offences listed in paragraph 5, as defined by the law of the issuing State; and
   (b) punishable in the issuing State by a custodial sentence or a detention order for a maximum period of at least three years.
5. The offences referred to in paragraph 4 are:
   - participation in a criminal organisation;
   - terrorism as defined in Annex 45;
   - trafficking in human beings;
   - sexual exploitation of children and child pornography;
   - illicit trafficking in narcotic drugs and psychotropic substances;
   - illicit trafficking in weapons, munitions and explosives;
   - corruption, including bribery;

- fraud, including that affecting the financial interests of the United Kingdom, a Member State or the Union;
- laundering of the proceeds of crime;
- counterfeiting currency;
- computer-related crime;
- environmental crime, including illicit trafficking in endangered animal species and endangered plant species and varieties;
- facilitation of unauthorised entry and residence;
- murder;
- grievous bodily injury;
- illicit trade in human organs and tissue;
- kidnapping, illegal restraint and hostage-taking;
- racism and xenophobia;
- organised or armed robbery;
- illicit trafficking in cultural goods, including antiques and works of art;
- swindling;
- racketeering and extortion;
- counterfeiting and piracy of products;
- forgery of administrative documents and trafficking therein;
- forgery of means of payment;
- illicit trafficking in hormonal substances and other growth promoters;
- illicit trafficking in nuclear or radioactive materials;
- trafficking in stolen vehicles;
- rape;
- arson;
- crimes within the jurisdiction of the International Criminal Court;
- unlawful seizure of aircraft, ships or spacecraft; and
- sabotage.

Article 600
Grounds for mandatory non-execution of the arrest warrant

The execution of the arrest warrant shall be refused:

(a) if the offence on which the arrest warrant is based is covered by an amnesty in the executing State, where that State had jurisdiction to prosecute the offence under its own criminal law;

(b) if the executing judicial authority is informed that the requested person has been finally judged by a State in respect of the same acts, provided that, if a penalty has been imposed, it has been enforced, is in the process of being enforced or can no longer be enforced under the law of the sentencing State; or

(c) if the person who is the subject of the arrest warrant may not, owing to the person's age, be held criminally responsible for the acts on which the arrest warrant is based under the law of the executing State.

Article 601
Other grounds for non-execution of the arrest warrant

1. The execution of the arrest warrant may be refused:

(a) if, in one of the cases referred to in Article 599(2), the act on which the arrest warrant is based does not constitute an offence under the law of the executing State; however, in relation to taxes or duties, customs and exchange, the execution of the arrest warrant shall not be refused on the grounds that the law of the executing State does not impose the same kind of tax or duty or does not contain the same type of rules as regards taxes or duties, customs and exchange regulations as the law of the issuing State;

(b) if the person who is the subject of the arrest warrant is being prosecuted in the executing State for the same act as that on which the arrest warrant is based;

(c) if the judicial authorities of the executing State have decided either not to prosecute for the offence on which the arrest warrant is based or to halt proceedings, or if a final judgment which prevents further proceedings has been passed upon the requested person in a State in respect of the same acts;

(d) if the criminal prosecution or punishment of the requested person is statute-barred under the law of the executing State and the acts fall within the jurisdiction of that State under its own criminal law;

(e) if the executing judicial authority is informed that the requested person has been finally judged by a third country in respect of the same acts provided that, if a penalty has been imposed, it has been enforced, is in the process of being enforced or can no longer be enforced under the law of the sentencing country;

(f) if the arrest warrant has been issued for the purposes of execution of a custodial sentence or detention order and the requested person is staying in, or is a national or a resident of the executing State and that State undertakes to execute the sentence or detention order in accordance with its domestic law; if consent of the requested person to the transfer of the sentence or detention order to the executing State is required, the executing State may refuse to execute the arrest warrant only after the requested person consents to the transfer of the sentence or detention order;

(g) if the arrest warrant relates to offences which:
   (i) are regarded by the law of the executing State as having been committed in whole or in part in the territory of the executing State or in a place treated as such; or
   (ii) have been committed outside the territory of the issuing State, and the law of the executing State does not allow prosecution for the same offences if committed outside its territory;

(h) if there are reasons to believe on the basis of objective elements that the arrest warrant has been issued for the purpose of prosecuting or punishing a person on the grounds of the person's sex, race, religion, ethnic origin, nationality, language, political opinions or sexual orientation, or that that person's position may be prejudiced for any of those reasons;

(i) if the arrest warrant has been issued for the purpose of executing a custodial sentence or a detention order and the requested person did not appear in person at the trial resulting in the decision, unless the arrest warrant states that the person, in accordance with further procedural requirements defined in the domestic law of the issuing State:

(i) in due time:

(A) either was summoned in person and thereby informed of the scheduled date and place of the trial which resulted in the decision, or by other means actually received official information of the scheduled date and place of that trial in such a manner that it was unequivocally established that the person was aware of the date and place of the scheduled trial ;

and

(B) was informed that a decision may be handed down if that person did not appear for the trial;

or

(ii) being aware of the date and place of the scheduled trial, had given a mandate to a lawyer, who was either appointed by the person concerned or by the State, to defend him or her at the trial, and was indeed defended by that lawyer at the trial;

or

(iii) after being served with the decision and being expressly informed about the right to a retrial or appeal in which the person has the right to participate and which allows the merits of the case, including fresh evidence, to be re-examined, and which may lead to the original decision being reversed:

(A) expressly stated that the person did not contest the decision;

or

(B) did not request a retrial or appeal within the applicable time frame;

or

(iv) was not personally served with the decision but:

(A) will be personally served with it without delay after the surrender and will be expressly informed of the right to a retrial or appeal in which the person has the right to participate and which allows the merits of the case, including fresh evidence, to be re-examined, and which may lead to the original decision being reversed;

and

(B) will be informed of the time frame within which the person has to request such a retrial or appeal, as mentioned in the relevant arrest warrant.

2. Where the arrest warrant is issued for the purpose of executing a custodial sentence or detention order under the conditions in point (i) (iv) of paragraph 1 and the person concerned has not previously received any official information about the existence of the criminal proceedings against him or her, that person may, when being informed about the content of the arrest warrant, request to receive a copy of the judgment before being surrendered. Immediately after having been informed about the request, the issuing authority shall provide the copy of the judgment via the executing authority to the person concerned. The request of the person concerned shall neither delay the surrender procedure nor delay the decision to execute the arrest warrant. The provision of the judgment to the person concerned shall be for information purposes only; it shall not be regarded as a formal service of the

judgment nor actuate any time limits applicable for requesting a retrial or appeal.

3. Where a person is surrendered under the conditions in point (i) (iv) of paragraph 1 and that person has requested a retrial or appeal, until those proceedings are finalised the detention of that person awaiting such retrial or appeal shall be reviewed in accordance with the domestic law of the issuing State, either on a regular basis or upon request of the person concerned. Such a review shall in particular include the possibility of suspension or interruption of the detention. The retrial or appeal shall begin within due time after the surrender.

Article 602
Political offence exception

1. The execution of an arrest warrant may not be refused on the grounds that the offence may be regarded by the executing State as a political offence, as an offence connected with a political offence or as an offence inspired by political motives.
2. However, the United Kingdom and the Union, acting on behalf of any of its Member States, may each notify the Specialised Committee on Law Enforcement and Judicial Cooperation that paragraph 1 will be applied only in relation to:
   (a) the offences referred to in Articles 1 and 2 of the European Convention on the Suppression of Terrorism;
   (b) offences of conspiracy or association to commit one or more of the offences referred to in Articles 1 and 2 of the European Convention on the Suppression of Terrorism, if those offences of conspiracy or association correspond to the description of behaviour referred to in Article 599(3) of this Agreement; and
   (c) terrorism as defined in Annex 45 to this Agreement.
3. Where an arrest warrant has been issued by a State having made a notification as referred to in paragraph 2 or by a State on behalf of which such a notification has been made, the State executing the arrest warrant may apply reciprocity.

Article 603
Nationality exception

1. The execution of an arrest warrant may not be refused on the grounds that the requested person is a national of the executing State.
2. The United Kingdom, and the Union, acting on behalf of any of its Member States, may each notify the Specialised Committee on Law Enforcement and Judicial Cooperation that that State's own nationals will not be surrendered or that the surrender of their own nationals will be authorised only under certain specified conditions. The notification shall be based on reasons related to the fundamental principles or practice of the domestic legal order of the United Kingdom or the State on behalf of which a notification was made. In such a case, the Union, on behalf of any of its Member States or the United Kingdom, as the case may be, may notify the Specialised Committee on Law Enforcement

and Judicial Cooperation within a reasonable time after the receipt of the other Party's notification that the executing judicial authorities of the Member State or the United Kingdom, as the case may be, may refuse to surrender its nationals to that State or that surrender shall be authorised only under certain specified conditions.

3. In circumstances where a State has refused to execute an arrest warrant on the basis that, in the case of the United Kingdom, it has made a notification or, in the case of a Member State, the Union has made a notification on its behalf, as referred to in paragraph 2, that State shall consider instituting proceedings against its own national which are commensurate with the subject matter of the arrest warrant, having taken into account the views of the issuing State. In circumstances where a judicial authority decides not to institute such proceedings, the victim of the offence on which the arrest warrant is based shall be able to receive information on the decision in accordance with the applicable domestic law.
4. Where a State's competent authorities institute proceedings against its own national in accordance with paragraph 3, that State shall ensure that its competent authorities are able to take appropriate measures to assist the victims and witnesses in circumstances where they are residents of another State, particularly with regard to the way in which the proceedings are conducted.

Article 604
Guarantees to be given by the issuing State in particular cases

The execution of the arrest warrant by the executing judicial authority may be subject to the following guarantees:

(a) if the offence on which the arrest warrant is based is punishable by a custodial life sentence or a lifetime detention order in the issuing State, the executing State may make the execution of the arrest warrant subject to the condition that the issuing State gives a guarantee deemed sufficient by the executing State that the issuing State will review the penalty or measure imposed, on request or at the latest after 20 years, or will encourage the application of measures of clemency for which the person is entitled to apply under the law or practice of the issuing State, aiming at the non-execution of such penalty or measure;

(b) if a person who is the subject of an arrest warrant for the purposes of prosecution is a national or resident of the executing State, the surrender of that person may be subject to the condition that the person, after being heard, is returned to the executing State in order to serve there the custodial sentence or detention order passed against him or her in the issuing State; if the consent of the requested person to the transfer of the sentence or detention order to the executing State is required, the guarantee that the person be returned to the executing State to serve the person's sentence is subject to the condition that the requested person, after being heard, consents to be returned to the executing State;

(c) if there are substantial grounds for believing that there is a real risk to the protection of the fundamental rights of the requested person, the executing judicial authority may require, as appropriate, additional guarantees as to the treatment of the requested person after the person's surrender before it decides whether to execute the arrest warrant.

Article 605
Recourse to the central authority

1. The United Kingdom and the Union, acting on behalf of any of its Member States, may each notify the Specialised Committee on Law Enforcement and Judicial Cooperation of, in the case of the United Kingdom, its central authority and, in the case of the Union, the central authority for each State, having designated such an authority, or, if the legal system of the relevant State so provides, of more than one central authority to assist the competent judicial authorities.
2. When notifying the Specialised Committee on Law Enforcement and Judicial Cooperation under paragraph 1, the United Kingdom and the Union, acting on behalf of any of its Member States, may each indicate that, as a result of the organisation of the internal judicial system of the relevant States, the central authority or central authorities are responsible for the administrative transmission and receipt of arrest warrants as well as for all other official correspondence relating to the administrative transmission and receipt of arrest warrants. Such indication shall be binding upon all the authorities of the issuing State.

Article 606
Content and form of the arrest warrant

1. The arrest warrant shall contain the following information set out in accordance with the form contained in Annex 43:
   (a) the identity and nationality of the requested person;
   (b) the name, address, telephone and fax numbers and e-mail address of the issuing judicial authority;
   (c) evidence of an enforceable judgment, an arrest warrant or any other enforceable judicial decision having the same effect that fall within the scope of Article 599;
   (d) the nature and legal classification of the offence, particularly in respect of Article 599;
   (e) a description of the circumstances in which the offence was committed, including the time, place and degree of participation in the offence by the requested person;
   (f) the penalty imposed, if there is a final judgment, or the prescribed scale of penalties for the offence under the law of the issuing State; and
   (g) if possible, other consequences of the offence.
2. The arrest warrant shall be translated into the official language or one of the official languages of the executing State. The United Kingdom and the Union, acting on behalf of any of its Member States, may each notify the Specialised Committee on Law Enforcement and Judicial Cooperation that a translation in one or more other official languages of a State will be accepted.

Article 607
Transmission of an arrest warrant

If the location of the requested person is known, the issuing judicial authority may transmit the arrest warrant directly to the executing judicial authority.

Article 608
Detailed procedures for transmitting an arrest warrant

1. If the issuing judicial authority does not know which authority is the competent executing judicial authority, it shall make the requisite enquiries, in order to obtain that information from the executing State.
2. The issuing judicial authority may request the International Criminal Police Organisation ('Interpol') to transmit an arrest warrant.
3. The issuing judicial authority may transmit the arrest warrant by any secure means capable of producing written records under conditions allowing the executing State to establish the authenticity of the arrest warrant.
4. All difficulties concerning the transmission or the authenticity of any document needed for the execution of the arrest warrant shall be dealt with by direct contacts between the judicial authorities involved, or, where appropriate, with the involvement of the central authorities of the States.
5. If the authority which receives an arrest warrant is not competent to act upon it, it shall automatically forward the arrest warrant to the competent authority in its State and shall inform the issuing judicial authority accordingly.

Article 609
Rights of a requested person

1. If a requested person is arrested for the purpose of the execution of an arrest warrant, the executing judicial authority, in accordance with its domestic law, shall inform that person of the arrest warrant and of its contents, and also of the possibility of consenting to surrender to the issuing State.
2. A requested person who is arrested for the purpose of the execution of an arrest warrant and who does not speak or understand the language of the arrest warrant proceedings shall have the right to be assisted by an interpreter and to be provided with a written translation in the native language of the requested person or in any other language which that person speaks or understands, in accordance with the domestic law of the executing State.
3. A requested person shall have the right to be assisted by a lawyer in accordance with the domestic law of the executing State upon arrest.
4. The requested person shall be informed of the person's right to appoint a lawyer in the issuing State for the purpose of assisting the lawyer in the executing State in the arrest warrant proceedings. This paragraph is without prejudice to the time limits set out in Article 621.
5. A requested person who is arrested shall have the right to have the consular authorities of that person's State of nationality, or if that person is stateless, the consular authorities of the State where that person usually resides, informed of the arrest without undue delay and to communicate with those authorities, if that person so wishes.

Article 610
Keeping the person in detention

When a person is arrested on the basis of an arrest warrant, the executing judicial authority shall take a decision on whether the requested person should remain in detention, in accordance with the law of the executing State. The person may be released provisionally at any time in accordance with the domestic law of the executing State, provided that the competent authority of that State takes all the measures it deems necessary to prevent the person from absconding.

Article 611
Consent to surrender

1. If the arrested person indicates that he or she consents to surrender, that consent and, if appropriate, the express renunciation of entitlement to the speciality rule referred to in Article 625(2) must be given before the executing judicial authority, in accordance with the domestic law of the executing State.
2. Each State shall adopt the measures necessary to ensure that the consent and, where appropriate, the renunciation referred to in paragraph 1 are established in such a way as to show that the person concerned has expressed them voluntarily and in full awareness of the consequences. To that end, the requested person shall have the right to a lawyer.
3. The consent and, where appropriate, the renunciation referred to in paragraph 1 shall be formally recorded in accordance with the procedure laid down by the domestic law of the executing State.
4. In principle, consent may not be revoked. Each State may provide that the consent and, if appropriate, the renunciation referred to in paragraph 1 of this Article may be revoked in accordance with the rules applicable under its domestic law. In such a case, the period between the date of the consent and that of its revocation shall not be taken into consideration in establishing the time limits laid down in Article 621. The United Kingdom and the Union, acting on behalf of any of its Member States, may each notify the Specialised Committee on Law Enforcement and Judicial Cooperation that it wishes to have recourse to this possibility, specifying the procedures whereby revocation of the consent is possible and any amendments to those procedures.

Article 612
Hearing of the requested person

Where the arrested person does not consent to surrender as referred to in Article 611, that person shall be entitled to be heard by the executing judicial authority, in accordance with the law of the executing State.

Article 613
Surrender decision

1. The executing judicial authority shall decide whether the person is to be surrendered within the time limits and in accordance with the conditions

defined in this Title, in particular the principle of proportionality as set out in Article 597.

2. If the executing judicial authority finds the information communicated by the issuing State to be insufficient to allow it to decide on surrender, it shall request that the necessary supplementary information, in particular with respect to Article 597, Articles 600 to 602, Article 604 and Article 606, be furnished as a matter of urgency and may fix a time limit for the receipt thereof, taking into account the need to observe the time limits provided for in Article 615.
3. The issuing judicial authority may forward any additional useful information to the executing judicial authority at any time.

Article 614
Decision in the event of multiple requests

1. If two or more States have issued a European arrest warrant or an arrest warrant for the same person, the decision as to which of those arrest warrants is to be executed shall be taken by the executing judicial authority, with due consideration of all the circumstances, especially the relative seriousness of the offences and place of the offences, the respective dates of the arrest warrants or European arrest warrants and whether they have been issued for the purposes of prosecution or for the execution of a custodial sentence or detention order, and of legal obligations of Member States deriving from Union law regarding, in particular, the principles of freedom of movement and nondiscrimination on grounds of nationality.
2. The executing judicial authority of a Member State may seek the advice of Eurojust when making the choice referred to in paragraph 1.
3. In the event of a conflict between an arrest warrant and a request for extradition presented by a third country, the decision as to whether the arrest warrant or the extradition request takes precedence shall be taken by the competent authority of the executing State with due consideration of all the circumstances, in particular those referred to in paragraph 1 and those mentioned in the applicable convention.
4. This Article is without prejudice to the States' obligations under the Statute of the International Criminal Court.

Article 615
Time limits and procedures for the decision to execute the arrest warrant

1. An arrest warrant shall be dealt with and executed as a matter of urgency.
2. In cases where the requested person consents to surrender, the final decision on the execution of the arrest warrant shall be taken within ten days after the consent was given.
3. In other cases, the final decision on the execution of the arrest warrant shall be taken within 60 days after the arrest of the requested person.
4. Where in specific cases the arrest warrant cannot be executed within the time limits laid down in paragraph 2 or 3, the executing judicial authority shall

immediately inform the issuing judicial authority of that fact, giving the reasons for the delay. In such cases, the time limits may be extended by a further 30 days.

5. As long as the executing judicial authority has not taken a final decision on the arrest warrant, it shall ensure that the material conditions necessary for the effective surrender of the person remain fulfilled.
6. Reasons must be given for any refusal to execute an arrest warrant.

Article 616
Situation pending the decision

1. Where the arrest warrant has been issued for the purpose of conducting a criminal prosecution, the executing judicial authority shall either:
   (a) agree that the requested person should be heard according to Article 617; or
   (b) agree to the temporary transfer of the requested person.
2. The conditions and the duration of the temporary transfer shall be determined by mutual agreement between the issuing and executing judicial authorities.
3. In the case of temporary transfer, the person must be able to return to the executing State to attend hearings which concern that person as part of the surrender procedure.

Article 617
Hearing the person pending the decision

1. The requested person shall be heard by a judicial authority. To that end, the requested person shall be assisted by a lawyer designated in accordance with the law of the issuing State.
2. The requested person shall be heard in accordance with the law of the executing State and with the conditions determined by mutual agreement between the issuing and executing judicial authorities.
3. The competent executing judicial authority may assign another judicial authority of its State to take part in the hearing of the requested person in order to ensure the proper application of this Article.

Article 618
Privileges and immunities

1. Where the requested person enjoys a privilege or immunity regarding jurisdiction or execution in the executing State, the time limits referred to in Article 615 only start running when, or if, the executing judicial authority is informed of the fact that the privilege or immunity has been waived.
2. The executing State shall ensure that the material conditions necessary for effective surrender are fulfilled when the person no longer enjoys such privilege or immunity. 3. Where power to waive the privilege or immunity lies with an authority of the executing State, the executing judicial authority shall request that authority to exercise that power without delay. Where power to waive the privilege or immunity lies with an authority of another State, third

country or international organisation, the issuing judicial authority shall request that authority to exercise that power.

Article 619
Competing international obligations

1. This Agreement does not prejudice the obligations of the executing State where the requested person has been extradited to that State from a third country and where that person is protected by provisions of the arrangement under which that person was extradited concerning the speciality rule. The executing State shall take all necessary measures for requesting without delay the consent of the third country from which the requested person was extradited so that the requested person can be surrendered to the State which issued the arrest warrant. The time limits referred to in Article 615 do not start running until the day on which the speciality rule ceases to apply.
2. Pending the decision of the third country from which the requested person was extradited, the executing State shall ensure that the material conditions necessary for effective surrender remain fulfilled.

Article 620
Notification of the decision

The executing judicial authority shall notify the issuing judicial authority immediately of the decision on the action to be taken on the arrest warrant.

Article 621
Time limits for surrender of the person

1. The requested person shall be surrendered as soon as possible on a date agreed between the authorities concerned.
2. The requested person shall be surrendered no later than ten days after the final decision on the execution of the arrest warrant.
3. If the surrender of the requested person within the time limit in paragraph 2 is prevented by circumstances beyond the control of any of the States, the executing and issuing judicial authorities shall immediately contact each other and agree on a new surrender date. In that event, the surrender shall take place within ten days of the new date thus agreed.
4. The surrender may exceptionally be temporarily postponed for serious humanitarian reasons, for example if there are substantial grounds for believing that the surrender would manifestly endanger the requested person's life or health. The execution of the arrest warrant shall take place as soon as those grounds have ceased to exist. The executing judicial authority shall immediately inform the issuing judicial authority and agree on a new surrender date. In that event, the surrender shall take place within ten days of the new date agreed.
5. Upon the expiry of the time limits referred to in paragraphs 2 to 4, if the requested person is still being held in custody, that person shall be released. The executing and issuing judicial authorities shall contact each other as soon as it appears that a person is to be released under this paragraph and agree the arrangements for the surrender of that person.

Article 622
Postponed or conditional surrender

1. After deciding to execute the arrest warrant, the executing judicial authority may postpone the surrender of the requested person so that the requested person may be prosecuted in the executing State or, if the requested person has already been sentenced, so that the requested person may serve, a sentence passed for an act other than that referred to in the arrest warrant in the territory of the executing State.
2. Instead of postponing the surrender, the executing judicial authority may temporarily surrender the requested person to the issuing State under conditions to be determined by mutual agreement between the executing and the issuing judicial authorities. The agreement shall be made in writing and the conditions shall be binding on all the authorities in the issuing State.

Article 623
Transit

1. Each State shall permit the transit through its territory of a requested person who is being surrendered provided that it has been given information on:
   (a) the identity and nationality of the person subject to the arrest warrant;
   (b) the existence of an arrest warrant;
   (c) the nature and legal classification of the offence; and
   (d) the description of the circumstances of the offence, including the date and place.
2. The State, on behalf of which a notification has been made in accordance with Article 603(2) to the effect that its own nationals will not be surrendered or that surrender will be authorised only under certain specified conditions, may, refuse the transit of its own nationals through its territory under the same terms or submit it to the same conditions.
3. The States shall designate an authority responsible for receiving transit requests and the necessary documents, as well as any other official correspondence relating to transit requests.
4. The transit request and the information referred to in paragraph 1 may be addressed to the authority designated pursuant to paragraph 3 by any means capable of producing a written record. The State of transit shall notify its decision by the same procedure.
5. This Article does not apply in the case of transport by air without a scheduled stopover. However, if an unscheduled landing occurs, the issuing State shall provide the authority designated pursuant to paragraph 3 with the information referred to in paragraph 1.
6. Where a transit concerns a person who is to be extradited from a third country to a State, this Article applies mutatis mutandis. In particular, references to an 'arrest warrant' shall be treated as references to an 'extradition request'.

Article 624
Deduction of the period of detention served in the executing State

1. The issuing State shall deduct all periods of detention arising from the execution of an arrest warrant from the total period of detention to be served in the

issuing State as a result of a custodial sentence or detention order being passed.

2. All information concerning the duration of the detention of the requested person on the basis of the arrest warrant shall be transmitted by the executing judicial authority or the central authority designated under Article 605 to the issuing judicial authority at the time of the surrender.

Article 625
Possible prosecution for other offences

1. The United Kingdom and the Union, acting on behalf of any of its Member States, may each notify the Specialised Committee on Law Enforcement and Judicial Cooperation that, in relations with other States to which the same notification applies, consent is presumed to have been given for the prosecution, sentencing or detention of a person with a view to the carrying out of a custodial sentence or detention order for an offence committed prior to the person's surrender, other than that for which that person was surrendered, unless in a particular case the executing judicial authority states otherwise in its decision on surrender.
2. Except in the cases referred to in paragraphs 1 and 3, a person surrendered may not be prosecuted, sentenced or otherwise deprived of liberty for an offence committed prior to that person's surrender other than that for which the person was surrendered.
3. Paragraph 2 of this Article does not apply in the following cases:
   (a) the person, having had an opportunity to leave the territory of the State to which that person has been surrendered, has not done so within 45 days of that person's final discharge or has returned to that territory after leaving it;
   (b) the offence is not punishable by a custodial sentence or detention order;
   (c) the criminal proceedings do not give rise to the application of a measure restricting personal liberty;
   (d) the person could be liable to a penalty or a measure not involving the deprivation of liberty, in particular a financial penalty or a measure in lieu of a financial penalty, even if the penalty or measure may give rise to a restriction of the person's personal liberty;
   (e) the person consented to be surrendered, where appropriate at the same time as the person renounced the speciality rule, in accordance with Article 611;
   (f) the person, after the person's surrender, has expressly renounced entitlement to the speciality rule with regard to specific offences preceding the person's surrender; renunciation must be given before the competent judicial authority of the issuing State and be recorded in accordance with that State's domestic law; the renunciation must be drawn up in such a way as to make clear that the person concerned has given it voluntarily and in full awareness of the consequences; to that end, the person shall have the right to a lawyer; and
   (g) the executing judicial authority which surrendered the person gives its consent in accordance with paragraph 4 of this Article.
4. A request for consent shall be submitted to the executing judicial authority, accompanied by the information referred to in Article 606(1) and a translation

as referred to in Article 606(2). Consent shall be given where the offence for which it is requested is itself subject to surrender in accordance with the provisions of this Title. Consent shall be refused on the grounds referred to in Article 600 and otherwise may be refused only on the grounds referred to in Article 601, or Article 602(2) and Article 603(2). The decision shall be taken no later than 30 days after receipt of the request. For the situations laid down in Article 604 the issuing State must give the guarantees provided for therein.

Article 626
Surrender or subsequent extradition

1. The United Kingdom and the Union, acting on behalf of any of its Member States, may each notify the Specialised Committee on Law Enforcement and Judicial Cooperation that, in relations with other States to which the same notification applies, the consent for the surrender of a person to a State other than the executing State pursuant to an arrest warrant or European arrest warrant issued for an offence committed prior to that person's surrender is presumed to have been given, unless in a particular case the executing judicial authority states otherwise in its decision on surrender.
2. In any case, a person who has been surrendered to the issuing State pursuant to an arrest warrant or European arrest warrant may be surrendered to a State other than the executing State pursuant to an arrest warrant or European arrest warrant issued for any offence committed prior to the person's surrender without the consent of the executing State in the following cases:
   (a) the requested person, having had an opportunity to leave the territory of the State to which that person has been surrendered, has not done so within 45 days of that person's final discharge, or has returned to that territory after leaving it;
   (b) the requested person consents to be surrendered to a State other than the executing State pursuant to an arrest warrant or European arrest warrant; consent must be given before the competent judicial authorities of the issuing State and be recorded in accordance with that State's domestic law; it must be drawn up in such a way as to make clear that the person concerned has given it voluntarily and in full awareness of the consequences; to that end, the requested person shall have the right to a lawyer; and
   (c) the requested person is not subject to the speciality rule, in accordance with point (a), (e), (f) or (g) of Article 625(3).
3. The executing judicial authority shall consent to the surrender to another State in accordance with the following rules:
   (a) the request for consent shall be submitted in accordance with Article 607, accompanied by the information set out in Article 606(1) and a translation as referred to in Article 606(2);
   (b) consent shall be given where the offence for which it is requested is itself subject to surrender in accordance with the provisions of this Agreement;
   (c) the decision shall be taken no later than 30 days after receipt of the request; and
   (d) consent shall be refused on the grounds referred to in Article 600 and otherwise may be refused only on the grounds referred to in Article 601, Article 602(2) and Article 603(2).

4. For the situations referred to in Article 604, the issuing State shall give the guarantees provided for therein.
5. Notwithstanding paragraph 1, a person who has been surrendered pursuant to an arrest warrant shall not be extradited to a third country without the consent of the competent authority of the State which surrendered the person. Such consent shall be given in accordance with the Conventions by which that State is bound, as well as with its domestic law.

Article 627
Handing over of property

1. At the request of the issuing judicial authority or on its own initiative, the executing judicial authority shall, in accordance with its domestic law, seize and hand over property which:
   (a) may be required as evidence; or
   (b) has been acquired by the requested person as a result of the offence.
2. The property referred to in paragraph 1 shall be handed over even if the arrest warrant cannot be carried out owing to the death or escape of the requested person.
3. If the property referred to in paragraph 1 is liable to seizure or confiscation in the territory of the executing State, that State may, if the property is needed in connection with pending criminal proceedings, temporarily retain it or hand it over to the issuing State on condition that it is returned.
4. Any rights which the executing State or third parties may have acquired in the property referred to in paragraph 1 shall be preserved. Where such rights exist, the issuing State shall return the property without charge to the executing State as soon as the criminal proceedings have been terminated.

Article 628
Expenses

1. Expenses incurred in the territory of the executing State for the execution of an arrest warrant shall be borne by that State.
2. All other expenses shall be borne by the issuing State.

Article 629
Relation to other legal instruments

1. Without prejudice to their application in relations between States and third countries, this Title, from the date of entry into force of this Agreement, replaces the corresponding provisions of the following conventions applicable in the field of extradition in relations between the United Kingdom, on the one side, and Member States, on the other side:
   (a) the European Convention on Extradition, done at Paris on 13 December 1957, and its additional protocols; and
   (b) the European Convention on the Suppression of Terrorism, as far as extradition is concerned.
2. Where the Conventions referred to in paragraph 1 apply to the territories of States or to territories for whose external relations a State is responsible to which this Title does not apply, those Conventions continue to govern the relations existing between those territories and the other States.

Article 630
Review of notifications

When carrying out the joint review of this Title as referred to in Article 691(1), the Parties shall consider the need to maintain the notifications made under Article 599(4), Article 602(2) and Article 603(2). If the notifications referred to in Article 603(2) are not renewed, they shall expire five years after the date of entry into force of this Agreement. Notifications as referred to in Article 603(2) may only be renewed or newly made during the three months prior to the fifth anniversary of the entry into force of this Agreement and, subsequently, every five years thereafter, provided that the conditions set out in Article 603(2) are met at that time.

Article 631
Ongoing arrest warrants in case of disapplication

Notwithstanding Article 526, Article 692 and Article 693, the provisions of this Title apply in respect of arrest warrants where the requested person was arrested before the disapplication of this Title for the purposes of the execution of an arrest warrant, irrespective of the decision of the executing judicial authority as to whether the requested person is to remain in detention or be provisionally released.

Article 632
Application to existing European arrest warrants

This Title shall apply in respect of European arrest warrants issued in accordance with Council Framework Decision 2002/584/JHA[1] by a State before the end of the transition period where the requested person has not been arrested for the purpose of its execution before the end of the transition period.

1 Council Framework Decision 2002/584/JHA of 13 June 2002 on the European arrest warrant and the surrender procedures between Member States (OJ EU L 190, 18.7.2002, p. 1).

APPENDIX C

Arrest Warrant Form: Annex 43 of the TCA

Annex 43
Arrest Warrant

This warrant has been issued by a competent judicial authority. I request that the person mentioned below be arrested and surrendered for the purposes of conducting a criminal prosecution or executing a custodial sentence or detention order.[1]

(a) Information regarding the identity of the requested person:
Name:
Forename(s):
Maiden name, where applicable:
Aliases, where applicable:
Sex:
Nationality:
Date of birth:
Place of birth:
Residence and/or known address:
Language(s) which the requested person understands (if known):
Distinctive marks/description of the requested person:

1 This warrant must be written in, or translated into, one of the official languages of the executing State, when that State is known, or any other language accepted by that State.

Photo and fingerprints of the requested person, if they are available and can be transmitted, or contact details of the person to be contacted in order to obtain such information or a DNA profile (where this evidence can be supplied but has not been included)

(b) Decision on which the warrant is based:

1. Arrest warrant or judicial decision having the same effect:

Type:

2. Enforceable judgement:

Reference:

(c) Indications on the length of the sentence:

1. Maximum length of the custodial sentence or detention order which may be imposed for the offence(s):

2. Length of the custodial sentence or detention order imposed:

Remaining sentence to be served:

(d) Indicate if the person appeared in person at the trial resulting in the decision:

1. ☐ Yes, the person appeared in person at the trial resulting in the decision.

2. ☐ No, the person did not appear in person at the trial resulting in the decision.

3. If you have ticked the box under point 2, please confirm the existence of one of the following, if applicable:

☐ 3.1a. the person was summoned in person on . . . (day/month/year) and thereby informed of the scheduled date and place of the trial which resulted in the decision and was informed that a decision may be handed down if he or she does not appear for the trial;

OR

☐ 3.1b. the person was not summoned in person but by other means actually received official information of the scheduled date and place of the trial which resulted in the decision, in such a manner that it was unequivocally established that he or she was aware of the scheduled trial, and was informed that a decision may be handed down if he or she does not appear for the trial;

OR

☐ 3.2. being aware of the scheduled trial, the person had given a mandate to a legal counsellor, who was either appointed by the person concerned or by the State, to defend him or her at the trial, and was indeed defended by that counsellor at the trial;

OR

☐ 3.3. the person was served with the decision on . . . (day/month/year) and was expressly informed about the right to a retrial or appeal, in which he or she has the right to participate and which allows the merits of the case, including fresh evidence, to be re-examined, and which may lead to the original decision being reversed, and

☐ the person expressly stated that he or she does not contest this decision;

OR

☐ the person did not request a retrial or appeal within the applicable timeframe;

OR

☐ 3.4. the person was not personally served with the decision, but
- the person will be personally served with this decision without delay after the surrender; and
- when served with the decision, the person will be expressly informed of his or her right to a retrial or appeal, in which he or she has the right to participate and which allows the merits of the case, including fresh evidence, to be re-examined, and which may lead to the original decision being reversed; and
- the person will be informed of the timeframe within which he or she has to request a retrial or appeal, which will be ...... days.

4. If you have ticked the box under point 3.1b, 3.2 or 3.3 above, please provide information about how the relevant condition has been met:

(e) Offences:

This warrant relates to in total: offences

Description of the circumstances in which the offence(s) was (were) committed, including the time, place and degree of participation in the offence(s) by the requested person:

Nature and legal classification of the offence(s) and the applicable statutory provision/code:

I. The following applies only in case both the issuing and the executing State have made a notification under Article 599(4) of the Agreement: if applicable, tick one or more of the following offences, as defined by the law of the issuing State, punishable in the issuing State by a custodial sentence or detention order for a maximum period of at least three years:

☐ participation in a criminal organisation,

☐ terrorism as defined in Annex 45 to the Agreement,

☐ trafficking in human beings,

☐ sexual exploitation of children and child pornography,

☐ illicit trafficking in narcotic drugs and psychotropic substances,

☐ illicit trafficking in weapons, munitions and explosives,

☐ corruption, including bribery,

☐ fraud, including that affecting the financial interests of the United Kingdom, of a Member State or of the Union,

☐ laundering of the proceeds of crime,

☐ counterfeiting of currency,

☐ computer-related crime,

☐ environmental crime, including illicit trafficking in endangered animal species and in endangered plant species and varieties,

☐ facilitation of unauthorised entry and residence,

☐ murder, grievous bodily injury,

☐ illicit trade in human organs and tissue,

☐ kidnapping, illegal restraint and hostage-taking,

☐ racism and xenophobia,

☐ organised or armed robbery,

☐ illicit trafficking in cultural goods, including antiques and works of art,

- ☐ swindling,
- ☐ racketeering and extortion,
- ☐ counterfeiting and piracy of products,
- ☐ forgery of administrative documents and trafficking therein
- ☐ forgery of means of payment,
- ☐ illicit trafficking in hormonal substances and other growth promoters,
- ☐ illicit trafficking in nuclear or radioactive materials,
- ☐ trafficking in stolen vehicles,
- ☐ rape,
- ☐ arson,
- ☐ crimes within the jurisdiction of the International Criminal Court,
- ☐ unlawful seizure of aircraft, ships or spacecraft,
- ☐ sabotage.

II. Full descriptions of offence(s) not covered by Section I above:

(f) Other circumstances relevant to the case (optional information):
(NB: This could cover remarks on extraterritoriality, interruption of periods of time limitation and other consequences of the offence)

(g) This warrant pertains also to the seizure and handing over of property which may be required as evidence:

This warrant pertains also to the seizure and handing over of property acquired by the requested person as a result of the offence:

Description of the property (and location) (if known):

(h) The offence(s) on the basis of which this warrant has been issued is (are) punishable by/has(have) led to a custodial life sentence or lifetime detention order:

the issuing State will upon request by the executing State give an assurance that it will:

- ☐ review the penalty or measure imposed – on request or at least after 20 years,

and/or

- ☐ encourage the application of measures of clemency to which the person is entitled to apply for under the law or practice of the issuing State, aiming at a non-execution of such penalty or measure.

(i) The judicial authority which issued the warrant:

Official name:

Name of its representative:[2]

Post held (title/grade):

File reference:

Address:

Tel. No.: (country code)

(area/city code)

Fax No. (country code)

(area/city code)

E-mail:

Contact details of the person to contact to make necessary practical arrangements for the surrender:

Where a central authority has been made responsible for the transmission and administrative reception of arrest warrants:

2 In the different language versions a reference to the 'holder' of the judicial authority will be included.

Name of the central authority:

Contact person, if applicable

(title/grade and name):

Address:

Tel. No.: (country code)

(area/city code)

Fax No. (country code)

(area/city code)

E-mail:.

Signature of the issuing judicial

authority and/or its

representative:

Name:

Post held (title/grade):

Date:

Official stamp (if available):

APPENDIX D

AW validity checklist

______________v________

Date AW issued	
Date AW certified	
Is it an accusation or conviction warrant? [Box B] Is the warrant as a whole unclear?	
Date of offence [Box E]	
Place of offence [Box E]	
Description of offence [Box E] Is the description sufficiently particularised?	
Accusation: maximum sentence [Box C]	
Conviction: sentence imposed [Box C] Is the sentence sufficiently particularised?	
Extradition offences? [Box E] Would the conduct constitute an offence in the UK? If so, is it punishable in requesting state by at least 12 months (accusation) or did requested person receive sentence of at least 4 months (conviction)? Check location of conduct.	
Conviction: Was the requested person present at trial? [Box D]	

APPENDIX E

AW first appearance checklist

Check identity	
Consider section 4: date and time of arrest; AW provided?	
Has the requested person been given a copy of the AW? If not, judge may discharge	
Has the requested person been brought as soon as practicable before the appropriate judge? If not, judge must discharge	
Explain extradition procedure – court not interested in whether/by whom offence was committed, but whether procedural requirements met; timescale	
Explain consent and specialty	
Is the requested person serving a sentence in the UK or subject to a domestic charge?	
Are there any issues to raise?	
Consider bars	
Conviction in absence?	
Human rights	
Physical/mental health	
Why does the requested person think s/he shouldn't be extradited?	
In appropriate cases, fill out the legal aid form	
Explain appeal process	

APPENDIX F

Bail checklist

Circumstances of arrest: where was the requested person arrested (i.e. home? work?) Does s/he accept any statements said to have been made by him/her?	
When did the requested person come to the UK and why?	
Has the requested person been back to the requesting state?	
Was the requested person aware of criminal proceedings and if so, was s/he present and why did s/he leave?	
Does the requested person have family? Where are the family based and what are their circumstances? Are they dependent? Any responsibilities as a sole carer?	
Is the requested person employed? If so, what are his or her hours of work? How far is the place of work from home?	
What is the requested person's housing situation?	
Does the requested person have community ties?	
Are details on police national computer print out correct? Is there any explanation for failing to attend on previous occasions?	
Has the requested person instructed lawyers in requesting state?	
What is his/her immigration status?	

Where are his/her identity documents? If not in the requested person's property, can someone else find them to surrender them to the court/police?	
Does the requested person know whether a surety or security may be available? If so, obtain telephone numbers.	
Where is the nearest police station to the requested person's home address located? Would a reporting condition at any particular time be problematic?	
If a curfew were imposed, what hours would be practicable for the requested person?	
What is the requested person's mobile telephone number?	

APPENDIX G

Updated Guidance on use of CVP in Extradition Courts

The increased use of live links during the pandemic has become an invaluable tool in keeping our courts running by maintaining a safe working environment.

Following a clear indication by the Lord Chief Justice, my predecessor gave a blanket direction that extradition prosecutors and defence lawyers could appear by CVP as the default position. I reviewed that direction and renewed it until the 12th April 2021.

Since that review, a number of things have moved on; the incidence of disease has decreased, the vaccination programme has continued with over 31m adults now vaccinated to some degree and the next stage of the Prime Minister's 'road map' out of lockdown is due to be implemented also on 12th April. At this point, in England at least, all non-essential retail can reopen and the hospitality industry may again provide service outdoors.

In addition, the LCJ has issued an updated announcement and so I consider I should further review the default position. Thus, from Tuesday 13th April [2021], the default position can no longer be that all parties attend remotely but rather the court will consider each application on the statutory interests of justice test.

I am not minded to issue detailed guidance as it may fetter judicial discretion, but I would imagine that a significant factor in any determination on the interests of justice would be whether the hearing is contested or not. Those matters which are contested are broadly unlikely to be suitable for live link directions without specific reasons being provided to satisfy the test. It is considered that the interests of justice are normally best served by punctual and efficient hearings, these are harder to achieve with parties attending remotely. Factors which fall to be considered are wide and include vulnerabilities and distances to travel but also include caring responsibilities and the efficient disposal of the courts business.

In the absence of a direction from the court, parties are expected to be present in the courtroom.

Procedural Guidance

All applications for CVP must contain the full name, court number, whether AM or PM and be sent either directly to the judge sitting and IJ office or just the IJ office who will notify the judge, depending on whether the judge has indicated he or she is happy to receive direct correspondence.

Applications must be made the previous working day unless an overnight case or an unexpected intervening act means that it is impossible to do so, for example, the advocate tests positive for covid 19 in the evening before the hearing and the first chance to notify the court that they are unable to attend and require CVP is the morning of the hearing.

All applications must contain sufficient information for the court to properly determine the interests of justice test, applications that simply state that CVP is requested without more may be refused. If the application is premised on the health of the advocate of a member of their family, the court will not ordinarily enquire as to detail of said illness and privacy can be maintained. That said, sufficient information must be provided for the court to assess whether or not it remains in the interests of justice.

The granting of CVP is still subject to the court's review and may be rescinded if the efficient disposal of cases is in some way impacted negatively by the use of the equipment, there are difficulties in hearing or seeing an advocate or they have such difficulty, or if no information comes to light that would have not in the first instance merited the granting of the application.

Paul Goldspring

Senior District Judge (Chief Magistrate) for England and Wales

14th April 2021

APPENDIX H

Case management form

It is now a standard direction in extradition cases at Westminster Magistrates' Court that you provide the following details that may be relevant in these proceedings. The information you provide must be accurate as it may be checked, and it may be referred to at later hearings.

About you

Please print your full name and date of birth:

1. Are you the person requested in the warrant? **Y/N**

2. Have you any serious physical or mental health problems that may be relevant to these proceedings? **Y/N**
   If so, please describe them

3. Are you currently working? **Y/N**
   If so, please state whether employed or self employed

About your family

1. Please give names and dates of birth (or ages) of any family member dependent on you in the United Kingdom.

2. Do any of your UK dependants have serious physical or mental health problems relevant to these proceedings? **Y/N**
   If so, please describe them:

3. If your extradition is ordered will any other person be able to care for your dependant(s)? **Y/N**
   If not, why not?

Your connection with the United Kingdom

1. Do you live here? **Y/N**
   If so, since when?

Your connection with the Requesting State

1. Are you a citizen of the requesting state? **Y/N**

2. If not, have you been there? **Y/N**
   If so, when were you last there?

3. If you have now been arrested on a conviction warrant, were you present at the conviction hearing? **Y/N**

4. When did you first know of these proceedings?

5. Have you been granted asylum from the requesting state? **Y/N**
   If so, when?

6. What hardship do you believe you would suffer in the requesting state, if returned?

7. Is there any other good reason why you should not be extradited?

SIGNED BY REQUESTED PERSON

....

DATE ....

INFORMATION FROM LAWYER

Name

....

(please print)

Name of firm of solicitors

....

(please print)

Have you had sufficient time to advise your client on potential challenges? **Y/N**
If not, please explain:

What potential issues have been identified for these proceedings?

APPENDIX I

Readiness Check for Full Extradition Hearing

CASE PROGRESSION: READINESS FOR FULL EXTRADITION HEARING

Case Name		
Case No.		
Date of Full Extradition Hearing		
Venue	Westminster Magistrates' Court	

We are currently making enquiries on readiness for the full extradition hearing and whether it will be effective.

1. **Can you confirm your readiness for the full extradition hearing**? Choose an item.

2. **Issues:**
   - Are there specific issues preventing readiness? Choose an item.
   - If yes, what are the issues? How if possible, could the court assist with this / these issues?

3. **Bringing the date of the hearing forward:**

If a slot becomes available and we can accommodate the hearing earlier would parties be in agreement with bringing the date forward? Choose an item.

- If yes, what is your preferred date and time (please select up to five choices):

Slot	Click or tap to enter a date.	Click or tap to enter a date.	Click or tap to enter a date.	Click or tap to enter a date.	Click or tap to enter a date.
10am	☐	☐	☐	☐	☐
2pm	☐	☐	☐	☐	☐

4. **Interpreter:**

Does the Requested Person need an interpreter? If yes, what language?	Choose an item.	**Language**
Does the Requested person speak any other languages? If yes, please list as many as possible.	Choose an item.	

CASE PROGRESSION: READINESS FOR FULL EXTRADITION HEARING

5. Cloud Video Platform (CVP):

- Is CVP required? Choose an item.
- If yes, the number of attendees? Choose an item.

Reason/s for CVP request: Please give a written explanation as to why this is needed and their names and email addresses.

Name of attendee wishing to appear by CVP	Email address

6. Any other relevant information:

(including media interest)

Form completed by:			
Organisation			
Email address			
Telephone / Mobile			
Date		Case no:	

Please return your completed form to Westminster.ij@justice.gov.uk

CASE PROGRESSION: READINESS FOR FULL EXTRADITION HEARING

Additional Information

APPENDIX J

CPS internal process for dealing with forum bar cases

1. This process is to assist extradition and domestic prosecutors who have cause to apply the Guidelines on the Handling of Cases where the Jurisdiction to Prosecute is shared with Prosecuting Authorities Overseas ('the Guidelines') or where he/she is dealing with a case where there appears to be a forum issue.

2. The extradition and domestic units within CPS will share information unless it is inappropriate or unlawful to do so in accordance with general principles.

3. The Extradition Unit will inform requesting states or judicial authorities generally or on a case by case basis that this information will be shared in cases where forum may be an issue.

4. Decisions on forum will be taken by a domestic prosecutor as the Extradition Unit acts for the foreign state making the extradition request.

5. The Extradition Unit will provide advice on how forum might apply in extradition if requested by a domestic prosecutor.

6. Where a domestic prosecutor who is involved in a case where the guidelines are engaged, makes a decision on appropriate jurisdiction he or she will make a record of the decision using the template Record of a decision of Concurrent Jurisdiction. This record should include a note of the extent to which the prosecutor has been able to consider the specified matters set out in the forum bar and any relevant information regarding each. Where public interest or other considerations determine that sensitive information cannot be shared publically it should be recorded elsewhere.

7. If on the basis of information contained in the extradition request it is obvious that that forum will be in issue the Extradition Unit lawyer will check CMS to see if a domestic case has been registered involving the same defendant and conduct. It will also be necessary to contact directly the relevant Central Casework Division and Complex Casework Units to find out if a domestic prosecutor is or has been engaged in the case.

8. Four separate scenarios may be envisaged.

No domestic prosecutor is or has been engaged

9. If it appears that no prosecutor is or has been seized of the case but it appears to be a case where one might expect contact under the guidelines, the

Deputy Head of Division (Extradition) will notify the Head of Special Crime and Counter Terrorism Division to decide if any further action is required.

10. If forum is raised and there has been no domestic involvement, the Extradition Unit lawyer will inform the judge. The Extradition Unit lawyer will assist the court with the specified matters as far as is possible. If further information is requested by the court, a domestic prosecutor may need to confirm that the CPS is not engaged domestically and that they have no evidence to consider.

A decision to charge in this jurisdiction

11. Where a domestic prosecutor has decided that it is appropriate to charge requested person with corresponding offences, Section 8A or 76A of the Act applies the extradition proceedings must be adjourned.

A decision that England and Wales is not the most appropriate jurisdiction

12. Where a prosecutor has engaged the guidelines without making a formal Code Test decision and it has been decided that a prosecution should be conducted elsewhere he/she will inform the Extradition Unit and provide the template containing a record of that decision. If forum is raised in the subsequent extradition, the Extradition Unit lawyer will inform the court of the domestic prosecutor's decision and will assist on the specified matters using the template and any relevant material from the extradition papers.

13. In the event that the extradition court needs further information, the Extradition Unit lawyer will consider whether it is necessary to seek an adjournment so that the prosecutor who made the relevant decision may be made a party to the proceedings.

A decision to issue a prosecutor's certificate

14. A prosecutor can issue a certificate where he/she has made a decision whether or not to prosecute on the basis of the Full Code Test or where it is appropriate to do so because of concerns about the disclosure of sensitive material. A prosecutor considering the issuance of a certificate must consider in doing so, his/her ability to protect that material during any appeal proceedings under s19E.

15. If it appears to the prosecutor with conduct of the domestic prosecution that it may be appropriate to issue a certificate, he/she will draft a briefing note outlining why a certificate is appropriate together with a draft certificate using the template Forum Bar Prosecutor's Certificate. This should be sent in the first instance, via the CCP, to the Head of Special Crime and Counter Terrorism Division (SCCTD) (or in her absence the Head of Central Fraud Division (CFD)). The prosecutor's certificate will be considered, authorised and given under the signature of the Head of SCCTD, the Head of CFD or the Principal Legal Advisor in consultation with the Director of Public Prosecutions.

16. If authorisation is given, the prosecutor will provide the signed certificate to the Extradition Unit lawyer to enable him/her to provide a copy to the court and to serve it on other parties as appropriate.

17. Any appeal against a 'relevant certification decision' should be conducted by the domestic unit which is dealing or has been dealing with the case.

Role of the Extradition Unit lawyer in the forum hearing

18. Where the fugitive provides sufficient information for the court to determine that the forum bar is engaged,[1] the court may require the Extradition Unit lawyer to provide further information to assist in deciding whether a substantial measure of the relevant activity[2] occurred within the United Kingdom and/or information about any of the specified matters listed at ss (3). If the Extradition Unit lawyer is unable to assist from the information contained in the extradition request or the template provided by a domestic prosecutor (if engaged), further enquiries should be made of the requesting state or the relevant prosecutor.

19. Where appeal proceedings are being conducted by a prosecutor following the issuing of a prosecutor's certificate, the Extradition Unit lawyer should assist by providing the records of any extradition hearing and any relevant advice about law and procedure.

1 In the absence of judicial guidance, the CPS believes that the provisions in the Act require the fugitive to produce sufficient information to engage the forum bar before further information is sought from the requesting state.

2 This is not currently defined. We are advised that it is intended to be the definition determined by Wallace Duncan and adopted in Sheppard and Whittle however this is likely to be the subject of legal argument in due course.

Index